Paolo Foradori | Simona Piattoni | Riccardo Scartezzini (eds.)

European Citizenship:
Theories, Arenas, Levels

 Nomos

Foto: Quelle: Credit © European Community, 2007

Die Deutsche Nationalbibliothek verzeichnet diese Publikation in
der Deutschen Nationalbibliografie; detaillierte bibliografische
Daten sind im Internet über http://www.d-nb.de abrufbar.

Die Deutsche Nationalbibliothek lists this publication in the
Deutsche Nationalbibliografie; detailed bibliographic data is
available in the Internet at http://www.d-nb.de .

ISBN 978-3-8329-2940-4

1. Auflage 2007
© Nomos Verlagsgesellschaft, Baden-Baden 2007. Printed in Germany. Alle Rechte,
auch die des Nachdrucks von Auszügen, der fotomechanischen Wiedergabe und der
Übersetzung, vorbehalten. Gedruckt auf alterungsbeständigem Papier.

Preface

Riccardo Scartezzini

What can hold the European polity together? In June of 2003, a group of scholars met in Acquafredda di Maratea, thanks to a generous European Science Foundation (ESF) grant, to try and answer this rather fundamental question, which has been at the center of scholarly and public debates in recent times. With my colleague from the University of Trento, Simona Piattoni, and long-time friend and colleague, Salvador Giner, we felt the need to discuss this question in detail. To our great satisfaction, we managed to enlist an impressive group of scholars with whom to reflect upon this issue, by exploring its many facets in a series of small panels during a five-day conference in a lovely Mediterranean setting.

The process of European integration has been attributed to different dynamics: the visions of postwar political leaders set on preventing any further intra-European bloodshed; the functional imperatives of ever-expanding markets requiring commensurate institutions; the interests of political leaders pursuing national interests through international agencies. An analysis of the driving forces of the process of European integration, however, does not exhaust the search for the social grounds upon which the European polity might be based. The exploration of these principles is the contribution that this conference intended to make.

The key concept of this book is "citizenship" in its social, cultural, economic, and political aspects. In the European mind, citizenship is still primarily associated with the nation-state, as, not in the least, the rejection of the European Constitutional Treaty has shown. The introduction of the concept of European citizenship in the Maastricht Treaty immediately posed questions of content and meaning. What is the relation between national and EU citizenship? Can citizenship be given any meaningful content beyond the narrow confines of the nation-state? What is the relation of EU citizenship to identity? The introduction of EU citizenship may not have been taken serious by some, yet it would appear an essential element in any trans-national polity, such as the EU, which is no longer characterised by the strict intergovernmentalism of an international organisation. As the EU has assumed an important role in ever more areas, European democracy requires European citizenship, in the sense of a well-defined list of rights and duties as they apply to the various levels of the European polity.

However, the discussion about (EU) citizenship frequently is bedevilled by an understanding of the concept that reflects the specific historical trajectories of European societies, and therefore cannot serve as a useful guide to policy, unless, of course, one should argue that Europe is destined to tread one of the national paths. Yet, the existence of the EU itself is proof to the contrary. The historical and geographic specificity of the common understanding of citizenship is reflected in three main aspects. (1) Citizenship is exclusive: one cannot simultaneously be a citizen of

5

more than one state or state-like entity. (2) Citizenship is unitary: its meaning and content are identical for all the members of the same body politic. (3) Citizenship is static: it is the reflection of some pre-existing traits and habits and its core meaning thus is not subject to evolution. Citizenship, in this view, provides the foundation for political and social interaction, and will expand its scope only as the balance of forces in the political and social environment evolves. Although its content may change, as shown by the addition of a catalogue of social rights during the 19th and 20th centuries, these dynamics are generally underplayed as the fuller application of a non-changing principle. Indeed, even for T. H. Marshall (1992), the addition of social rights seems to have marked the completion of a historical trajectory and not just another phase in a concept which could, in principle, keep changing its content and meaning.

As the chapters in this volume show, such an understanding bears no justification, but is merely the reflection of the specific historical trajectories travelled by European societies. The concept of citizenship as exclusively linked to the state and homogenous across the national territory, served the needs of European nations increasingly in need of mobilising their citizenry in order to prevail in the manifold military conflicts of the 19th and 20th century. The emphasis on the static nature of the concept sprang from the same roots, as ideas, institutions and concepts that are seen to be in evolution can never make a claim to absolute truth and demand absolute allegiance as religious beliefs can. Put differently, the common understanding of citizenship bears the marks of the belligerent history of the European nation state.

For those who hold that the inevitable endpoint of the process of European integration is a "United States of Europe", in which the national conception of citizenship will merely be transposed to a higher level, the limitations listed above need not be of consequence. Yet, each single contribution in this volume makes clear that European citizenship can only be conceptualised and practised in the form of a novel and distinct re-combination of the multifarious elements of the concept.

Engaging with Habermas' influential notion of "constitutional patriotism", for example, Føllesdal, Laborde and Delanty demonstrate the need for a conceptualisation of citizenship which also allows for an attachment to local political cultures. Foradori's analysis of the EU as a *sui generis* power on the international scene implies that one of the main mechanisms through which European nation-states have historically fostered feelings of national identity, namely the emphasis on the unique cultural traits of the nation, cannot be employed by the EU.

What the contributions in this book thus have in common is that they distance themselves from any state-centered specific understanding of citizenship, in order to allow the concept's incomparably richer theoretical possibilities, historical roots and possible applications, to come into view again.

The volume is structured in three parts. The chapters grouped in the first part of the book mainly are of a conceptual nature and demonstrate the theoretical inaccuracies of an understanding of citizenship as exclusively linked to a single polity. In the first chapter, Giner shows that the current developments in the direction of a cosmopolitan citizenship can be interpreted as a revival of older republican theories which stressed a universally shared dignity in all human beings. Underlying the contribu-

6

tions by Føllesdal, Laborde and Nida-Rümelin is the demonstration that citizenship does not need to rest on a national identity. Føllesdal's contingent complier, Laborde's civic patriot and the cooperative outlook of Nida-Rümelin's citizen all depart form the rational insight of the benefits of cooperation. Thus it becomes possible to see citizenships as a relation articulated at different levels, from the sub-national to the trans-national. The relevant question, as far as the European component of citizenship is concerned, then becomes what types of institutions are required to uphold this cooperation, and not how to create a common identity.

The chapters grouped in the second part display a stronger empirical orientation. They attempt to shed light on some aspects of the dynamics of the concept of citizenship by analysing how it operates within a set of current arenas. The focus here is on the role of civil society in shaping a legitimate European form of governance, and on the institutional dimensions in which a discourse on citizenship-formation is being developed. Smisman's focus is on the EU's attempt to give a concrete trans-national content to the participatory aspect of European citizenship by means of networking. His overall conclusion, however, is a sceptical one, as the current practice of networking seems able to guarantee neither adequate citizen participation nor the fundamental rights European citizens expect to be guaranteed in a trans-national polity. Egeberg further probes into the evolutionary nature of actual citizenship by a careful empirical examination of how feelings of belonging are shaped by the institutional traits of the environments in which actors operate. Nicoletti elaborates on the notion of "international civil society" and the question of responsiveness in a multi-level polity which seeks to assure citizen participation and public accountability. In chapter 8, Scartezzini shows, how the EU's attempts at instituting citizenship re-invents the concept's meanings and practices.

The third section of the book further elaborates the notion of citizenship as articulated on multiple levels and provides it with historical content. Leontidou analyses the urban dimension of the foundation of a European citizenship and a description of European cities as cultural units with memories of citizenship as city States in the past. Piattoni identifies the limitations, in terms of actors' representativeness and decisions' legitimacy, of European governance systems and speculates whether multi-level political representation (with an emphasis on the regional level) can amend those limitations. Delanty examines citizenship as it extends beyond the nation-state to global contexts and cosmopolitan discourses, and the implications of this for the question of identity and more generally the problem of culture. Finally, Foradori analyses the development of a specific EU international actorness and identity, and looks at the consequences of the progressive militarization of the EU for the *civilian power* model.

Together, these analyses of the dimensions, arenas and level of European citizenship give a multi-faceted picture of citizenship that tries to overcome the restrictiveness of the conventional national notion without, however, suggesting any self-enclosed supranational alternative.

In drawing together the many conversations that we had since the conference, it is my particular pleasure to thank all the colleagues who have collaborated with me on this project, particularly Paolo Foradori and Simona Piattoni who have worked at the production of this volume.

Contents

About the Authors

Gerard Delanty Professor of Sociology/Head of School of Sociology and Social Policy, Department of Sociology, University of Liverpool, Eleanor Rathbone Building, Bedford Street South, University of Liverpool, Liverpool L69 7ZA, UK. Email: delanty@liverpool.ac.uk

Morten Egeberg is Director of ARENA - Centre for European Studies, and Professor of Political Science at the University of Oslo, Norway. Email: morten.egeberg@arena.uio.no

Andreas Follesdal, Professor, Director of Research, Norwegian Centre for Human Rights, University of Oslo. Email: andreas.follesdal@arena.uio.no

Paolo Foradori, Lecturer in Sociology of European Integration, Department of Sociology and Social Research, University of Trento (Italy). E-mail: paolo.foradori@soc.unitn.it

Salvador Giner, (MA, PhD. University of Chicago), Emeritus Professor of Sociology, University of Barcelona. President, Academy of Sciences and Humanities of Catalonia, Barcelona. Email: sginer@teleline.es

Cécile Laborde, Senior Lecturer in Political Theory, University College London UK. Email: c.laborde@ucl.ac.uk

Lila Leontidou Professor of Geography and European Culture and Dean of the School of Humanities, Hellenic Open University, *11-13 Ravine street, 115 21 Athens, Greece*. E-mail: leontidou@eap.gr; leontidou@geo.aegean.gr.

Michele Nicoletti, Professor of Political Philosophy at the Faculty of Humanities and the School of International Studies, University of Trento, Italy. Email: michele.nicoletti@unitn.it

Julian Nida-Rümelin, Professor, Chair for Political Theory and Philosophy, University of Munich. Homepage: www.Julian.Nida-Ruemelin.de

Simona Piattoni, (PhD MIT) Associate Professor of Political Science and Director of the Master's Programme in European and International Studies at the University of Trento, Italy. Simona.piattoni@unitn.it

Riccardo Scartezzini, Professor of Sociology of International Relations, Director of the Jean Monnet European Centre, University of Trento, Italy; riccardo.scartezzini@unitn.it

Stijn Smismans, (PhD EUI) is Senior Researcher and Lecturer of European law at the Faculty of Sociology of the University of Trento. Homepage: http://users.pandora.be/stijnsmismans

List of abbreviations

AC:	Advisory Committee on Safety and Health at Work
CFSP:	Common Foreign and Security Policy
COPS:	Political Security Committee
COREPER:	Committee of Permanent Representatives
DG:	Directorate General
ECSC	European Coal and Steel Community
EDC:	European Defence Community
EHCR:	European Convention of Human Rights
EP:	European Parliament
ESDP:	European Security and Defence Policy
ESF:	European Science Foundation
EU:	European Union
EUMC:	EU Military Committee
MEP	Member of the European Parliament
OH&S:	Occupational Health and Safety
OMC:	Open Method of Co-ordination
QMV:	Qualified Majority Voting
RAM:	Revolution of Military Affairs

Part 1 – Theory: Competing Conceptualizations of Citizenship

1. Paths to Full Citizenship

Salvador Giner

1.1. The Political Discovery of Human Dignity

The condition of citizenship, in its fullness, is one of the highest achievements of modern civilization. When upheld, it entails the widespread recognition of the dignity of all human beings. Many other achievements, from universal access to education, the right to health care and assistance, the free expression of opinions worship and thinking, to the equal right to participate in the polity, are derived from that core condition.

Citizenship has had a long and troubled history. No one would maintain today that citizenship, an ancient invention, reappeared in the modern world after an unbroken line of subterranean transmissions between generations. Nor that, after a centuries-long silence, European classical citizenship experienced a rebirth with the coming of modern times. Ever since Benjamin Constant (1819) sharply and convincingly distinguished between the 'liberty of the ancients' and that of the 'moderns', we have learned to treat classical citizenship as essentially distinct from the modern kind. Though Thucydides (and through him, Pericles), other Greeks and Cicero had much influence on later thinkers, contemporary emphasis has been on a realistic distinction between the ancient world's more circumscribed conceptions of citizenship – which excluded women, slaves, foreigners and others - and the modern form, which burst out openly and without too many ambiguities during two coetaneous modern revolutions at the end of the 18th century, i.e. the American and the French,. Historical rigour has induced us to emphasize difference and stress discontinuity.

This cautious approach often extends to those late-medieval and Renaissance political theorists who did develop a proto-theory of modern citizenship. Some of us may feel inclined to consider this too strict in view of the considerable influence early modern political theorists - such as Machiavelli and Bodin - exercised upon their immediate posterity. This attitude becomes somehow untenable when we consider the extent to which their teachings about the nature of the body politic powerfully influenced the thought of those who did elaborate the theory of the citizen destined to succeed in the modern world. Late-medieval theories of the body politic as the secular home of free and sovereign men under the rule of law and devoted to the public cause are doubtlessly at the root of the republican conception of citizenship and the citizenry. Yet, they ceased to be generally heeded once a much more individualistic conception of the polity came to prevail after Locke. A much stronger revival of that earlier republican tradition – which also found an echo during the English Puritan Revolution as well as in America and France during their own revolutions - had to await the late 20th century. Emphasizing fraternity (solidarity)

21

and civic virtue, rather than other basic elements of democracy, such as individual freedom, the republican Machiavellian conception of the body politic lost much force during the long period of liberal hegemony in the West.

Despite all precedents, a single and robust historical current of continuous theorising about man as citizen thus cannot be identified. Nevertheless, from the Renaissance onwards a conception arose of political man as a citizen, which influenced the full-blown version known to us.

The theory of a universally shared dignity in all human beings having substantial political consequences has its roots in some late Renaissance thinkers, such as the founders of *ius gentium* Francisco de Vitoria and Hugo Grotius. Yet, it was in the work of Thomas Hobbes and Samuel Pufendorf where it was put forward in a manner that was bound to be decisive, duly re-cast, in the doctrines of the American and French revolutionists. Thus Hobbes' *De Cive* of 1642, assumed the universal political sovereignty of each and everyone, in other words, the universal political dignity of man, his or her capacity to share in the polity and to be the natural subject of rights. For Hobbes, however, the solution to the problem of order produced by his vision of an original state of generalized and fragmented sovereignty (as a historical point of departure) had to find the well-known answer he was later to develop in the *Leviathan* and the *Behemoth*. The Hobbesian need for the sword and the obedience to a supreme sovereign, however, should not blind us to the fact that he built his political philosophy on the basis of a radical and universal conception of all men as free and equal subjects of rights.

For his part, Samuel Pufendorf, in his work *On the Duty of Man and Citizen according to Natural Law*, published three decades later in 1673, reached somewhat similar conclusions, since, as Hobbes, he started from a theory of self-preservation. Unlike Hobbes, Pufendorf, however, emphasized the general need for moral standards in human intercourse, not necessarily imposed by an all-powerful monarch or arbiter. He went further than Hobbes in his emphasis on the citizens' need for sociability and developed his immensely influential notion that to every right of the citizen corresponds a duty to the polity. Until then, classical thinkers from Cicero to Machiavelli had given priority to the citizens' obligations to their fatherland or their polity, not to their rights. Later the emphasis would shift to rights, especially in liberal thinking. Only much later, with the rise of the welfare state, a balanced view of rights and duties – almost in the spirit of the by then nearly forgotten Pufendorf - would reappear. Neither Hobbes nor Pufendorf developed the liberal theory of the citizen, but both, in their similarly named treatises *On the citizen* and *On the Duty of Man and Citizen*, established the theoretical ground for a universal consideration of all members of a political community as morally, and therefore politically, equal and autonomous individuals similarly entitled to be considered sovereign.

There is a subtle thread leading from the worldly, secular affirmation of man's dignity during the Renaissance – in Pico della Mirandola's 1486 *Oratio de hominis dignitate* or in Machiavelli's *Discourses* – to Pufendorf's vision of natural law, via the earlier efforts of Vitoria and Grotius to universalize that condition to all mankind. What had first been an ontological and moral discovery that had to be philosophically asserted and explained, soon became a legal and political affirmation with important consequences for a conception of society. Yet, no thinker or school managed to find a viable solution. Hobbes' illiberal proposals seemed to negate his initial conceptions about the natural equality and humanity of all. Order mattered more to him than liberty. (In fact, Hobbes thought that whatever freedom was to be had was a by-product of order.) Others remained lost in a quagmire of good intentions based on the abstractions of natural law and on the innate sociability of human beings. Only the later and vigorous rise of liberal thought would eventually allow the establishment of a viable modern society based on a plausible theory of citizenship.

1.2. The One-Dimensional Citizen and the Nation State

The history of the rise of citizenship, both as a conception and as a legal and political institution, has often been told. I shall not repeat it here. All that must be recalled in the present context is that with John Locke a theory of the citizen arose that was destined to dominate the more democratic of the modern nations until the outbreak of the Great War in 1914. According to it, the citizen is the subject of a state and a member of a political community. A citizen is any individual member of that community in a given territory and under one single constitution and government. As such, he or she is deemed to possess certain freedoms and substantial rights, such as the right to enjoy whatever goods and properties he or she legally owns, or to express whatever opinions the citizen wishes to make known. The generalization of that 'classical' condition of citizenship did not extend to other levels of the citizen's existence: she or he may be rich or poor; possess greater or lesser life chances in terms of education or work, or indeed gender.

The rise of this conception was simultaneous with, if not preceded by, certain historical processes, which, likewise do not call for a detailed description here. Some democratic theorists themselves, such as Tocqueville, were keen to describe their social origin and thus presented citizenship not only normatively but also as a result of a historical process within a given civilization. Tocqueville showed how citizenship naturally arose out of the structures of North American colonial society with its several immigrant collectivities, the pluralism of religious churches and sects, and the consolidation of self-governing communities at great distance from the metropolis. Citizenship was for them the common clay of a varied and plural society. He also showed how another polity, likewise made up of citizens but with a quite different tradition, arose out of the previous undermining of the feudal order by the French monarch, the imposition of a single system of law, and other factors favourable to its development. The two conceptions of citizenship – the Anglo-Saxon and the French - were thus seen more as a result of distinct and alternative historical processes than as the result of abstract theories.

This sociological tradition –with its Tocquevillian roots - has continued until our days. Thus, Norbert Elias saw the production of citizens as a part of the 'process of civilization' in which the establishment of good manners of social intercourse, no longer restricted to a caste or aristocratic class, played a crucial role. In the West

23

there has been a long historical trend which may be identified as the long 'socio-genesis' of the citizenry. Elias was not altogether explicit about the intimate relationship between manners and citizenship, but the causal connection is clear enough in his work, as is his more subtle analysis of the process of self-distancing (and its contrary attitude, 'engagement') which is an essential property inherent in a truly modern individual, a citizen by definition. The individual citizen's personal aims and ambitions, privacy and intentions, can only be promoted under modern conditions. These allow the citizen to distance him- or herself from tribe, caste, and class, and to mind his or her own business, untroubled by others or by the state. A *Gesellschaft* environment is necessary for citizens to thrive as such. *Gemeinschaften* (communities) may survive and even thrive in the modern world, with their intense personal commitments, loyalties and engagements, but only under the anonymous, egalitarian and impersonal rules of the *Gesellschaft* are truly modern citizens to be found. (Once again, the abyss that separates ancient citizenship from its modern version is evident.)

The first citizens produced by the Western 'process of civilization', to make use of Norbert Elias' notion, were one-dimensional political animals. Thus, the new modern polity granted them a narrow, though vital, series of legal and political rights that could be understood as one single set of possibilities. Citizens were one-dimensional political animals in the sense that certain other dimensions of their lives as members of society were not contemplated by the liberal and individualistic law of the land. The tensions created by this one-sided development of citizenship soon produced a massive critical reaction among those who discovered what were soon to be defined by the radicals on the left as the inner contradictions of the bourgeois dominated world, born out of the early development of liberal democracy.

Not only did rich citizens, or educated ones, enjoy vastly better life chances – in terms of class, status, and power - than poor, uneducated ones, but also the law itself often excluded the latter from the very status of citizens that the new liberal universe granted them as a matter of principle. Reformism and the continuous expansion of the franchise in several key liberal and constitutional countries partly solved the problem. But not sufficiently. The bitter criticism (anarchist, socialist and even radical liberal) against the 'bourgeois state' was directed at the massive contradiction between rights and real life-chances. The Marxian critique of the democratic, industrial and bourgeois world became the most rigorous and well grounded and the most efficient of all criticisms. In retrospect, we are able today to view very favourably the great moral depth of the invention of political citizenship, as established in a period roughly covering the years between the Glorious Revolution in England and the American and French Revolutions. Yet, it is also true that, as a one-dimensional conception, it remained manifestly unsatisfactory for many serious rational observers from very diverse schools of thought.

The doctrines such as bolshevism or fascism that, sooner or later, condemned one-dimensional citizenship wholesale and saw no hope at all in its institutionalization in the modern polities, were themselves bound to fall into the state of barbarism that would eliminate all possibilities of growth and evolution for the initial conception of man as citizen. In other words, totalitarian doctrines that complained about

24

the poverty or emptiness of the (modern classical) conception of the citizen were themselves to blame, and not liberal philosophy, for the downfall of that much superior conception. They destroyed citizenship.

The socialist (and especially the Marxian) critique was well grounded, but many of its followers continued to condemn the 'bourgeois state' even when it was decidedly reformist. Some even castigated, over many decades during the 20th century, all manner of socialist reformism as a treason to their principles or as an expression of 'collaboration with the class enemy', to recall the now stale language of the period. Such an approach blinded a large part of the left-wing critique to the real possibilities for change embodied in the liberal conception.

The conservative and at times reactionary critique was no less blind than radical thinking to the real limitations of classical, one-dimensional citizenship. Although Alexis de Tocqueville should not be included in the conservative tradition without qualifications, his initial analysis of some pernicious consequences of democracy for the flourishing of truly free, creative and distinctive individuals are at the root of that critique. The highly influential theory of mass-society (including the process of 'massification', the alleged rise of 'mass man', and the development of mass-politics and mass-culture) stemmed from the notion that liberal democratic society, though geared in principle to the institution of liberty and citizenship, produced in the end un-free, unimaginative and manipulable individuals. The theory was completed a decade before the Second World War when José Ortega coined the expression 'mass man' and Karl Mannheim that of 'mass society'. Its ramifications in several directions and its considerable intellectual authority and cultural influence would last for decades.[1] The disillusioned conservative interpretation of citizenship, embodied in the mass-society conception of modernity, fuelled the sceptical mood prevalent among many analysts of the modern world. In the 21st century, it continues to inspire much criticism of crucial phenomena such as the political culture generated by the mass media, which is seen as inimical to the consolidation of a free and responsible citizenry.

At one point the conservative doctrine of the degradation of the citizen into a mere 'mass man' crucially influenced and distorted the left-wing critique of modernity put forward by intellectual movements such as that of the Frankfurt school. Thus, 'one-dimensional man' as described by an emblematic Frankfurt school treatise - very widely read at a crucial moment of Western democratic discontent in the sixties and early seventies - not only corresponded to the afore-mentioned 'mass man' conception of the modern un-free citizen, but was also a caricature of the 'one dimensional citizen' prevalent until then at the political and legal levels. Norbert Elias' notion of the solitary *homo clausus,* also generated by late modern society in the fullness of the modern civilization process, was another expression of the same malaise (Elias 1970: 119, 125, 130-132, 135). The independent, assertive, creative

1   For a detailed account cf. S. Giner (1976)

citizen created by the liberal revolution had become manipulable, gullible, vulgar and lonely.

1.3. The Multi-Dimensional Citizen

For quite a long time, one-dimensional or classical liberal citizenship was circum-scribed to a few countries. In America itself liberal citizenship was still undergoing expansion in the 1960's when blacks and other, formerly excluded peoples were gaining access to voting and other rights in many areas.. Fascism in Italy and Ger-many, and Stalinist Communism, wiped it out for a substantial period of time in Europe, while countries such as Portugal, Greece and Spain reinstated it only in the 1970s. Its uneven expansion has nevertheless continued until the present day.

It was under the very pressure created by the obvious shortcomings of its tradi-tional one-dimensional version that citizenship grew in several directions. By doing so, it transformed itself into a far more complex political and moral institution, more adequate to the dignity of the human beings it was intended to uphold. It should be obvious then that critical analyses of liberal, one-dimensional citizenship, interesting though some of them were, failed to understand and predict the historical growth and transformation of the liberal citizen into a multi-dimensional one.

In 1949, T. H. Marshall was the first sociologist to view modern citizenship as a historical process undergoing several stages of development as it deepened its roots within a few national societies. He argued that citizenship possessed three dimen-sions, civil, political and social. Legal institutions first protected civil citizenship – assuring the right to property and guaranteeing some basic freedoms for many indi-viduals. Political citizenship, for its part, grew apace with the development of de-mocracy. Finally, social citizenship extended with the growth of the welfare state, which further integrated most citizens into the wider society by making education, economic opportunities, health care, and other services available to most people within each state. Contemplating the process from an essentially British perspective, Marshall (1973) saw in the 18th, 19th and 20th centuries the three successive moments of that development. His reflections meant the transition, within the citizenship doctrine, from a one-dimensional to a three-dimensional conception of citizenship.

Much has been written about Marshall's seminal essay. Most criticism has ac-cepted his 'developmental' interpretation while often refining his idea of the differ-ent stages, each wider than the former, through which citizenship has passed in a number of Western countries. Few have noticed that, as a welfare-state theorist, he was too generous in his appreciation of the capacity of the liberal order to undermine social class all by itself. (Contrary to his main thesis, citizenship, in some specific senses, may generate new forms of class inequality.) Despite Marshall's consider-able faith in the social democratic reformism of the post-war British Labour Party, his approach unveiled a tendency that was mostly confirmed by the known facts in a number of countries.

In the early 21st century, it is impossible to maintain that the historical process of the unfolding of citizenship has been smooth or even similar in Western countries. In some countries such as the United States, Great Britain and a few others, vigorous conservative attempts to reinstate a minimalist state and market forces, and to revert to 'civil' and 'political' citizenships at the expense of 'social' citizenship, succeeded for some time in arresting the further development of economic redistribution and social justice through the welfare state, though never dismantling it. Eastern European countries had already enjoyed a noticeable development of welfare provisions and social equality under Soviet dictatorships, and only later were able to enjoy the civil liberties and political advantages of liberal, or even civil, citizenship. In other words, the process varied everywhere. Not only did it not always follow the Marshallian sequence, but in some important cases it even followed a reverse path. (To complicate things further, welfare states differed from each other in many ways, something which has inspired exercises, often more scholastic than really enlightening, in public welfare taxonomy.)

Without wishing to enter into a discussion of the several waves of citizenship expansion, a considerable degree of consensus exists around the notion that a fuller institutionalization of citizenship in a modern democratic society entails, at least:

- (a) A set of legal rights: personal security, freedom of expression, equality before justice, rights of property according to the law;
- (b) Another set of political rights, such as voting rights, or the right of political representation;
- (c) Certain so-called social rights, represented by pensions, health care, and subsidies from the public services to the citizens in need of them;
- (d) Participation rights, as established by law, in citizens' councils, industrial co-determination, and other circumstances, in which diverse stake holders have a right to voice their legitimate needs;
- (e) Ethnic or other community rights[2], from aborigines in Australia and North American Indians to European stateless nations –or even strongly distinct regions- within the European Union of nation states, (These collectives, historically, linguistically, or otherwise defined, demand recognition in strict terms of citizenship into the larger political community.) The basic kinds of rights (and corresponding duties, such as military service, tax obligations, school attendance, and others) could be grouped differently.

By looking at the diverse criteria available today in the literature, one may perhaps accept that there are essentially five sufficiently distinct kinds of citizenship rights and duties: legal, political, solidarity, communal and cultural.

- *Legal rights,* correspond to what is often described as 'civil' rights. They cover rights such as privacy and ownership and establish duties such as the payment of taxes.

---

2   For current classifications see Isin & Turner (2002) Chapters 2, 4, and 6.

- *Political rights*, not only include the traditional rights of voting, public demonstration, and running for office or holding it, but also those of promoting social movements in civil society – besides political parties - to achieve legitimate aims.
- *Solidarity rights* are those that allow fraternity to flourish. The right to receive help from the public sphere is one of them, as is the right of citizens to organize in favour of the common good, or of any issue that they freely deem necessary to confront for the common good and general interest of the people.
- *Communal rights* are those that allow members of a social unit to participate in the decisions that affect their life and orientation. Collective bargaining between employers and employees, councils of urban dwellers and co-determination in the firm, are examples.
- *Cultural rights*. Ethnic, language, belief and other cultural rights within a plural society need not be in opposition and contradiction to the universalistic orientation of citizenship. Citizenship is the guarantee that the citizenry may group in any form they wish, as long as that is not harmful to the common good.

1.4. Advanced Citizenship and the Republican Citizen

Republicanism is a conception of the political community with very old historical roots. Yet, only relatively recently a number of theorists, as well as many concerned citizens, have made substantial efforts to consolidate it as an alternative to other democratic conceptions of the polity. The proponents of republicanism have sharply distinguished it from most forms of communitarianism, on the one hand, and from mainstream liberalism, on the other. Further distinctions, as between republicanism and traditional democratic socialism, have also been drawn.

An account of contemporary republicanism is not called for in the present context. It shares some features with liberalism (Dagger 1997), first and foremost the emphasis on personal freedom and individual initiative, though fewer with communitarianism. Its main emphasis is upon fraternity or solidarity - hence its proximity to redistribution and social justice - and upon its vision of the citizen as a participating, active political animal, inspired by a certain degree of civic virtue and a sense of responsibility for the common good, as developed in the public sphere or *res publica*[3], by a process of civic deliberation. These elements are essential for a republican conception of the good society.

What is striking about this conception, over and beyond any sympathy one may feel towards it, is its affinity to the mature, multi-dimensional interpretation of the modern citizen. I would not go so far as to claim that all friends of the described 'advanced' or mature citizen are implicit and unconscious republicans. I limit myself

---

3   '*Res Publica*' in the old Ciceronian sense of public sphere or 'matters of common concern' for all citizens, not in the modern sense of 'republic'.

to point out the 'elective affinities' that exist between the two, that is, between doctrinal or theoretical republican citizenship and what may be called a fuller, or advanced, citizenship. The latter's demands for the implementation of solidarity rights and policies, especially towards those who are underprivileged or 'precarious' citizens, coincide with those of republicanism (Moreno 2000). The same can be said of its emphasis on participation rights in industry, communal life, the public conversation and the political sphere. These coincidences are undeniable facts. The burden of proof that they are not lies not on republican theory. It is those who are sceptical about the intimate links between republicanism and advanced multi-dimensional citizenship who must show that they are separate and wholly independent from each other.

There may be elements in some of the schools of thought into which republicanism can be divided that are irrelevant to such affinities: constitutional patriotism – in so far as it is a republican attitude - and civic patriotism come to mind. Yet, there are others, which are crucial to both advanced citizenship and republicanism, that warrant the 'convergence' position adopted here, according to which the rise of advanced citizenship and republicanism are intimately linked, indeed mutually dependent.

The common ground between theoretical and real-life advanced republicanism extends to another feature. Both advanced citizenship theory and republican practices in modern democracies consider that rights and obligations are the result of conflict. Both stem from a 'conflict theory position'. For the advanced conception of citizenship, certain rights may exist as the 'natural rights' of human beings as citizens, but all rights are also understood as conquered. Rights are implemented only after battles. Vindications, claims and counterclaims have generated them in a given political community. From the electoral franchise of the working and lower classes to the incorporation of all races or women into de body politic, and later of several significant minorities (homosexuals, for instance), all rights and corresponding duties stem from social, cultural, political and economic movements (Turner 1986) and their corresponding struggles.

Rights may stem from abstract principles in some significant cases, but they are always the result of history, of human beings in action, frequently against each other or struggling over scarce or restricted goods. Rights are rights won. Emancipation, freedom from domination, equality, moral recognition, all are historical victories, not always easily won. In some democracies, struggles involving rights of citizenship have led to civil wars, in others, conquered civic or political rights have been the outcome of very serious efforts by different social movements involving a fair amount of violence. (The black people's right to gain access to all public spaces, the women's vote, equal pay for women and men, are just three well known examples). In some cases, revolts against exclusion from rights have been fairly bloodless and yet also very tense and protracted. From Australian aborigines to North and South American Indians, incorporation of so-called indigenous peoples into the wider democratic polity has been the result of a struggle or a series of struggles. Slavery would not have been abolished without the abolitionist movement that preceded it.

Caste in India was eroded only because of a struggle for national independence and citizenship.

Occasional coincidences of republican universal citizenship with other doctrines – either communitarian or liberal - should not blur the picture. It would be pretentious to claim that there are no areas of overlap between the three great interpretations of contemporary democracy, liberalism, communitarianism and republicanism. Yet, whatever the common ground shared with other orientations, republicans, as con-flict-oriented theorists though certainly peace-loving democrats, have stressed the conflict component in the constitution of liberty more so than anyone else.

Civic virtue itself must be understood as a result of a political socialization proc-ess in which demands for a certain amount of public moral restraint combine with demands for active participation in public life. The latter can only be fulfilled if a considerable number of citizens are active, not passive, members of the polity. Re-publicans do not imagine their citizens to be saints. Hence the measured and circum-scribed sense in which the notion of civic virtue - responsible participation in the public realm - is used in their language. By the same token, however, active ('virtu-ous') citizens can neither be fanatic militants nor professional party members. Many social movements, altruistic organizations and civil society associations are, in this sense, implicit republicans (Giner & Montagut 2005). So are many of those who voice their critical opinions with due independence, or who seek to participate in deliberative democracy, or at least to participate and have their voice heard in the public debate.

The assertion that voluntary associations in civil society are a dimension of re-publican practices hides no desire whatsoever to reduce and assimilate the so-called 'Third Sector', now so powerfully significant, into contemporary republicanism. Yet, it would be quite wrong for republican theory to take any serious distance from it. For republicanism, civic altruism is of the essence. An affinity with voluntary associations, altruistically oriented towards solving certain social problems and the mitigation of social evils in the public sphere, is an obvious feature of republican-ism. Such voluntary associations involve the public practice of civic virtue. They are not party-political, but they represent the presence of the private in the public sphere. Non-party, public concerns that manifest themselves in altruistic action are thus an expression of civic virtue[4]. The fact that most are far from morally perfect, or that some lend themselves to the enticements of corruption, political manipulation or slackness in their alleged dedication to altruism, does not invalidate this assertion. Above all, a republican view of advanced citizenship is neither utopian nor naïve. It measures the quality of democracy by the presence of altruism, solidarity and good public behaviour in a given polity but, once again, does not equate civic virtue with saintliness.

---

4   I have called it *lo privado publico*, see Giner (1994); for a Italian equivalent see. Donati (2004)

The rise of advanced, multi-dimensional citizenship has gone hand-in-hand with certain forms of peaceful civil-society activism, precisely because rights are won, and civil and other rights are created and developed through struggles, many of them fortunately highly civilized, though certainly not always easy for those involved in them.

The growth of advanced citizenship has not been smooth anywhere. Moreover, its full consolidation has encountered serious difficulties even in those countries whose democratic political order, constitution and culture seemed to be most favourable to its flourishing. Class-inequality, the 'corporate society' and mass politics through media manipulation, are just three of the obvious contemporary foes of republican citizenship. None of those forces is sufficient to completely arrest in its tracks the consolidation of full citizenship, but no critical account could be complete without reference to them.

The structure of society entails that there are parallel social structures of freedom and of citizenship. The dialectic between class (a main feature of the social structure) and citizenship is not straight forward, or zero-sum. The consolidation of a society of citizens also allows the growth of new social classes and privileges if it is not accompanied by fair but vigorous redistribution policies. Laissez faire policies by themselves may foster the growth of new barriers of privilege.

The rise of a corporate society – bureaucratization, corporatism, the predominance of firms, trade unions, monopolies, oligopolies - breeds a vast network of organized interests that openly runs counter to the agile, fluid and open nature of a society with a minimally empowered citizenry, based on a minimum of deliberative and solidarity practices. The democratic deficit from which a number of societies suffer stems largely from the disproportionate role played by lobbies and organized interests in the public decision process.

Mass-culture and the mass media add a new dimension to the public sphere, the arena where a truly deliberative and republican democracy may flourish. The manipulation of public opinion and the simplification of complex issues by the media are one of the great challenges facing the progress of a free, conscious and well-educated citizenry.[5]

These developments are serious hindrances to the consolidation of a truly advanced citizenship. Admitting their enormous power and influence will allow any pessimist to consider the future of full citizenship a dark one. Yet, the admission of equally powerful trends towards the growth and deepening of citizenship – at least in key regions of the world such as contemporary Europe- is also based on hard evidence.

The task of the analytical observer is to study the arena in which the complex struggle now takes place between a vibrant, demanding and democratic citizenry and the contemporary forces that lead to new forms of domination and un-freedom.

---

5   There is a dearth of republican theory facing the problems that mass-culture and the mass media pose for the practice and advancement of civic virtue or advanced citizenship.

1.5. Cosmopolitan Citizenship and its Discontents

Citizenship is expansive. First confined to the nation state, it progressively sank its roots among all the members of the political community, incorporating class after class, region after region, profession after profession, in a process that was neither smooth nor easy or identical for each element involved. More often than not, the trend towards an always-wider citizenry eroded linguistic, racial or cultural communities. It also inevitably generated bitter resistance to laws and measures that were often unfair and occasionally cruel to each distinct community affected by such expansion. The deviations and aberrations of forcefully imposed republicanism (from 17th century Puritanism and French revolutionary Jacobinism to 20th century Stalinism) are well-known and unpalatable memories. (In fact, they entailed the obliteration of genuine republicanism itself.) The history that has led to the incipient establishment of advanced citizenship dawning today is not entirely pleasant.

The modern expansive wave of citizenship has not stopped at the borders of the states in which it was born. It has begun to overflow old frontiers. This already began to happen when citizenship was still sinking its roots within its own polities, when it had not yet completed its course within them. Many blacks in the USA, for instance, were still fighting for their rights as citizens in the 1960's and the abolition of *apartheid* in South Africa came much later; while in Europe, as mentioned before, some countries like Portugal, Greece and Spain, definitely freed themselves from dictatorship only in the mid 1970's. In the early 21st century, important ethnic minorities in Western Europe (France, November 2005) were angrily expressing their frustration at the lack of *de facto* recognition as full citizens. Examples could be multiplied. The outcome of the trend remains uncertain, so that the prediction of an unstoppable current of democratic incorporation into citizenship – both inside and beyond state borders - cannot possibly be made with complete confidence. Not only are traditional barriers still in place in many countries, but also the obstacles to a much fuller citizenship for certain categories of citizens don't seem to recede.

Nevertheless, the transformation of national into cosmopolitan citizenship is not just a pious thought or, as in its early formulations from St Augustine to Immanuel Kant and Karl Marx, a well-argued moral and philosophical ideal. Current globalization trends entail modifications and reformulations of institutions of democratic governance such as citizenship (Brodie 2004) in the direction of trans-national laws, regulations and provisions. Moreover, the realization that the national state can no longer be considered the perfect guardian of the rights of its citizens has generated, especially in the decades after the Second World War, a series of movements towards the denationalization of citizenship and the consolidation of a truly cosmopolitan citizenship, grounded on the conviction that civil rights are universal and not bounded by the limits of caste, faith or race. The United Nations' declarations of universal rights were a turning point in this process, as was the creation of the International Court of Justice at The Hague in 1945. The same can be said of the establishment of significant, though unofficial, international tribunals of human rights, stemming from civil society initiatives, and the creation and constant growth of respected citizens' organizations such as Amnesty International.

To be certain, the trans-national protection and defence of rights ought not to be confused with civic participation and active citizenship and the rights of members of cultural or ethnic communities to be recognized as such. They are essentially different, but they are also closely related. The one presupposes the other. Active, multi-dimensional, cosmopolitan citizenship cannot thrive without the proper institutional, legal, and sufficiently denationalized framework.

The growth of cosmopolitan citizenship is still incipient. Yet, it is also undeniable. We do not know whether it will fully triumph in the end. In several parts of the world, not the least in contemporary Europe, it has made substantial progress. Yet, even in that part of the world, neo-tribal warfare and ethnic-religious hatred in the Balkans unleashed the fury of fratricidal warfare at end of the 20th century. Hideous crimes against humanity were committed. Today, powerful democratic nations, under the fear of fanatical terrorism, behave undemocratically abroad and violate basic human rights. Echoes of the imperialistic and undemocratic misbehaviour of the Athenians toward other sister democratic city-states during the Peloponnesian War have not died out. This tragic contradiction, forever recorded by Thucydides, was repeated in our own time. Under such conditions, the flourishing of world fraternity and world citizenship seems very hard to achieve. They look perilously like the once distant abstractions of Kant's plans for a perpetual peace among civilized peoples, peoples of citizens, not vassals.

As these reflections come to a close, I wish to remind the reader that in this chapter I have not wished to enter into the philosophically very significant issue of the coming of a hypothetical state of 'plenitude' as regards citizenship. Perhaps the current and welcome proliferation of citizen's rights, entitlements and attributes to the entire citizenry – though unevenly and certainly not in all countries - may bring about a situation in which a new, unexpected, turning point in the history of citizenship is reached. Historically, the fullness of any civilizational process – be it feudalism, monarchical absolutism, communism, or any other political order- has always led to a serious crisis of the system. My own suspicions about this hypothetical reversal of fortunes cannot be developed here. Especially considering that so much is still to be done until the poor, the downtrodden, the socially disadvantaged and the unfairly excluded are duly integrated into the community of the free and equal (Giner 2005). Yet, considering the possible future difficulties of a full citizenship under the inflationary weight of its own critical mass of duties and rights may one day not be an idle philosophical exercise.

All we may witness today, in the midst of current difficulties, is some palpable progress towards effective cosmopolitan citizenship. Its supporters have become more sophisticated in some respects: while subscribing to the universalism that is inherent in any notion of multi-dimensional citizenship, they have realized that it does not necessarily have to be inimical to certain expressions of communitarianism. Human beings cannot live without communitarian ties. (Even the thinkers of the brotherhood of man, of the universal rights of all human beings and the desirable and necessary denationalization of citizenship, see themselves as members of the community of humankind, of an ideal species of detribalized rational animals[6].) It is in the active and constant search for this harmony between our legitimate and necessary loyalties and identifications on the one hand, and our universally shared conditions with all other humans, on the other, that the successful destiny of citizenship lies in the future. When humans remain radically apart from each other, independent identity makes us poorer and more dangerous to each other. Yet, when we share our common humanity as political and moral animals, difference and identity turn us into decent human beings.

6   *Pace* arguments to the contrary, such as Walzer (1994)

2. Duties of Union Citizenship in a Stable, More Democratic European Union – A Liberal Contractualist Defence

Andreas Follesdal

"A lady asked Dr. [Benjamin] Franklin Well Doctor what have we got a republic or a monarchy. A republic replied the Doctor, if you can keep it."

James McHenry, representative of Maryland at the Constitutional Convention in Philadelphia, 17 September 1787

2.1. Introduction

Ever since Union citizenship was introduced in the Maastricht Treaty, its content and role has been opaque and challenged by scholars[7]. The Constitutional Treaty for Europe confirmed that Union Citizenship provided little clarification. Union citizenship is not meant to replace national citizenship, but is held by every national of a Member State:

"Citizens of the Union shall enjoy the rights and be subject to the duties provided for in the Constitution. They shall have:

(a) the right to move and reside freely within the territory of the Member States;

(b) the right to vote and to stand as candidates in elections to the European Parliament and in municipal elections in their Member State of residence, under the same conditions as nationals of that State;

(c) the right to enjoy, in the territory of a third country in which the Member State of which they are nationals is not represented, the protection of the diplomatic and consular authorities of any Member State on the same conditions as the nationals of that State;

(d) the right to petition the European Parliament, to apply to the European Ombudsman, and to address the institutions and advisory bodies of the Union in any of the Constitution's languages and to obtain a reply in the same language. These rights shall be exercised in accordance with the conditions and limits defined by the Constitution and by the measures adopted thereunder.
"

Article 1-10 2 Council of the European Union 2004

---

7   Indeed, some hold that they were already part of the *acquis communaitaire* before Maastricht. (La Torre 1998, Meehan 1993,Wiener 1998).

Beyond this somewhat anaemic list of rights, duties are still barely mentioned, and the point of the office of citizenship is still obscure. Crucial questions are left unanswered. What should be required of citizens and on what grounds? For instance, what need, if any, is there to insist that they share European values and objectives, and respect diverse national values, cultures and histories? May Union citizens be required to learn about, respect and even be socialized to, the facts, beliefs and common European values, and each other's 'national culture'? Should they be made to accept the values and objectives stated in the Preamble?

"the cultural, religious and humanist inheritance of Europe,... CONVINCED that, while remaining proud of their own national identities and history, the peoples of Europe are determined to transcend their former divisions and, united ever more closely, to forge a common destiny," (Preamble)

A political theory of Union Citizenship has little to build on in order answer such questions about the most defensible role and contents of the office of Union citizenship. The following remarks present and defend some components of such an account.[8] Union citizenship is interpreted as one means to provide much needed assurance and trust in a multi-level political order with democratic procedures. This fits with the received view among scholars, that Union Citizenship was introduced in an attempt to create a closer bond between Europeans and the Union institutions.[9]

Section 1 sketches the increased need for complex forms of trust among ever more interdependent Europeans. Section 2 draws on the literature on Assurance Games to explain one important role of citizens' socialization to certain civic duties. Section 3 identifies some elements of such civic duties in the EU on the basis of a distinct Liberal Contractualist normative theory. Section 4 contrasts this account with the views of Habermas and David Miller.

2.2. Citizenship and Trust in Multilevel Political Orders

Few defend the present list of rights as sufficient for a conception of Union citizenship. Indeed, some critics observe that the package of rights is too meagre even as a PR stunt (Preuss 1995, Laffan 1996. Weiler 1996). Defenders may rebut that a full account must also include the whole legal and constitutional order laid out in the Constitutional Treaty, with the Charter of Fundamental Rights (now in Part Two of

---

8   Other answers, largely complementary to the present one, include Meehan 1993, and a well-grounded historical account in Wiener 1998.

9   The inclusion of Union Citizenship in the EC Treaty apparently came from a Memorandum of the Spanish Government presented to the Intergovernmental Conference on Political Union in 1990. (Shaw 1997a, Weiler 1996). The Commission also claimed in *Opinion October 21 1990* that a European citizenship was necessary to strengthen democratic legitimacy. Cf. Closa 1992.

the Constitution), and other rights scattered in the Constitutional Treaty.[10] However, many of these rights are not exclusive to Union citizens, and others are exercised as national citizens.

When it comes to duties, the Constitutional Treaty only mentions that they exist, without specification.[11] This temporary silence is understandable given the governments' aim to foster citizens' affective attachment to the Union. Some scholars question the need and wisdom of creating such attachments in the first place. Yet, a political order cannot be sustained unless citizens have duties and civic virtues in addition to rights. Every political order must foster a

> 'sense of community' and [with] ... institutions and practices strong enough and widespread enough to assure, for a 'long' time, dependable expectations of 'peaceful change' among its population" (Deutsch et al. 1957, 5.)

What should those duties and civic virtues be? The following remarks explore the implications of an understanding of the role of Union Citizenship as an important trust-building mechanism for European integration.

In this view, Union citizenship should be fostered, and be built on certain shared civic values and duties, i.e. "some thin but effectual sense of community ".[12]

Such a sense of community is sorely needed in the European Union, as in other multi-level political orders; especially with the increased use of majority and qualified majority decisions.

2.2.1. Multi-Level Political Orders

For our purposes, a federation is a political order where competences are constitutionally split between sub-units and central authorities. The Constitutional Treaty would have enhanced these features of the EU, since it specified more carefully the exclusive competences of the Union institutions and the member states. The EU has features clearly at odds with 'confederal' models: Central legislation has direct effect, not only over Member States but also over citizens. Decisions by qualified majority voting (QMV) in the Union bodies bind the citizenry and Member States, even when they vote against. This is not to deny that there are also confederal ele-

---

10 For instance, the right to elect Members to the European Parliament (Art. I-20.2; I-46), which in turn elect the Commission President (Art. I-27) and can censure the Commission; the powers of the European Council (Art. I-22), and the Council of Ministers (I Art. I-23) enjoyed by accountable government officials of the Member States; and through the role of national parliaments to apply the Principle of subsidiarity (Protocol 2), and protections against one's government breach of the values of the Union, Art. I-2 (Art I-59).

11 "Citizens of the Union shall enjoy the rights conferred by this Treaty and shall be subject to the duties imposed thereby." EC Treaty Art 17.2, cf. Laffan 1996, Shaw 1997b, Bauböck 1999, 38.

12 MacCormick 1997, cf. Weiler 1996, Guild 1996.

ments, but the federal features should make us heed some lessons from comparative federalism about multi-level systems (Follesdal 2005).

These political orders are typically marked by higher levels of deep or 'constitutional' conflicts among groups. Indeed, conflicts within or among previous unitary states often gave rise to such multi-level solutions rather than complete separation or centralisation.[13] In addition, the division of powers among levels in their constitutional structure is inherently unstable and contested with risks of both complete centralization and secession. Many scholars point to the need for widely shared dispositions among citizens and elites to maintain such political orders over time. Citizens need a shared sense of belonging to two political communities as citizens of two commonwealths[14:] i.e., loyalty to members of their own sub-unit, and an 'overarching loyalty' to other citizens in the political order.

I submit that European institutions must seek to foster such dispositions. In particular, these dispositions must alleviate certain kinds of mistrust likely to arise in the European setting. The particular needs for trust have developed over time, as new multi-level arrangements were introduced to address new common problems among states seeking to prevent nationalistic wars and common decisions by majority rule.

2.2.2. European Institutions as Creators and Consumers of Trust

The institutions of what now is the European Union were in part deliberately created to resolve several collective action problems. They sought to provide trust, and thereby both acknowledged and reshaped European citizens' and politicians' ends and preferences. From the post-war beginnings, these arrangements were typical of 'coming together' federal arrangements to secure common interests by pooling sovereignty. One express goal of the 1952 European Coal and Steel Community (ECSC) was to provide assurance that even hostile states could not pose serious threats to neighbours, by putting crucial resources under common command:

> "The solidarity in production thus established will make it plain that any war between France and Germany becomes not merely unthinkable, but materially impossible." (Schuman 1950)

The ECSC would reduce mistrust about Germany's future actions by publicly shifting the opportunity space and payoffs for agents with aggressive ends, and by fostering and supporting agents' peaceful ends: "the leaven from which may grow a wider and deeper community between countries long opposed to one another by sanguinary divisions." (ibid). The ECSC thus facilitated certain contingent strategies of cooperation. It acknowledged fear of some agents' aggressive ends and sought to shape incentives and socialisation efforts in response to possible aggressive strate-

---

13 Lemco 1991, Franck 1968, Linz 1999, McKay 2001, McKay 2004, Simeon & Conway 2001, Filippov, Ordeshook, & Shvetsova 2004; Norman 1994, Stepan 1999.

14 Hume 1882, MacCormick 1995.

gies. The ECSC treaty enhanced trust concerning the others' cooperative strategies and their cooperative ends regarding peace, while simultaneously acknowledging that fears of aggression were not unfounded.

The ECSC and later treaties also addressed collective action problems among actors with shared preferences for a common market that would secure economic expansion, low unemployment and rising standards of living. Defection in Prisoner's dilemma situations had to be prevented since each government would have a dominant strategy to protect its own industries from competition. Monitored and enforced treaties provide means for credible commitments and reduced risks of suckers' payoff by making such commitments conditional on general compliance through ratification of monitored agreements.[15]

These common market treaties thus facilitate cooperation by reducing the incentives to free ride. Such arrangements enhance trust in others' future compliance by sanctioning non-compliance. Consider the four freedoms. If only some member states maintain a free market while other states hinder competition, the compliers stand to lose whatever benefits of free trade they had hoped for. This is of course especially risky if the regulations - even when generally complied with - threaten the member states' capacity to maintain social policies or other vital interests of citizens (Scharpf 1997a, Pierson 1998). In such cases, general compliance can obviously not be expected on the basis of guaranteed benefits for all, but must instead require that participants trust each other. This, in turn, requires the ability to commit oneself and convince others of this.

Other sources of mistrust are common to such *'coming together'* agreements and *holding together* federations among groups marked by strong cleavages. Common decisions pose great risks for minorities who must trust that the majority will not threaten their central interests. Common decisions may still be preferable, but only with safeguards. There are at least two forms of protection that render common decision mechanisms trustworthy. One is similar to individual human rights entrusted to an independent judiciary, which protects individuals against certain common decisions. Likewise, groups may enjoy immunity and local autonomy over such policy issues as language and culture. Another mechanism is to keep issues on the common agenda, but depart from ordinary majoritarianism in favour of voting procedures favouring minorities. These arrangements prevent or greatly constrain an inconsiderate majority's ability to harm territorially based minorities.[16] Note that these risks are different from standard free riding. The danger is not that others will not comply with the rules, but that the rule-makers will fail to respect the central interests of minorities – which may be regarded as a meta-rule of democracy. These arrangements acknowledge the possibility that majorities may not always take into account the plight of minorities, due to ignorance, self-interest, or other factors.

---

15   Majone 1998: 103; Moravcsik 1998. Though third party enforcement may not be required, cf. Ostrom 1991.

16   cf. Madison 1961.

There is a risk that these protections send a wrong signal, i.e. that citizens in a democracy need not consider the impact on others. Just as vetoes, immunity or skewed voting weights may "simply send the wrong signals. They miscue people - voters and politicians alike - to think in narrow terms of personal and sectional interests." (Goodin 1996: 340)

EU institutions not only create trust but also increase the need for trustworthiness. Even with protections against majority abuse, the increased use of (qualified) majority rules creates some risks and requires trust among Europeans. The (qualified) majority must be trusted not to abuse its power and the loosing minority must be trusted to comply with decisions that run counter to its best judgment:

> "the bare basics of democratic theory tell us that formal or informal state vetos will not disappear without prejudice to legitimacy before citizens can be reassured either that they will most likely belong to cross-states majorities or that citizens and decision-makers of other Member States will have sufficiently 'internalized' their concerns." (Nicolaidis 2001: 454.)

Consider how the EU increasingly requires individuals and their representatives to adjust or sacrifice their own interests and those of their voters for the sake of other Europeans.

There are at least four aspects of Union regulations where trust in the compliance and commitment of other citizens or officials seems crucial. Trust is necessary for compliance with existing rules; for the creation of new regulations; for establishing and adjusting new institutions and rules of the game; and for court adjudication.

Trust in others' stable compliance is paramount for achieving and sustaining existing practices. In stable democracies, the majority can expect minorities to respect political decisions that go against their better judgment. One reason for such trust is no doubt that the losers can assume that today's majority will comply even if they lose out tomorrow; and because both sides are confident that the majority will not disregard the losers' concerns (Taylor 1969, Barry 1991).

Increased use of majoritarian decisions in the Union will require further trust among Europeans. It will be put to the test when individuals are required to act contrary to the majority of their fellow countrymen out of respect for majority decisions made in European institutions (Scharpf 1997a: 21). Union citizens must combine and order their two citizenships:

> I am simultaneously a European citizen in terms of my European transnational affinities to shared values which transcend the ethno-national diversity. So much so, that in a range of areas of public life, I am willing to accept the legitimacy and authority of decisions adopted by my fellow European citizens in the realization that in these areas we have given preference to choices made by my outreaching demos, rather than by my in-reaching demos. (Weiler & Mayer 1995: 14)

Moreover, consider soldiers who must fight for European values and objectives under a common defence policy. They and other citizens must trust that the forces are not turned against themselves. In addition, citizens and politicians of each Member State must trust that the rest of the Union complies with common decisions, rather than to free ride on the sacrifice of others.

Secondly, the population at large must also trust the legislators and executive branch. For instance, if the population suspects the Commission of abuses of trust,
40

acceptance and compliance with its decisions are at stake (Wessels 1999: 268). The mundane areas of everyday compliance with Union regulations also require mutual trust between citizens and Union officials, insofar as the public must be assured that decisions have indeed been made with their interests in mind (Weiler 2001, 69).

The creation of laws and regulations also requires complex forms of assurance among legislators in multilevel systems. Representatives in supranational or inter-governmental bodies must juggle their commitment to their national electorate with sufficient consideration for the weal and woe of other Europeans. Moreover, they must not be fooled by less scrupulous representatives, nor must they lose the trust of their voters. Much trust of this kind is required in intergovernmental negotiations: a representative may change her political goals or policy preferences in light of new information, for instance at Commission committees[17], but such shifts may provoke suspicion among voters. Such incidents of "public reasonableness" are still sound and applaudable when all can be trusted to participate (Macedo 1990).

A third area where trust is important is when institutions and constitutions are created or modified. Such changes are to be expected, especially in light of the track record of multinational federations whose competence allocation faces frequent challenges. Since these are high stakes, citizens and their representatives must be reasonably secure that their interests will be considered and respected by other par-ticipants. Participants must trust that they all seek changes guided in part by consid-erations of legitimacy and that none only pursue their unbridled national interests.

A fourth area where trust is necessary concerns the adjudication of Community regulations by domestic courts and the European Court of Justice. Citizens must trust the court to interpret the legislation correctly according to the fundamental values and objectives of the Treaties and the Constitutional Treaty. Otherwise, citi-zens and officials may question and even withhold their own costly compliance.

To summarize, there are several important challenges of trust when seeking to maintain a legitimate European political order. Both ordinary European citizens and officials must have grounds for trust, that is, they must have mutual expectations that most others will comply with common laws and regulations, and that they create new institutions and rules guided by a common commitment to maintain a fair European order. We now turn to consider how the institution of Union Citizenship may be a solution to some of these challenges.

2.3. The Roles of institutions in Facilitating Trustworthiness

One possible justification for Union Citizenship is as a stabilising devise to foster flag and maintain the mutual, legitimate trust and trustworthiness required amongst Europeans and toward their politicians. I first sketch multiple ways that institutions

---

17   As reported by Egeberg 1999, Egeberg & Trondal 1999, Trondal 2000.

can foster trustworthiness.[18] Of particular concern is how they can enhance political trust and trustworthiness in a normatively legitimate EU among people who are 'contingent compliers'. Contingent compliers are prepared to comply with fair rules as long as they believe that others will do so as well, e.g. out of a sense of justice. They may, for instance, be motivated by what John Rawls (1971: 336) called a *Duty of Justice* (cf. Scanlon 1998: 339):

> "that they will comply with fair practices that exist and apply to them when they believe that the relevant others likewise do their part; and to further just arrangements not yet established, at least when this can be done without too much cost to ourselves."

EU institutions and Union citizenship can provide important forms of assurance among contingent compliers.

The assurance problems among contingent compliers were addressed already by Rousseau (1978: 2.4.5, Madison 1787). Recent work on the theory of games and research on social capital has shed further light on how institutions can bolster expectations concerning others' actions to affect the complex assurance problems that face contingent compliers.[19]

Social institutions can promote trust and trustworthiness in various ways. They can reduce the likelihood that others default by shifting the trusted's incentives. They can reduce the costs of disappointed trust; for instance by imposing restrictions on the scope of legal political decisions through human rights protecting minorities.[20]

A contingent complier decides to comply with rules and institutions and otherwise cooperates with officials' decisions because she: a) perceives the government as trustworthy in making and enforcing normatively legitimate policies; and b) she has confidence that other actors, both officials and citizens, will do their part.

Institutions can provide assurance of at least seven relevant kinds. With regard to the first condition - perception of the government pursuing normatively legitimate policies- ,

- Civil society can foster the development and dissemination of a plausible public political theory that provides normative legitimacy by laying out and defending the objectives and normative standards of the political order: democracy, subsidiarity, solidarity, and human rights.
- Institutions must be sufficiently simple and transparent to allow assessment.

---

18 For a more detailed account that draws on Margaret Levi's helpful discussions see Follesdal 2006.

19 Sen 1967, Taylor 1987, Elster 1989: 187; Ostrom 1991, Scharpf 1997b, Rothstein 1998; Levi 1998a. Recent normative contributions addressing the standards of normative legitimacy on the explicit assumption of such contingent compliance include Rawls 1971, Goodin 1992, Thompson & Gutmann 1996: 72-73; Miller 2000. For Social Capital, cf. Loury 1977; Coleman 1990: chap. 8; Putnam 1993; Putnam 1995; Levi 1998b; Newton 1999.

20 I here modify Margaret Levi's model of contingent consent (Levi 1998a: chap. 2, Braithwaite & Levi 1998.). See also Goodin 1992.

- Institutions must generally be seen to be sufficiently effective and efficient according to the normative objectives and standards. Institutions may also help provide public assurance of general compliance.
- Institutions can be seen to socialize individuals to be conditional compliers, for instance in the educational system, or in political parties that foster reasonably consistent and responsive policy platforms.
- Institutions can include mechanisms that can be trusted to monitor whether policies or authorities actually solve the problems they were designed to address.
- Institutions can provide sanctions that modify or reinforce citizens' incentives, so as to increase the likelihood that others will also comply.
- Institutions can include mechanisms that can be trusted to monitor the compliance of citizens and authorities with the legal rules.

I venture that Union citizenship can play a crucial role in providing assurance of the fourth kind. Reassurance among conditional compliers requires more than actual compliance by a large proportion of individuals. Each individual must also have reason to believe that sufficiently many others will continue to comply in the future, since compliance by each is conditional on the expected compliance of others.

Institutions can socialize individuals to the Duty of Justice[21] and other relevant norms and virtues. When this socialization happens in public institutions, it provides public assurance and reminders that all, or most, citizens, including politicians, share these norms about what justice requires and what it means to be a citizen.[22] There would seem to be at least two main arenas of such socialisation: the public education systems through curriculum requirements, and political parties.

Party contestation is crucial for socialization and preference formation. Many scholars point to the importance of federation-wide parties competing at several levels of the multi-level political order (Cf. Linz 1999). Such competition fosters political debate and formation of public opinion about the best means and objectives of policies that heed and accommodate the interests of both the sub-unit population and that of other Union citizens. These debates allow voters to form their preferences concerning complex policy issues on the bases of alternative party platforms,

---

21 Which Margaret Levi calls 'ethical reciprocity', "a norm requiring that individuals in a given population cooperate with government demands, but only as long as others are also contributing." (1998: 24-25)

22 Perhaps individuals should be socialised so that their perceptions and preferences make certain behaviour – compliance, or conditional compliance with legitimate rules - seem obvious and appropriate, or is simply taken for granted, rather than basing actions on calculation (Stinchcombe 1986, March & Simon 1993). These features have been explored by "New Institutionalism" (March & Olsen 1989), honing insights found among authors as different as Aristotle, J. J. Rousseau, J. S. Mill and J. Rawls (Rousseau 1972: 4; Rousseau 1993; Mill 1969: 139; Mill 1958: chap. 3; Mill 1970: 23; Rawls 1971). For instance, institutions can foster compliance by generating and enabling what L. C. Becker (1969) calls "noncognitive" trust, a sense of security about others benevolence and compliance that is not focussed on specific people or institutions, nor a matter of conscious strategic choice.

all of which claim to be committed to the interests of all members of the union. They thus socialize citizens toward an 'overarching loyalty' and reduce the risk that political power will be used with disregard for some sub-units (Linz 1999).

2.4. A Liberal Contractualist Account of Union Citizenship Duties

We now consider aspects of the content of Union citizenship duties and virtues. We start by sketching aspects of liberal contractualism, and then consider what virtues or dispositions institutions may and must foster in the citizenry in order to maintain a normatively legitimate multi-level political order.

The topic of civic virtues of Union citizenship may seem particularly problematic for the liberal tradition in political philosophy, which is often accused of failing to allow political obligation even to one political community. Liberalism is said by thoughtful authors to focus on universal principles to the disregard of particular ties to one's own community. If so, it may endorse citizens' acquiring the universalistic values of Art I-2 that are found in most decent societies:

"respect for human dignity, freedom, democracy, equality, the rule of law and respect for human rights, including the rights of persons belonging to minorities.

These values are common to the Member States in a society in which pluralism, non-discrimination, tolerance, justice, solidarity and equality between women and men prevail."

However, what need, if any, is there for the shared European and diverse national values, culture, and history? May Union citizens be required, as part of Union citizenship, to learn about, respect, and even be socialized to, the facts, beliefs and values of their own and others' 'national culture'? And should they be made to accept further values and practices of "the cultural, religious and humanist inheritance of Europe,... remaining proud of their own national identities and history." Does liberalism justify socialization of the kind required for trust?

Liberal Contractualism draws on a fundamentally liberal, Kantian perspective, according to which public power should be exercised in ways that can be justified to the people living under it insofar as they share a sense of justice, understood as a highest-order interest in living together with others on terms they could not reasonably reject (Scanlon 1982: 116, Scanlon 1998, Barry 1989: 8).

Contractualist theories hone this vague commitment by invoking the notion of hypothetical consent (O'Neill 1989). The principles of legitimacy we should hold institutions to are those that the affected persons would unanimously consent to under conditions that secure and recognise their status as appropriately free and equal, thus manifesting "our respect for the reasonableness of others" (Macedo 1990). Many of the recent contributions to this tradition have followed John Rawls in addressing urgent topics of justice facing unitary states - "sovereign states with central administration" (Rawls 1993: xxii). European integration raises concerns beyond that focus, and requires us to develop aspects of federal political theory (cf. Follesdal 2003).

I submit that Liberal Contractualism can account for the need for Citizenship as a stabilizing device that creates and sustains trust within the multilevel political order along the lines sketched above. This conception of Union citizenship is more complex than 'Constitutional Patriotism', yet does not require that citizens endorse all aspects of the 'national' public cultures, be it the European or that of their own state.

Union citizens should not only be socialized to human rights and democratic decision-making plus a variety of liberal virtues, but they should also share a 'thin' political theory with normative conceptions of the person and the multi-level political order. Citizens should also be acquainted with 'particularistic' aspects of European culture, values and history. The justification is not only instrumental, i.e. to motivate endorsement of the universalistic values of Art I-2, but also because "this is our culture". Yet, this account denies that a shared national identity at the member state or European level is required as the main source of trust.

Union citizenship can help foster and secure the stability of a legitimate multi-level political order by providing a sufficient basis for ensuring that the legitimate institutions endure, in the sense that government policies, if normatively legitimate, enjoy general compliance and adapt as necessary over time (cf. Choudhry 2001: 383).

Both legal rights and obligations, and non-legal practices and dispositions of those holding the office of citizenship, are required to achieve requisite trust in general compliance with a fair political order. Our focus here is on the dispositions and substantive obligations of citizens that should be fostered and upheld by institutions in order to maintain a normative legitimate multi-level political order over time. Many illegitimate orders, such as dictatorships, are stable. Our question is limited to legitimate orders, and the stabilizing role that citizenship obligations play in maintaining them.

What is both necessary and permissible for citizens to accept, or support, the requisite stability enforced by domestic or European public power? I submit that citizens must be habituated to three sets of commitments. First, they must act on principles of legitimacy for the political institutions and for the constitutional norms. Second, beyond "Constitutional Patriotism", Union citizens must share fragments of a justification of the principles of legitimacy, such as offered by a conception of the proper roles of individuals - including their responsibilities as citizens – and of the multi-polar European political order. This order must be perceived by citizens as a complex system of co-operation that expresses the inhabitants' equal standing. Third, they must be committed to become familiar with the prevailing institutions, the public political culture, and other cultural practices, at both European and Member State levels. These three aspects are required for citizens to make credible commitments and ensure conditional compliance with legitimate European institutions. Some clarifying comments are in order.

2.4.1. Normative Principles of Legitimacy for the Multi-Level Political Order

Normative principles of legitimacy, duly worked out for multi-polar polities, serve several roles in accounting for stability. One is to provide critical standards for assessing existing institutions. Public agreement on standards of legitimacy allows a public determination of whether an existing order merits compliance by conditional compliers while maintaining the possibility of a critical stance and facilitating agreement on how to improve existing institutions and policies.

Citizens must be committed to act on such principles. This commitment to act always in accordance with principles does not provide the sole motivation for individuals' actions.

I take it that the values of the Union (I Art. I-2) and some of its objectives (I Art. I-3) are included among such principles, especially democracy, the rule of law, human rights, pluralism, tolerance, justice, equality, solidarity and non-discrimination, social justice and protection, and solidarity among the sub-units. The challenge is not to list them, but to specify and order such norms. The elaboration of the substantive content of such principles for the European political order must be provided elsewhere.

One might argue that it is only a common commitment to actual institutions that is required, and not a commitment to such principles. Thus, Andrew Mason holds that "liberal regimes can be sustained by a sense of belonging to them" (Mason 1999: 279). This commitment to the actual institutions does not seem to extend to the individuals participating in them, nor to a national identity or to such principles of legitimacy.

In response, three remarks. First, the interpretation of institutionalised practices is seldom uncontested, and certainly not over time. Such interpretations will partly be made and assessed by appeal to the 'spirit of the laws'; to more general principles, or some other standards. So even on their own terms, such accounts would include some role for shared values or ideals. Second, trust in the future compliance of others must rest on something more than the observation of present compliance. Accordingly, something more seems needed to provide general assurance that there is indeed 'a sense of belonging', in the sense of a commitment to future compliance. Such assurance is bolstered if the compliance of others is not only a matter of the present acceptance of existing norms of appropriateness or of a stalemate between factions not sufficiently powerful to overrule the others. A shared public commitment to principles provides part of such assurance among contingent compliers, although public knowledge of the different reasons various people have may indeed provide sufficient assurance.

However, a third area where assurance is needed seems to require common grounds. In a political order, laws and policies must continually be made and revised. Individuals need assurance that others will use their political power as voters and politicians to further what they regard as just arrangements and vote for laws sometimes out of consideration for the common good rather than unbridled self-interest. Shared reasons, for instance in the form of such common principles, can provide assurance of the requisite kind among legislators when new rules and institutions are to be created. The requisite assurance can be fostered by way of publicly shared principles for adjusting and creating these new practices so that legislators can trust others to seek institutions that satisfy these principles.

Against such accounts, one might point to present disagreements about conceptions of equality and justice. Andrew Mason concludes from the fact of disagreement that shared reasons are unnecessary because different conceptions of these principles do not hinder compliance. Citizens may value the same institutions but not share the principles because there are contested conceptions of the ideals of equality, justice or freedom (Mason 1999, 281.) However, the issue of trust does not concern compliance in the present but expectations of others' future behaviour. Disagreements indicate that future compliance is not secure, particularly so when the laws and policies change. In such circumstances, individuals may not be able to appear trustworthy and this may threaten general compliance.

2.4.2. Conceptions of Citizens and of the European Political Order

Second, in addition to principles of legitimacy, citizens must share the immediate grounds for such principles. Liberal Contractualism would seek to provide a justification of such principles based on normative conceptions of the individual, of the ends of the political unity, and a conception of the proper relationship between individuals and the political order.

Individuals are to be regarded as free and equal members of a system of cooperation coercively maintained by public force. Authority is to be allocated according to a Principle of Subsidiarity, duly defined.

Such conceptions play the equivalent role of Rawls' well-known conception of society as a system of co-operation among individuals, regarded for such purposes as free and equal participants. However, that particular conception is insufficient or inappropriate for the European Union as a non-unitary political order with Member States and Community institutions splitting and sharing sovereignty.

Some indication of standards for the proper allocation of competences between sub-units and the common political authority must be provided – for instance in the form of a justified specification of a principle of Subsidiarity.[23] Leaving those important issues aside, we focus here on the conception of citizen used to justify the principles of legitimacy. Which virtues and duties should citizens have, even in a political order where religious and philosophical disagreements counsel extreme caution in using public power to promote contested virtues?

---

23   See Follesdal 1998 for a detailed discussion of plausible versions of 'subsidiarity'.

2.4.2.1. Duty of Justice – Justifying the Political Obligation to One's Own Political Order

Liberal Contractualism follows Rawls and Waldron in holding that citizens should be brought up to have certain political virtues, including "toleration and mutual respect, and a sense of fairness and civility" (Rawls 1971: 122). Two central duties are those of justice and of mutual respect – what I take Waldron to describe as the 'responsibilities of citizenship' - including willing compliance with a normatively legitimate order and paying appropriate attention to the interests and views of others (Waldron 2000).

A central assumption is that citizens should be brought to have a sense of justice; an effective desire to comply with existing, fair rules; and the willingness to give one another that to which they are entitled, "predicated on the belief that others will do their part" (Rawls 1971: 336, 505, 567). They comply, that is, with the "Duty of Justice".[24]

Note that this Duty of Justice explains the ties to one's own political order, insofar as it is just and generally complied with. This has been a concern for several critics of 'Constitutional Patriotism', since it seems that a commitment only to certain principles provide citizens with insufficient bonds and allegiance to their own political institutions (Kymlicka & Norman 1994). Liberal Contractualism avoids this alleged weakness since the Duty of Justice requires citizens to have political obligations to their own just institutions that exist and apply to them. Union citizens must be committed not only to abstract principles but also to the concrete institutions that embody these principles. These institutions are specified in the constitutions of one's Member State and the treaties of the European Union, and the political obligation requires citizens to comply with their results, namely concrete organisations, laws and the central political practices, insofar as they are legitimate.[25]

To illustrate: among such concrete duties might well be those suggested by Elizabeth Meehan[26] - if they are normatively legitimate. Meehan suggests the duty to

---

24 For an elaboration and defence, see Waldron 1993 and his discussion of the "Duty of Civic Participation", Waldron 2000; and T. M. Scanlon's Principle of Established Practices (Scanlon 1998: 339). Becker's notion of 'conscientiousness' (Becker 1996: 56) appears to be similar.

25 I believe similar interpretations are possible regarding Jürgen Habermas' claim that *Constitutional Patriotism* is a sufficient common base. While Liberal Contractualism differs from Constitutional Patriotism in ways explored above and below, they share a focus on the constitutional order (Habermas 1996: 500; Habermas 1990: 257), and seek to minimise the reliance on contested values in response to the challenge of pluralism (Habermas 1998: 225, Habermas 1992: 16). For an exploration of this account, see De Greiff (2000). I do not deny that alternative interpretations of Habermas seems possible, e.g. when he writes that the requisite "identity of a political community, which may not be touched by immigration, depends *primarily* upon the constitutional principles rooted in a political culture and *not* upon an ethical cultural form of life as a whole." (Habermas 1992: 17, my emphasis).

26 Meehan 1993, cf. fruitful discussion in Shaw 1997a.

obey lawful rules, participate in military defence and pay taxes. She also includes a duty to be willing to work and, more contestable, a duty to vote. If such moral or even legal duties can be argued as necessary to sustain the legitimate European political order, they may be supported by the Duty of Justice. Liberal Contractualism may thus find itself in agreement with much of classical and recent republicanism, which sees a politically active citizenry as necessary for maintaining a just political order (cf. Rawls 2001). The detailed duties will depend on the particulars of the citizens' own institutions.

A note on the need for compliance with the legitimate political culture is required. In order to exercise one's political rights responsibly, citizens need knowledge about the political culture, understood as the public practices regarding the responsible exercise of offices (Cf Laborde 2002).

Such familiarity and compliance - if not full acceptance - is needed for full and responsible participation in political institutions. Citizens must accept the prevalent public political culture – insofar as it is legitimate - at least sufficiently to understand the claims of others so as to consider them when voting.[27] This duty regarding the political culture is also supported by the Duty of Mutual Respect.

2.4.2.2. The Duty of Mutual Respect

The duty of mutual respect requires that citizens

> "show a person the respect which is due to him as a moral being, that is, as a being with a sense of justice and a conception of the good.... Mutual respect is shown in several ways: in our willingness to see the situation of others from their point of view, from the perspective of their conception of their good; and in our being prepared to give reasons for our actions whenever the interests of others are materially affected..... Thus to respect another as a moral person is to try to understand his aims and interests from his standpoint and to present him with considerations that enable him to accept the constraints on his conduct. Since another wishes, let us suppose, to regulate his actions on the basis of principles to which all could agree, he should be acquainted with the relevant facts which explain the restrictions in this way." (Rawls 1971: 337-8; cf Waldron 1987)

Why are these shared commitments to the grounds for common principles - conceptions of citizens and the political order – necessary for stability of a legitimate political order?

One important reason is that this provides a much needed justification for some such principles over others, and allows a critical yet argued stance towards one's constitutional tradition, thereby answering Weiler's challenge: "How, then, do we

---

27 The public political culture is of course often unduly skewed in favour of a majority's broader culture. Insofar as this hinders the responsible exercise of the office of citizenship, the duty of justice does not require acquiescence, but rather efforts to change this political culture.

both respect and uphold all that is good in our constitutional tradition and yet, at the same time, keep it and ourselves under sceptical check?" (Weiler 2001: 65)

In addition, and central to our present concerns, is the need for assurance. Consensus on principles of legitimacy is insufficient to convince others of one's trustworthiness regarding future compliance with these procedures. The others' present compliance by itself does not give us reason to trust that they will continue to respect democratic procedures. We also need assurance that they believe themselves to have reasons for continued compliance in the future.

Europeans also need mutual assurance when creating new institutions. In order to secure compliance over the long term, such changes and legal interpretations of rules must be accepted as legitimate expressions of equal respect among citizens of different Member States, rather than be seen as dictated by expediency or arbitrary consensus alone. The institutional changes and interpretations must therefore be seen to be guided by more than principles of an existing constitution. Disagreements about the proper division of competences between Member States and the Community institutions, for instance, may diminish support and compliance by citizens and government officials. Politicians may suspect civil servants sent to Brussels of harbouring inappropriately supranational loyalties, due to loyalty shifts by the civil servants (Trondal & Veggeland 2000). Shared conceptions of the roles of Member States and the Community, e.g. in the form of a suitably specified Principle of Subsidiarity, can serve to bolster trustworthiness and reduce such mistrust (Follesdal 1998).

2.4.3. Acquaintance with Local Norms, Cultural Practices and Others' Institutions

A third aspect of the Liberal Contractualist conception of citizenship is a commitment to be somewhat familiar with the local institutions, norms and cultural practices of other citizens. There are several reasons to require such familiarity.

Liberal Contractualism requires that citizens are prepared, to some extent, to become acquainted with the various cultures and ways of life enjoyed by fellow citizens, as well as the political institutions of other Member States - especially when urged to do so. This is because European legal institutions and policies may create unforeseen and burdensome conflicts with social practices and domestic institutions, in ways that can be avoided by creative yet legitimate legislation or policy measures. A willingness to accommodate to others' existing, legitimate and strongly held expectations is part of the Duty of Mutual Respect. This duty is more demanding in a multi-level political order where sub-units do not enjoy veto power, since citizens are rendered vulnerable to other Union citizens who live under other institutions and with different political cultures, - and who therefore may have greater difficulty realizing the impact of common decisions. A duty to consider the impacts across sub-units is therefore required to reassure all citizens of the responsibilities of majority rule in these multi-level political orders. All citizens should have some knowledge of the main cultures that existing in the political community to ensure that changes respect (though not necessarily abide by) the important expectations of such groups. Such knowledge, however, does not require acquiescence in the permanent maintenance of such cultural practices and institutions.

This duty undoubtedly puts burdens on citizens; indeed, this is one reason in support of subsidiarity and for permitting more economic inequality within non-unitary political orders (Cf. Follesdal 1998: 2001).

I submit that this brief account lends support and some specificity to Weiler's point about the special challenges of the responsibilities among Union citizens:

> We acknowledge and respect difference, and what is special and unique about ourselves as individuals and groups; and yet we reach across differences in recognition of our essential humanity. (Weiler 2001: 66.)

This account also suggests that we interpret the Constitutional Treaty as laying down citizens' duties when it states that the Union "shall respect its rich cultural and linguistic diversity, and shall ensure that Europe's cultural heritage is safeguarded and enhanced" (Art 3), and "shall respect the equality of Member States before the constitution as well as their national identities, inherent in their fundamental structures, political and constitutional, inclusive of regional and local self-government." (Art. 5.1)

If the institution of citizenship is to serve as an assurance mechanism, Union Citizens must be committed to principles of legitimacy; to conceptions of citizens and citizens' duties, and the role of the political order; and to be somewhat acquainted with the world views, practices and legal institutions of other Union citizens.

2.5. Alternatives and Challenges

We finally turn to consider some areas where this account seems to diverge from the normative political theories of Jürgen Habermas and David Miller.[28]

2.5.1. Habermas – Constitutional Patriotism

Several authors register the hope that a 'civic demos 'must be possible, based on a commitment to a common constitutional order specifying procedures for reaching politically binding decisions. Ethnically or culturally based 'belongingness' should worry us (Cf. Ackerman 1980: 69ff.; Preuss 1996: 275; MacCormick 1996: 150; MacCormick 1997: 341). Liberal Contractualism also shares the concern to avoid ethnic or other contested bases for social trust and European citizenship.

---

28 I here agree with Lacorne (2001) that we need to go beyond abstract constitutional patriotism.

Jürgen Habermas has long argued for the need to limit what citizens must share to a 'Constitutional Patriotism' that amounts to constitutional rights and principles understood as (some) human rights and "a consensus on the procedures for the legitimate enactment of laws and legitimate exercise of power" (Habermas 1993: 133). More recently, he has acknowledged that citizens must also accept aspects of the local, varying 'political culture' as a means to motivate such acceptance.

This wariness of particular cultures would presumably make Constitutional Patriots cautious of the claim in the Constitutional Treaty's Preamble, that the peoples of Europe should remain "proud of their own national identities and history..." Some might also suspect that the Constitutional Patriot's vision of Europe is one of strong centralisation, where the Union level political order focuses on universalist principles, leaving Member States with little authority. Leaving such issues aside, we focus on two challenges that Constitutional Patriotism raises to Liberal Contractualism.

Why go beyond Constitutional Patriotism and require agreement even on the *grounds* for constitutional principles? And why value local institutions and culture more than merely as instrumental motivation-enhancers for accepting universal principles?

2.5.1.1. Why Shared Grounds for Constitutional Principles?

I submit that the need for assurance under democratic interdependence explains why Liberal Contractualism requires more than agreement on the procedures for legislation and constitutional change.

To illustrate, consider Kurt Baier's notion of *Constitutional Consensus.* Baier (1989) holds that commitment to certain constitutional rules - what he calls a "Constitutional consensus" – should suffice for stability. All that is needed is consensus "on the procedures for making and interpreting law and, where that agreement is insufficiently deep to end disagreement, on the selection of persons whose adjudication is accepted as authoritative" (Baier 1989: 775). I take it that this is close to "Constitutional Patriotism".

However, constitutional principles cannot provide the mutual trust necessary for constitutional changes, or for institutional development and application on the basis of political judgement. Fundamentally competing conceptions of the appropriate procedures and the ends of the polity threaten the long-term stability of co-operation, as well as the ability to make credible commitments. Habermas holds that the problem of disintegration can be resolved by the "conviction that the democratic process itself can provide the necessary guarantees for the social integration of an increasingly differentiated society" (Habermas 1998d: 133). However, this claim is not obviously correct. Even though all currently accept the democratic process, trust in their future acceptance of it will be greatly enhanced by knowing their reasons. This sort of reassurance would require at least knowledge about the reasons others have for accepting these democratic procedures, even though one might not share such reasons.

Habermas himself offers certain arguments, based on criteria for an ideal speech situation, that might underpin such a commitment to procedures. His argument is contested because of both the premises and the argumentative steps[29], but public knowledge that citizens endorse such arguments provides some assurance of the requisite kind.

Assurance also requires more than such divergent arguments for principles of legitimacy. Current agreement about procedures is insufficient, since disagreement about their justification threatens the possibility of agreeing to *changes of procedures*. One might agree to the need for democratic procedures, and there may be a happy consensus on the actual procedures, but when changes in procedures are required, assurance must be provided by appeal to some other common grounds. Liberal Contractualism suggests such a shared basis in the form of a thin conception of the Union Citizen and the appropriate division of labour between the Community and Member States.

2.5.1.2. Why value Local Cultures- Only as Means for Supporting Universal Principles?

Habermas' defence of particular, national – and European – culture may strike some as too functional.

"They are valuable not in themselves, but because they embody or implement general principles of a universal nature. The particular features of a political community serve a functional role, because universal principles cannot serve as the cement of political integration unless they are situated in a historically informed and concrete way so that they can count as reasons for participating in schemes of political cooperation." (Choudhry 1999: 393)

Constitutional Patriotism appears not to value existing institutions and particular cultural practices - even those within the constraints of justice - simply because they're 'ours', but only because they motivate acceptance of universal principles. What gives them value is not their particularity but their motivational role for the constitutional principles that on their own lack 'driving force'.[30] If this is all that can be said, it is difficult to understand why these cultures have any claim to be respected and protected, rather than to be, say, slowly transformed into a common culture shared by all Europeans. This is of course not an objection, but only an implication; the point here is to clarify how Liberal Contractualism differs.

First, we can note that there may be further instrumental reasons for shared history and particular practices among Europeans, based on considerations of trust[31]:

29   Cf. Olafson 1990, Heath 1995, Larmore 1996: 205-21.
30   Cf. Laborde 2002 for another expression of this.
31   For references and discussion, cf. Follesdal 2000, Follesdal 2004

History - including the intentional building of 'collective memories' (Rothstein 1999) -

- 1) helps convey the long-standing mutual dependence among Europeans that underscores the need for assurance mechanism;
- 2) helps specify the not illegitimate expectations other Europeans have formed about the future actions of European agents, - the various norms of appropriateness - as explications of Europeans sharing a 'common fate'(cf. Breton 1995); and
- 3) can bolster the reputation of institutions and politicians as trustworthy. Among the more recent historical events relevant in the European setting are the Commission resignation, the reactions against Austria, and the handling of the mad cow disease (cf. Lacorne 2001, Follesdal 2002).

Liberal Contractualism also provides arguments for why existing institutions and the political culture have value, and that it matters, normatively, that they are *ours*. The point was made above. When justifying political obligation, we do so on the basis of the duty of justice, by appeal not only to 'abstract principles', but also by showing that a particular set of institutions does in fact exist, that their rules are publicly known and generally complied with, and that these rules apply to us. One relevant premise thus is that these institutions and practices are indeed ours. This commitment to existing practices requires a broad range of knowledge about the central, legitimate expectations of citizens affected by the common institutions (Gunsteren 1988: 736).

2.5.2. David Miller – Nationality Required for Solidarity Must Have Unique Characteristics

David Miller's account of citizenship focuses, as does Liberal Contractualism, on the role of trust, assurance and stability (E.g. Miller 2000: 86). However, he defends the need for a shared national identity with further substantive norms, beliefs or commitments, i.e. a more substantive common public culture. This may require "non-neutrality where the national culture itself is at stake." The national public culture must have substantive norms that serve to set members off from other peoples and has a unifying function:

> "When I say that national differences must be natural ones, I mean that the people who compose a nation must believe that there is something distinctive about themselves that marks them off from other nations, over and above the fact of sharing common institutions. This needs not be one specific trait or quality, but can be a range of characteristics which are generally shared by the members of nation A and serve to differentiate them from outsiders. ....
>
> These five elements together -- a community constituted by mutual belief, extended in history, active in character, connected to a particular territory, and thought to be marked off from other communities by its members' distinct traits -- serve to distinguish nationality from other collective sources of personal identity." (Miller 2000: 30-31)

Miller holds that such a national allegiance is required to develop the appropriate responsible citizenship, and to maintain the trust required for solidaristic arrangements characteristic of European welfare states.

The problematic aspect of Miller's notion of national identity is not that it is essentialist or static. Miller himself, in contrast, claims that it is malleable (Miller 2000: 35), and can be purged of elements that exclude minorities on the territory. He also interestingly notes that there can be nested nationalities, citing the Scottish and British nationalities (cf. Follesdal 2000). Still, while Miller (1995: 159) in principle is open to the development of a European identity, he is sceptical of the prospects of maintaining pan-European welfare regimes due to the lack of a substantive national identity among Europeans.

Leaving detailed criticisms aside, we consider some points where Liberal Contractualism differs from Miller's account.[32]

2.5.2.1. Substantive Socialization

Socialization to citizenship, in Miller's view, requires that all share the particularistic norms and beliefs of the relevant nationality. In particular, he seems to hold that the requisite social trust for social insurance schemes requires more in the way of shared national culture than liberalism permits. Yet, he does not specify what this shared public culture crucially consists of. It includes a constitution, and presumably civic nationalism, "in the sense that each acknowledges the authority of a common set of laws and political institutions."(Miller 1995: 190), and "a dense web of customs, practices, implicit understandings, and so forth." "Where some cultural feature -- a landscape, a musical tradition, a language -- has become a component part of national identity, it is justifiable to discriminate in its favour if the need arises." (Miller 1995: 41, 195) This would appear to include the promotion of a religion through the school system (Miller 1995: 195). However, it is difficult to get a precise sense of what he would include in the national identity beyond shared institutions. One reason may be that it is for the particular set of individuals to determine the content of the national identity (Miller 2000: 34).[33]

The role of this shared national public culture is to facilitate trust, apparently of the kind needed in assurance games (Miller 2000: 31-32).

---

32 I leave aside several topics of alleged disagreement between Miller's republicanism and Rawlsian Political Liberalism, which he sometimes criticizes under the label 'liberalism' in Miller 1995 and Miller 2000.

33 Though he seems to allow shared religion as a component (Miller 1995: 19).

Miller's account can be questioned on several grounds[34], but here we focus on the point that Miller dismisses other sources of solidarity too quickly. Stable redistributive arrangements that require trust need not draw on nationalism of the kind Miller suggests. What seems to be required are shared institutionalised practices among citizens with some public common political virtue, maintained by institutions crafted to provide the requisite reassurance. The Liberal Contractualist strategy sketched above requires agreement on certain principles, and on their immediate justification sufficient to ensure shared interpretation, application and stable compliance, without making controversial metaphysical assumptions or contested views about the proper ends of humans. I take John Rawls, Jürgen Habermas, and other liberal theorists to contribute to such projects. On such accounts the institutions need not build on individuals' shared norms of solidarity, existing prior to and outside of the institutions in civil society and associations. Instead, or in addition, institutions can also establish and maintain such principles and virtues.[35]

2.5.2.2. Exclusionary

Miller's conception of national identity requires that this common public culture has characteristics setting members apart from non-members. National divisions must be conceived as natural ones; "they must correspond to what are taken to be real differences between peoples."(Miller 1994: 140). It is not clear why this is necessary for providing assurance, except perhaps to help identify outside free riders. Moreover, Miller's discussion of nested nationalities would seem to require changes in this definition, since he agrees that "it is possible to have a smaller nationality nesting within a larger one" (Miller 2000: 185, n.26). Leaving such issues aside, the implications would seem dire for the development of European Citizenship. There are no obvious and attractive values accepted only by Europeans, yet acceptable as legitimate common grounds (Closa 1998, 425, Bauböck 1997, Norman 1995).

In contrast, Liberal Contractualism does not seek values at the level of abstract principles and ideals that are unique to one's own community.[36] The principles, and indeed the political theory, need not be unique to Europeans. The role of shared commitments is to ensure stability in the sense of compliance with existing institutions, and appropriate adjustment of institutions and constitutions. The fact that other just institutions exist elsewhere, or that they might be somewhat more just, by itself does not generate a duty on the citizens' part to abide by them. The concern is

---

34   For instance, insofar as there are deep ideological disagreements concerning the distributive requirements embedded in the national identity – e.g. between social democrats and Tories – it remains unclear whether there is indeed *one* national identity "that binds these parties together" (Miller 2000: 33).

35   Such claims are explored by Levi 1998a, b and Rothstein 1998.

36   *Pace* Miller 1995, Tamir 1993.

to ensure general compliance among citizens, not to set them apart or exclude others. This approach also recognises the need to identify and exclude non-compliers or free riders and, possibly, to restrict access to costly redistributive arrangements, but there seems little reason to do so on the basis of acceptance of a national public culture.

2.5.2.3. Pessimism Regarding a Fair Europe

Miller's account leads to a particular scepticism regarding the possibility of a stable, fair Europe, at least insofar as it involves redistributive arrangements across populations of different nationalities.[37] Such arrangements would require that someone created and maintained a shared 'European' nationality to sustain the institutions. Such a shared national identity is beyond what exists, and is likely to exist (though possible – cf. Miller 1995: 159). Miller's account of Union citizenship thus leads to pessimism concerning the possibility of achieving the Union's objective to "promote economic, social and territorial cohesion and solidarity among Member States" (Art I-3). Support for such arrangements would have to draw on a European national allegiance, which, according to Miller (2000: 26), could not withstand critical scrutiny. Furthermore, the deliberate creation of such an identity would be risky since many national identities are not supportive of just institutions at all. Many warn against versions of such a national identity at the European level. Indeed, some maintain that national identities are exactly what the EU promises deliverance from (Delanty 1995). Indeed, Miller notes that many regard any notion of a "European" national identity as backward. A Pan-European 'national' identity might well be a cure worse than the disease.

Liberal Contractualism, in contrast, holds that Miller's dire expectations for European redistributive arrangement are too hasty. This is not to say that time may not prove him right, for instance due to co-ordination traps (Scharpf 1988, 1999). Yet, the grounds Miller offers for his pessimism are insufficient. A European national identity of the kind Miller deems needed may be unwise and beyond reach, but just European redistributive institutions among Union citizens with a sense of justice may still secure the requisite assurance.

These remarks have sought to clarify how the Liberal Contractualist account of Union citizenship compares to the theories of Habermas and Miller, on some issues pertinent to the claims made in the Constitutional Treaty regarding shared European values and the respect due existing national cultures and institutions. I have also suggested that some pessimism regarding a future fair Europe is premature, for institutions may foster Union citizens and sufficient assurance among them.

---

37 For discussion of distributive requirements among sub-units, cf. Follesdal 2001.

2.6. Conclusions: Union Citizenship and Prospects for the EU

The present reflections have focussed on the role of some notions of Union Citizenship in securing trustworthiness, stable compliance and willing support among Europeans for European institutions and practices. Such perceived needs seem to have fuelled the call for Union citizenship in the first place.

Union Citizenship may well have been introduced to enhance trust among Europeans themselves and towards those who govern Europe. One way it does this is by drawing on and fostering only a very limited set of shared values and objectives, far less than that historically aimed for in European nation states. A limited normative basis is regarded as possible, partly because Liberal Contractualism, as some other political theories, postulates a different fundamental motivation for individuals' compliance than 'sentiments of affinity', namely a sense of justice.

Liberal Contractualism, as several other theories, assumes that institutions can socialise individuals into a "sense of justice". A central challenge is to ensure that national and EU institutions are "framed so as to encourage the virtue of justice in those who take part in them" (Rawls 1971: 261), so that individuals can come to see themselves as free and equal participants in a joint European scheme of co-operation that commands the willing compliance of most Europeans.

The development of the requisite European sense of commonality might be a dynamic process. Common institutions – in particular citizenship and enhanced political arenas for public contestation among political parties, and opportunities for European party families - can help create Union citizens, policies and sufficient monitoring to build trust.[38] Institutions must facilitate the shared communication and commitments necessary for legitimate majority rule (Habermas 1998a, MacCormick 1997: 353) and may be crucial for creating and confirming the appropriate will to live together (Preuss 1996). The constructive potential of institutions in shaping perceptions, ideas, preferences and options, suggests that pessimism based on the current absence of trust is premature.

The civic virtues of Union citizens should not only include a commitment to some very general principles of justice, or to abstract constitutional principles. Acting on a sense of justice entails interacting in our day-to-day lives with other individuals in accordance with their legitimate expectations about our behaviour, honouring their trust in our responses. The argument above accepts an account of the practices one is embedded in as a part of, but only one part of, a full justification of the institutions. Citizens' sense of justice includes a commitment to honour the legitimate expectations of other citizens on the basis of shared principles of legitimacy and a shared understanding of the appropriate relations between individuals and the European multi-polar polity uniting them.

---

38 Preuss 1995: 277-78; Streeck 1996: fn 64 and 74; cf. Putnam 1993, 184; Rawls 1999, 112; Follesdal & Hix 2005.

I have not claimed that there is agreement at present on any of these components of Union citizenship, nor that political philosophy should aim to provide answers that replace the need for democratic deliberation on such issues. On the contrary, the contribution of political philosophy is rather *to* the democratic debate, suggesting what it should be about. Liberal Contractualism suggests that agreement on all these three components seem necessary to maintain a maximally stable and legitimate European order and that democratic deliberation in Europe should have such agreement as a publicly stated objective.

Union Citizenship may facilitate this trust, yet it may backfire and fail to provide the desired support for existing institutions. Talk of 'citizenship' highlights the questions of the normative authority and trustworthiness of Union institutions. Why, if at all, should individuals and officials regard Community regulations as morally binding on their conduct, imposing on them a moral obligation to comply? The response must show how the offices and institutions of the European Union satisfy the normative standards befitting a multi-level political order among equals.

Insofar as the Constitution fails to satisfy such criteria of legitimacy in public scrutiny, the focus on Union Citizenship may serve to reduce rather than enhance the support and trust Europeans exhibit towards each other because their common institutions are considered illegitimate, hence not the subject of political obligation. Recall that Conditional compliance rests on standards of legitimacy that, if unfulfilled, may destabilise rather than consolidate the European political order.

Talk of citizenship may thus increase mistrust, rather than induce support. This should come as no surprise. Governments have often discovered that citizenship rights have "the potential for exacerbating, as well as diminishing the conflict of classes" (Goodin 1988). Just to mention some challenges: Introducing citizenship rights only for citizens of Member States immediately highlights the plight of permanently resident non-nationals (Follesdal 1999). The introduction of Union Citizenship also introduces fundamental inconsistencies in current citizenship practice both within many states and within the European Union as a whole (Bauböck 1994a: 220, Meehan 1993, Wiener 1998, Follesdal 1999).

More fundamentally, the institutions may not enjoy sufficient trust to promote long-term commitments. In particular, there are insufficient arenas for political deliberation and preference formation in Europe at present. Others' commitment to the common European weal seems required but not yet secured. I submit that this is one way to understand Dieter Grimm's (1995: 293-94) concern about the present absence of a European public sphere and other prerequisites for democratic rule, especially majoritarian arrangements. Institutions must face the double challenge of economising on trust while at the same time fostering the means for credible commitments among Europeans. For such reasons majority rule may best be introduced only gradually, as we indeed witness in the successive treaties.

The right response to this risk surely is not that the normative political ideals and standards of democratic governance should be scrapped. This would run counter to the traditional critical function of normative political theory in the Western tradition. Rather, the introduction of Union citizenship should bolster demands for institutional redesign and further development of the necessary public arenas, so as to secure continued, willing compliance with these coercive institutions. Such political craftsmanship must rest on awareness of not only the scope, but also the prerequisites and limits to institutional redesign (Olsen 2000, Joerges, Mény & Weiler 2000). It remains to be seen whether the political will and resources for such changes exist. Only better institutions, visibly securing a just and democratically responsive political order among citizens committed to a fair Europe, can secure long-term trust among Union Citizens.

3. A Structural – Non-Identical, Multi-Level, Cooperative and Institutional – Approach to European citizenship

Julian Nida-Rümelin

3.1. Introduction

The aim of this paper is to present a philosophical account of what European, and more generally supranational, citizenship could be. Modern political theory, ranging from the European enlightenment to the present, has not yet developed a conceptual frame within which supranational citizenship can be understood. The aim of this paper is to present an understanding of European citizenship that meets this challenge by going beyond established paradigms of political theory. This understanding of European Citizenship – and citizenship and civil society in general – is based on a specific concept of practical rationality that combines a deontological critique of consequentialism (Nida-Rümelin 1993) with elements of rational choice theory. I call this approach *structural rationality* (Nida-Rümelin 2001). It is *deontological* in character and therefore opposed to consequentialist (economic) rational choice, but at the same time it accepts the conceptual frame of decision theory if understood in a strictly *coherentist* and not in the standard consequentialist sense (Nida-Rümelin 2005:. 174-185). Cooperation as a specific form of human interaction forms the core of this approach of citizenship. This contribution is a philosophical one, with all its defects, i.e. lacking empirical content, being overly abstract and even worse, being based on a specific theory of rationality that you probably do not know. I will try to deal with these defects as far as is possible within such a limited space. In order to do this I lay more emphasis on the structure of my argument than on its details.

I propose an idea of European citizenship that is normative and descriptive at the same time. It is *normative* in the sense that citizenship is understood as a frame of cooperation, and cooperation is possible only if normative reasons are accepted by the agents. It is *descriptive* in so far as European citizenship is – at least partly – an empirical phenomenon. In other words, forms of cooperation actually exist in Europe that can be interpreted as elements of European citizenship in the sense that I am going to explain.

I proceed in four steps. First, I recollect three paradigms of citizenship or *status civilis*. Second, I briefly examine the question how citizenship and democracy are correlated. Third, I argue that citizenship and democracy should be understood as frames of cooperation, and fourth, I specify this account focussing on European citizenship.

3.2. Three Paradigms of Citizenship

It is easy to see that European citizenship constitutes a major challenge to modern political theory. Its dominating paradigms of citizenship are incompatible with the established institutional frame of the European Union. This allows for two reactions: dismiss the idea of European Citizenship, or develop a new conceptual approach that is able to incorporate European Citizenship. In order to show that European citizenship is indeed a major challenge to modern political theory, we take a short look, in this section, at the three dominating paradigms of Citizenship (*status civilis*, civic state): the Hobbesian, the Lockean and the Rousseauean.

The Hobbesian paradigm deduces the *status civilis* from two premises: rationality of men, which is the ability to choose efficient means for their ends, and three anthropological invariants: competition, diffidence and glory (Hobbes 1997, chap. 13). The civic state is constituted by establishing an actor endowed with the power to keep the citizens in awe and hence secure peace. There is only one level of Hobbesian citizenship: Hobbesian citizenship is constituted by the submission of every single individual to one central power. It is this central power and its effectiveness that transforms individuals into citizen. It is an asymmetric - all to one – relation between every individual and the central authority that secures civic peace. Citizenship in the Hobbesian *status civilis* is not constituted by a specific relation between one individual and the other. The expected flourishing of society after its establishment is not the result of civic cooperation but of limiting the ranges of competition, diffidence and glory. Since the anthropological traits of humans do not change from *status naturalis* to *status civilis*, the individuals remain atomic entities fostering their own good, competing with, distrusting and dominating other individuals, but now within the limits established by the central authority.

The Lockean (Locke 1690) civic state is based on two fundamental assumptions: the first assumption is that man is endowed with *individual rights*. This assumption has two parts: the first is a normative thesis concerning the Natural Law. Men are endowed with Lockean rights by nature and by God, which seems to be the same. The second part is an empirical thesis about human social psychology. Men tend to act according to the Natural Law and there is a wide normative consensus concerning these rights. All men are equal since they are equally endowed with these human rights and men tend to act in such a way that these individual rights are respected.

The second fundamental assumption is that men *act rationally within the constraints* imposed on action by individual rights. Nevertheless, the natural state is not peaceful because divergent views have to be expected concerning the limits of individual rights and how they should be sanctioned. The resulting conflicts tend to escalate and threaten individual liberty and well-being. The lawful state settles these conflicts and allows for competition within a property-owning lawful society. This civic competition does not include existential threats to the citizens if they are loyal, i.e. if they abide by the laws designed to secure the three basic natural rights – to live, not to be bodily harmed, to accumulate and keep one's own property. Civic loyalty requires the acceptance of juridical sanctions in case of law breaking.

62

As in the Hobbesian account, the Lockean civic state is established by a constitutive normative consensus, but whereas the Hobbesian consensus is confined to the concentration of state power and the exclusive normative authority of the sovereign[39], the Lockean consensus includes basic human rights that humans possess prior to their citizen status. Unlike the Hobbesian civic state, the Lockean is not merely constituted by an all-to-one relation regarding the central power. Mutual respect of natural liberties and human rights seem to be an essential part of Lockean citizenship. Strictly speaking, this is not true: mutual respect of natural liberties and human rights are already an essential element of the natural state and these normative elements thus are not peculiar to the civic state. Lockean rights can best be understood as constraints on individual optimizing. Optimizing is rational only within these constraints. The lawful state secures these constraints by making them explicit and by sanctioning them. Cooperation between individuals is not what constitutes Lockean citizenship.

The third paradigm of citizenship is the Rousseauean (Rousseau 1978). Contrary to the other two, it is historicist in a sense. The natural state threatens individual liberty because of the development of civilisation, which had its starting point when men began to strive for property. Natural liberty within the natural state disappeared in the continuing process of alienation from nature and growing economic dependency. In order to restore natural liberty it is necessary to establish the civic state as there is no way to return to the original human condition as part of a natural order. A civic state divides mankind into two forms of existence. The one is that of the *private man* with his personal interests and claims (the bourgeois). The other is that of the citizen (the *citoyen*) for whom personal interests and aims loose their relevance. The division is secured by establishing a method of collective decision making that makes individual interests irrelevant. This is possible only if political associations of any kind, for example parties and lobbies, are prohibited. Rousseauean citizenship is not based on the concentration of power, as in Hobbes, neither it is based on the preservation of individual liberty, as in Locke. It restores the original freedom for citizens if they leave behind their individual life and its constitutive preferences, attitudes and desires. Rousseau's citizens judge and decide as members of a political collective, their status as citizen makes them identical, there is no individual difference that can play a legitimate role within the political sphere. The common will is a result of insight and not of cooperation.

These three paradigms of citizenship are all *one-level accounts;* they establish – in different versions – a collective actor that is constitutive for citizenship. None of these paradigmatic accounts has a genuine idea of citizenship as a frame of cooperation. In essence, my argument is that if citizenship is understood as a cooperative frame, the one-level account, i.e. the idea that citizenship is constituted by a collective actor, can and should be given up. Genuine citizenship is based on cooperation.

---

39 One can debate the question whether these two characteristics in fact are identical as the traditional interpretation of Hobbes assumes.

Democratic political institutions are frames that uphold, foster and initiate social cooperation. Social cooperation is a multi-level phenomenon. It is compatible with multiple identities, regional, national and supra-national loyalties; it reinvents itself every day by the contingencies of interaction. If citizenship is understood as a frame of social cooperation, it is per definition non-identical and multi-level. This type of citizenship is the only adequate one for the case of European citizenship.

3.3. Citizenship and Democracy

Modern citizenship is democratic citizenship. The Hobbesian paradigm of the civic state is not a democratic one. The Rousseauean is likewise not a democratic one, although it takes a second look to verify this[40]. The Lockean civic state, however, is a democratic one, and consequently John Locke was much more influential in the process of developing the constitutions of western democracies than were Jean-Jacques Rousseau or Thomas Hobbes. There are diverging points of view on what democracy is now, and they have some impact on the concept of citizenship. I think one can quite sharply distinguish between *four paradigms of democracy* - even if nobody assumes that established democracies are mere exemplifications of one of these paradigms - each of which defines a core element of a democratic system.

The first paradigm emphasises the relation between individual actors and those agents who politically represent the citizens in the democratic state. The constituent element of democracy is the collective actor, and democracy is defined by the way the decisions of this collective actor are legitimized. The *theory of collective choice* tries to make the criteria that constitute a democratic collective act explicit.

The second paradigm of democracy considers the *market,* in the broader sense, to be constitutive. In the political market, political goods are supplied and demanded and different interest groups compete in it .It is the bargaining process which frames political decisions. Lobbies are no threat to a democratic order but essential elements. Associations of any kind allow for a rationalisation of the bargaining process.

The third paradigm of democracy could be labelled *forum.* Different speakers develop their ideas; the public listens and makes up its mind. If a democratic decision is to be taken, the arguments that were developed in this discourse are to be weighed against each other and the project with the best arguments obtains the majority's support. The forum-paradigm of democracy focuses on the deliberative aspects of a democratic decision process.

The fourth paradigm of democracy could be labelled *praxis.* This paradigm considers civil engagement to be constitutive of democracy. Without civil engagement, there can be no democracy. Civil engagement is the core of every democratic order. Some associate this paradigm with strong democracy (Barber 1984).

---

40   Cf. the role of the legislator in Rousseau (1978), second book, chap. 7.

The relations between the paradigms of the civic state and the paradigms of democracy are quite complex and can only be sketched here for the purposes of my argument. Our sympathy for democracy may suggest that there is no citizenship without democracy. However, one should keep these two concepts logically separate. Conceptually it is possible that there is genuine citizenship in a non-democratic state. It makes sense to include the most important paradigms of the civic state in the concept of citizenship.

Every civic state constitutes some kind of citizenship. The Hobbesian civic state does not exclude democratic decision procedures, but neither does it require them. Hobbesian citizenship is constituted by the establishment of a common power that keeps all citizens in awe to secure peace. Cooperation plays an important role in the deductive argument that leads to the establishment of the state. Everybody does his part in a collective action that ends the war of nature. As Hobbes tries to show, everybody has an interest in the establishment of a common power. There is no consensus regarding the method of collective decision making (which would be relevant for democratic citizenship) but there is a consensus on how to preserve peace in the civic state.

Likewise, Lockean citizenship is primarily constituted by institutions that make sure that different opinions on how to sanction violations of individual human rights do not result in violent conflicts. There is a consensus regarding the establishment of a lawful state because its establishment is in the interest of everybody, even if everybody preferred a condition in which he could freely decide while all others obeyed the law. Additionally, in the Lockean civic state democratic decision procedures help to solve political conflicts. Lockean citizenship is constituted primarily by a consensus on the lawful state and secondarily by a consensus on majority rule.

In Rousseau's civic state, the individuals regain their original freedom by becoming genuine citizens. To be a citizen means to adopt political objectives as those of the common will. Since there is only one common will, democratic decision procedures are irrelevant in the ideal Rousseauean polis. Everybody agrees with everybody on the common will. Differences of opinion can arise only because of epistemic deficiencies. Rousseauean citizenship is not a democratic one.

3.4. Frames of Cooperation

It seems to me that cooperation is essential for understanding genuine citizenship, i.e. that there is a conceptual link between citizenship and cooperation. The fact that all three paradigms of the civic state and its correlated citizenship are contractarian and, therefore, cooperative accounts, does not prove the correctness of this assumption, but it is at least a good indication that the assumption might be true.

Contrary to what standard rational choice theory assumes, cooperative action can be represented by the well-known Prisoner's Dilemma Game. To cooperate means to choose that strategy C which is dominated by another strategy and for which it is the case that, if all actors choose C (or contribute to a collective strategy which belongs to C) they all fare better than if they all choose the dominant strategy D (or: contribute to the collective strategy D). The two-person case matrix that represents such a situation is:

		Table 3.1	
		B	
		C	D
A	C	3/3	1/4
	D	4/1	2/2

Standard decision theory assumes that cooperation in a one-shot Prisoner's Dilemma is rationally impossible because it would require incoherent preferences. The argument goes as follows.

The matrix above can be interpreted such that A has a first priority for a collective decision in which he himself does not cooperate whereas the other one does cooperate. The second priority is that both cooperate. The third priority is that both do not cooperate and the worst case is that he himself cooperates whereas the other person does not. If these are the preferences of A, then A prefers not to cooperate irrespective of what the other person does. If the probability of the other person's decision is independent from what A chooses, it follows that it cannot be rational for A to cooperate, because cooperation would run against his own preferences. Put in different terms, cooperation would reveal that he at least prefers to cooperate if the other person cooperates, or that he cooperates even if the other person does not cooperate because otherwise no probability whatsoever for B to cooperate would render cooperation rational. However, by establishing the matrix given above we have assumed that this assumption does not hold.

This interpretation is indeed necessary given the presuppositions of standard rational choice theory. One of the presuppositions is that one cannot drive a wedge between choice and preference. In interpreting the matrix by the preference relation given above we conceptually excluded such a "wedge". If, however, we discriminate between preference relations regarding consequences of choice on the one hand, and preferences regarding strategies within a given structure of interaction, on the other hand, then such a wedge between choice and preferences becomes conceptually possible (Nida-Rümelin 2005).

I have argued at length elsewhere that consequentialism fails not only in ethics, but also in the theory of rational choice (Nida-Rümelin 1995). The theory of rational choice should be considered a theory of coherent preferences and coherent subjective probabilities and nothing else. The standard rational choice account, however, is consequentialist in character. It adds a specific interpretation that goes far beyond the coherentist assumptions of the utility theorem (von Neumann & Morgenstern 1944; Marschak 1950).

We should adopt a structuralist point of view, according to which it is possible to cooperate rationally even in a one-shot Prisoner's Dilemma, because the structural traits of interaction can play a crucial role for the rational decision. A cooperative attitude reveals itself by driving a wedge between choice and preference in situations of the Prisoner's Dilemma type. It is a Prisoner's Dilemma insofar as the consequences of the four possible combinations of individual action are ranked the way the matrix suggests. The cooperative attitude comes into the game given this structural background of individual preferences that constitutes the Prisoner's Dilemma. The cooperative attitude reveals itself in choice C. This choice does not result in inconsistent preferences because it reveals a preference for cooperation and does not change the preferences regarding consequences. A person who is motivated by a cooperative attitude rationally chooses C although choosing C does not optimize the consequences of her decision. Not optimizing consequences does not necessarily result in inconsistent preferences or irrationality. Whether it does or not depends on the conceptual frame and the structuralist account allows for rational choice that is not consequentialist choice.

Cooperative choice can be rational. However, since cooperative choice is defined as running counter to optimizing consequences given the personal preferences, co-operation requires a certain distance from my personal point of view. Even if I have no altruistic motives at all, it is my contribution to a collective strategy that renders cooperation rational. It is the embedding of my cooperative strategy in a collective cooperative strategy that is essential for driving the wedge between choice and preference. But distance from the personal point of view is what makes up the normative. Within the structuralist account, the difference between the Assurance Game and the Other Regarding Game can be interpreted as different degrees of cooperative attitude (Sen 2001). *All cooperate* is one equilibrium point in the Assurance Game besides the other equilibrium point *all do not cooperate*, whereas in the Other Regarding Game *all cooperate* is the only equilibrium point. In fact, one could not even understand what it means to say that in the Other Regarding Game persons can cooperate if the Prisoner's Dilemma structure does not survive in this process of transformation from Prisoner's Dilemma to Assurance Game to Other Regarding. The structuralist account allows the Prisoner's Dilemma to survive in this process insofar as the preferences regarding consequences can still be unchanged, even if the cooperative attitude becomes stronger from Prisoner's Dilemma to Assurance Game and from Assurance Game to Other Regarding (Nida-Rümelin 1997, chap. 8).

The cooperative attitude modelled by the Assurance Game can be described as *conditional cooperation*: The person wants to cooperate if she can expect the other person to cooperate too. But, if she cannot expect the other person to cooperate she does not want to be the fool. In the Other Regarding Game, however, the person has a strong cooperative attitude because she wants to do her part no matter what she expects the other persons to do. In a way, she cooperates as part of a fictitious sample of cooperative actions even if she does not expect that this preferred collective action becomes true. Kantian ethics requires choosing cooperation even if one cannot expect others to join. But Kantian ethics puts the individual choice in the broader frame of generalizeable maxims or normative laws: "To act only so that the will through its maxims could regard itself at the same time as giving universal law" (Kant 1990: 51). It would not be reasonable to assume that all citizens of a society are Kantian agents. Yet, cooperative attitudes to a certain degree are widespread, and the empirical situation thus is somewhere in-between the Prisoner's Dilemma and the Assurance Game, but rarely goes beyond the Assurance Game in the direction of the Other Regarding Game. It follows that institutions are essential to render the expectation that others might cooperate as well rational.

Without an institutional frame that upholds, fosters and initiates social cooperation, the concrete cooperative citizens' activities would not be stable, if they were to arise at all. Without institutional backing, social cooperation empirically limits itself to those actors closely associated with each other. This empirical result (Putnam 2001) converges with the result of dynamic game theory which has shown that cooperative strategies have a chance to survive the selection process only if there is a high probability for continued interaction (Axelrod 1984).

If citizenship is understood as one form of genuine cooperation, the aspects of cultural unity and diversity gain new relevance for the theory of citizenship. The multi-level approach of this structuralist perspective allows for a divergence between the personal point of view and the citizen's point of view. One might call this a rational reconstruction of the Rousseauean paradigm of citizenship. The private person (the bourgeois) is represented by the preferences regarding consequences. These preferences are constituted by his regarding the structures of interaction. They are strictly individualistic preferences, which may represent personal economic interests, but also personal cultural points of view or subjective morals. As a citizen, one takes one's own personal point of view, one's personal economic interests, one's personal cultural orientation, one's personal morals into account, knowing, however, that other citizens have other personal points of view, other economic interests, other religious orientations, other private morals. As a citizen, one develops preferences regarding choice, which take this structure or setting of divergent personal points of view into account.

Citizens cooperate by preserving and surpassing their personal points of view at the same time. Citizens take diversities of culture, religious orientation, economic interests, and life forms seriously. Citizens do not adopt a strategic attitude regarding the diversities. Citizens do their part in a broader cooperative frame that constitutes citizenship. Empirically established cooperative frames are multi-level forms of cooperation: Some are intimately connected with one's private life and others include interactions that are rarely face-to-face. Citizenship is that part of this cooperative frame that is based on political institutions.

3.5. European Citizenship

Let us see how these quite abstract considerations help to understand European citizenship better.

European citizenship is atypical insofar as the civic state is not established on the European level. There is no common power to keep them all in awe in the words of Thomas Hobbes, and there is not even a European executive power that upholds, fosters and initiates cooperation. Up to now, the civic state on the European level is guaranteed exclusively by the member states. Since the civic state is constitutive for any citizenship if our argument is valid, European citizenship is derivative.

All essential elements of a democratic order are already established in every member state of the European community. European democracy is complementary. It extends the democratic institutional frame on the national level in order to uphold, foster and initiate cooperation transnationally within the European community. This cooperation differs from mere economic exchange because it is backed by citizens' rights and institutional duties. It does not establish the civic state and it does not establish a citizen status, but it extends the cooperative frame transcending the borders of the member states.

Since citizenship is a form of cooperation backed up by political institutions, it is not confined to one level of political decision-making. Federalist democracies put more emphasis on the aspect of cooperation, whereas centralized democracies like France put more emphasis on the process of democratic decision making on one level, namely the national. Federalist systems tend to dissolve central democratic action, they tend to disperse political responsibility and as a result, quick and coherent political action becomes difficult. European citizenship apparently remains in the tradition of federalism. A federalist understanding of citizenship adds a further level of cooperation backed by political institutions. From the standpoint of centralized nation states, European citizenship cannot be an extension of the national *status civilis*. It can either be a threat or merely a non-genuine form of citizenship.

It is a threat because in this understanding there can be only one genuine citizenship constituted by democratically legitimised central political action. The structuralist account, which we advocated above, favours a federalist understanding of citizenship, and it seems to me that this is the more adequate understanding of European citizenship. It is able to integrate the universalist account of a common citizen's morality with communitarian elements of cultural and regional identities. The model of rational cooperation forms its basis.

The stillborn European constitution contained elements of such a structural account, for example in articles I-46 and I-47. The convention's constitution contained libertarian and cooperative elements, but the institutional parts made clear that the "United States of Europe", with the European level being constitutive for political agency, was not intended. The structural cooperative design of the European political institutions backs this interpretation. European Citizenship is best understood as a structural one: non-identical, multi-level, cooperative and institutional.

4. Some Reflections on European Civic Patriotism

Cecile Laborde

4.1. Introduction

There is a tension within contemporary liberal theories of citizenship. On the one hand, liberals have argued that in pluralist societies political institutions cannot draw their legitimacy from an appeal to thickly constituted shared values. On the other hand, there is a growing sense that citizens' attachment to their institutions – what may be called patriotism – can be instrumental in fostering the virtues essential to the legitimacy and stability of liberal democracy. Is it possible to reconcile the conflicting imperatives of respect for diversity and sustained democratic legitimacy? In Europe, an influential school of thought, loosely inspired by Jürgen Habermas' constitutional patriotism (*Verfassungspatriotismus*), has argued that patriotic commitment is legitimate, in so far as it is directed at universalist-orientated political constitutions and detached from particular cultural contexts. Does constitutional patriotism succeed in reconciling democratic legitimacy and cultural diversity? Although I am in broad sympathy with the constitutional patriotic project, I argue that the strategy of relative insulation of politics from identity, which it pursues at least in its 'neutralist' version, is self-defeating. It turns out to be deficient on the ground of legitimacy – a familiar criticism of constitutional patriotism – but also of inclusiveness – a less common and more damaging criticism. This is because constitutional patriotism fails to take seriously the need for cultural mediations between citizens and their institutions and the identity-shaping function of institutions.

The question I want to ask is, using Habermas' phrase (1996a: 281-294), how much does it take for distant people to "feel politically responsible for each other"? If we care about the intensity of political deliberation, the survival of social-democratic practices, and the combined pursuit of legitimacy and inclusiveness, what kind of patriotism do we need? Elsewhere I have made a case for civic patriotism within nation-states, a civic patriotism that recognizes the role of particularist political cultures in grounding universalist principles. Civic patriotism is both more 'situated' and more radical than 'neutralist' constitutional patriotism. It promotes a mainly political identity, whose political content makes it compatible with a variety of practices and beliefs, but whose thin particularistic form justifies citizens' commitment to specific institutions and their permanent criticism through processes of deliberative democracy. In this chapter, I first set out the case for civic patriotism, in contrast to both the 'neutralist' and the 'critical' versions of constitutional patriotism. I then assess the prospects for civic patriotism, redefined as a critical constitutional identity, to function as an appropriate form of identity for European citizens[41].

4.2. Constitutional Patriotism: Critical and Neutralist

The constitutional patriotic account begins with the relatively simple proposition that the relationship between patriotism and cultural diversity is problematic only if, as in nationalist rhetoric, the focus of patriotic loyalty is the dominant culture. If instead, patriotism is seen as fostering citizens' commitment to the 'abstract procedures and principles' (Habermas 1989: 261) outlined in the constitution, it becomes compatible with a variety of cultural beliefs and practices. The social bond in a liberal-democratic state should be, in the words of one of Habermas' followers, 'juridical, moral and political, rather than cultural, geographical and historical'(Ferry 1992b: 174). Allegiance to the political community thus becomes independent of individuals' ethnic and cultural origins, religious beliefs, and social practices. By thus detaching political loyalty from the dominant culture, constitutional patriotism attractively combines the universalist and inclusive ideals of liberalism with a recognition that citizens of a liberal-democratic polity must display at least some shared dispositions and commitments.

However, the elusive nature of these dispositions and commitments has attracted the scepticism of critics of constitutional patriotism. Three types of concerns have been raised. First, if universalist inclusiveness requires that constitutional principles be as abstract as possible, how can we justify the requirement that individuals commit themselves to this or that particular constitution or polity[42]? Second, is a commitment to liberal procedures and principles sufficient to actualize the sense of trust and solidarity essential to maintain the thick web of mutual obligations upon which the liberal-democratic state rests? (Miller 1995, Canovan 2000: 413-432, Thibaud 1992: 19-126) Third, is it possible to disentangle liberal principles from the particular cultural contexts in which they acquire their practical political significance (Bader 1997: 771-813)? Critics of constitutional patriotism thus have challenged both the feasibility and the desirability of the 'uncoupling' (to use Habermas' term) of political loyalty and cultural affinity. In truth, or so I shall suggest, Habermas himself has been much more aware of these problems, and his constitutional patriotism is considerably more subtle than the customary representation of his views suggests. Unfortunately, as I will argue, his followers have tended to develop two alternative

---

41 My account of European civic patriotism is partly influenced by a 'republican' reading of Habermas' constitutional patriotism and by the 'cosmopolitan communitarianism' articulated by Castiglione & Bellamy (1998). There are significant differences of emphasis between these 'neo-republican' approaches, but I believe that they exhibit a significant core of shared principles, distinct from traditional standard liberal and communitarian accounts.

42 For a classic Kantian solution to this problem, see Waldron (1993: 3-30).

interpretations of constitutional patriotism (a 'critical' and a 'neutralist' interpretation) both of which, in different ways, tend to neglect Habermas' central insight, namely, the role of particularistic political cultures in grounding universalistic principles.

Let me first briefly resituate constitutional patriotism in the context of Habermas' wider opus. Confronting his conservative opponents in the seminal *Historikerstreit* (Historians' Debate), Habermas argued that a German liberal democratic national identity could only be elaborated through critical confrontation with the nation's past (in particular the Holocaust). The constitutional patriotism he called for did not imply the denial of the particular historical legacy the Federal Republic of Germany inherited, but rather the adoption of a "scrutinizing attitude towards one's own identity-forming traditions" (Habermas 1989: 236). Constitutional patriotism, in his view, involves a selective appropriation of one's past. It demands that political communities come to terms, through remembrance and fortitude, with repugnant legacies, and also that they endorse 'the heritage of cultural traditions that is consonant with abstract universalist principles' (Habermas 1989: 262).

Such a 'situated' understanding of constitutional patriotism is in line with Habermas' emphasis on, what he calls elsewhere, the unavoidable 'permeation of constitutional states by ethics' (Habermas 1994: 106-148)[43]. Democratic political cultures are grounded in ethical-political communal self-interpretations, which reflect the identity of particular political communities. Deliberately produced law should strive to be "neutral…vis-à-vis the internal ethical differentiation" (Habermas 1994: 134-135) inherent in multicultural societies, and democratic political cultures should be dissociated as much as possible from the history and culture of the dominant group. It remains, however, that they will inevitably express "an interpretation of constitutional principles from the perspective of the nation's historical experience [which] to this extent, cannot be ethically neutral" (Habermas 1994: 134)[44]. This ethical (or cultural) coloration of constitutional principles is not to be lamented. It crucially provides a "motivational anchorage" for citizens exercising their collective rights of public autonomy, and underpins the development of a "we-perspective of active self-determination" (Habermas 1999: 263). Constitutional patriots, Habermas concludes, must show 'loyalty to the common political culture', not simply to abstract principles (Habermas 1994: 134; 1999: 278).

More recently, he has defined constitutional patriotism as a 'patriotism based upon the interpretation of recognized, universalistic constitutional principles within the context of a particular national history and tradition' (Habermas 1998b: 308). Habermas' constitutional patriotism, therefore, must firmly be situated within the tradition of republican patriotism for which love of country and love of justice can

---

43 By 'ethics', Habermas means the normative dimension of particular cultures and forms of life.
44 On this point see O'Neil 1997, esp. chapters 6 and 7, and McCarthy 1999: 175-208.

be mutually supportive[45]. The civic patriotism I defend here elaborates on some central insights of this tradition, while taking issue with the interpretation of constitutional patriotism that has become dominant in recent debates about nationalism and liberalism.

Habermasian constitutional patriots have tended to split into a 'critical' and a 'neutralist' group, both of which have been only selectively faithful to the complexity of the original articulation of Habermas' theory. Critical theorists have concentrated on the radical potential of constitutional patriotism as a subversive force, intent on 'de-centering' and de-stabilizing homogeneous, hegemonic national identities. Drawing on Habermas' defence of 'post-national' identities and on his discursive theory of democracy, they have drawn attention to the pervasive but shifting nature of identities; the unavailability of transcendental, 'neutral' universal principles; the conflictual and open-ended outcomes of struggles for recognition and the permanent 'failure of equivalence' between principles and institutions. Constitutional patriotism, in their view, should shun all forms of 'identification' and instead inform 'practices that resist identification'. Citizens should positively embrace difference, and combat the exclusionary proclivities of appeals to 'closed' (typically national) identities through reflexive, self-critical engagement with others in democratic forums of deliberation[46].

Critical constitutional patriots are right to point out the subversive impact of constitutional patriotism upon traditional conceptions of national identity, and to suggest that the achievement of genuine inclusiveness requires deliberative democracy. However, because of their sceptical stance towards universal rights and principles, they tend to underestimate their role in constraining agonistic discursive conflicts, whose outcomes may otherwise turn out not to be liberal, inclusive or egalitarian. Further, because of their dismissal of all forms of 'identification' and 'commitment' as potentially oppressive, critical constitutional patriots remain quite elusive about what exactly will motivate citizens to engage actively in the self-critical, other-regarding practice of deliberation in a democratic community. The critical theory of constitutional patriotism, in short, is both insufficiently 'constitutional' and insufficiently 'patriotic'. While its advocacy of a deliberative, discursive and a potentially radical form of political identity is central to the civic patriotism I articulate below, it cannot stand on its own as a sustained attempt to combine moral universalism with more particular and fairly stable commitments and loyalties.

'Neutralist' constitutional patriots, on the other hand, have been more faithful to Habermas' original intentions – the reconciliation of social inclusion and political legitimacy – but they have only partially succeeded in both areas. Unlike critical theorists, 'neutralists' have neglected the deliberative, critical dimension of constitutional patriotism and, like critical theorists they have underestimated the role of

---

45   This interpretation of Habermas is notably suggested by Viroli (1995: 169-177) and Müller (2000: 96-97).

46   See Markell (2000), pp. 38-63; Bartholomew (2000); Delanty (1996), pp. 20-32.

political culture in underpinning political loyalty and social solidarity. This is because the neutralist version of constitutional patriotism takes Habermas' injunction to 'uncouple' politics and culture (too) literally. For example, for Etienne Tassin (1994: 111), constitutional patriotism 'refuses any convergence between culture and politics'. In most recent discussions, constitutional patriotism is likened to a 'culture-blind' principled patriotism. This tallies with the influential liberal approach to the relationship between citizenship and identity, often interpreted as requiring the state to adopt a 'hands-off' approach in matters of cultural identity: justice requires abstraction from particular bonds and loyalties[47]. The 'politics/culture' dichotomy is seen as neatly overlapping with germane distinctions central to the liberal articulation of 'thin' principles of the 'right', neutral towards 'thick' conceptions of the 'good'. Constitutional patriotism is thus interpreted as valorising 'universalism' over 'particularism'[48]; 'principles' over 'identity'[49] and 'procedures' over 'substance'.[50]

In addition, constitutional patriotism is brought to bear on two other important developments within liberal thought, namely the dis-aggregation of democratic citizenship and legal rights, with the latter being increasingly grounded in the universalistic basis of personhood (Soysal 1994, Cohen 1999) and the search for a 'liberal' (i.e. non-cultural and universalistic) form of nationalism, of which constitutional patriotism is often presented as the 'purest' version[51].

This collusion between constitutional patriotism and forms of 'culture-blind' neutralist liberalism, evident in much recent literature, has helped to obscure the role played by political culture in grounding constitutional patriotism. 'Neutralists', as a result, have not satisfactorily resolved the question of the articulation between universalist principles and particularist cultures. Attracta Ingram, for example insists that the distinguishing feature of constitutional patriotism is the attempt to substitute 'loyalty to universal values' for 'shared identity'. But, she later unexpectedly refers to the need for 'a shared political culture' expressing 'a solidarity rooted in regard for the concrete institutions that belong to our distinct political heritage' (Ingram 1996: 3, 14, 15). The problem, of course, is that the very concept of political culture blurs the distinction between (universalist) norms and (particularist) cultures. While implicitly admitting that universalistic principles need to be anchored in particular

---

47 For the charge that contemporary liberalism is committed to this misconceived form of cultural neutrality, see Carens, (2000: 8-14); Kymlicka, (1995: 3-4) and Tamir (1993: 147-150).

48 'Constitutional patriotism de-ethnicizes citizenship by replacing cultural attachments, which by definition are specific, with allegiance to institutions and symbols which are potentially universalizable.' (Lamoureux 1995: 132)

49 'Sharing universal values of democracy and respect for justice and rights [as opposed to sharing an] identity, in the sense of shared language, associations and culture.' (Ingram 1996: 3)

50 'Constitutional patriotism does not entail loyalty to a specific substantial community, but has the sole meaning of being loyal to the democratic procedures of the constitution.' (Mertens 1996: 336)

51 For theories of liberal nationalism more partial towards traditional 'cultural' bonds, see Miller (1995) and Tamir (1993).

contexts, neutralist constitutional patriots have been reluctant to explicitly discuss the degree and form of particularistic attachment that could legitimately be fostered for fear that appeal to particularism was ipso facto a concession to illiberal nationalism.

Is there a path between the Scylla of thick collective identity and the Charybdis of thin shared values? I shall suggest that there is, and that it is possible to combine the liberal and inclusive insights of constitutional patriotism with an awareness of the role played by political culture in the actual functioning of democratic politics – thus reconnecting with the deepest insights of Habermas' on deliberative and republican democracy, on post-conventional identity, on the German historians' debate, and on the substantive content of a European identity. Civic patriotism seeks to promote a mainly political identity, whose predominantly political nature makes it compatible with a variety of practices and beliefs, but whose thin particularistic content justifies citizens' critical commitment to specific institutions and practices. While committed to an essentially political construction of the social bond, civic patriotism acknowledges that the boundaries between the historical, cultural and political levels of identity are in practice much more porous than neat analytical distinctions allow. Political institutions and practices cannot be entirely separated from their wider cultural background. Further, liberal democracies need not shed their particular political culture in the name of moral universalism. Citizens can share a commitment to universal principles (civil liberties, equal rights, democratic self-government, etc.), and to the particular institutions and practices which actualize them – if and when they do. In other words, citizens strive to sustain their political culture and institutions because (and when) these represent their way of collectively realizing universalist ideals.[52].

This is by no means an intrinsically uncomfortable posture. Civic patriots have always subordinated their allegiance to a country to their love of liberty, even if it is their allegiance to this or that particular polity which coloured their understanding of liberty (Viroli 1995; Nabulsi 1999). In other words, a patriot should not say 'my country right or wrong', but rather, 'my country for the values it represents (or should represent).' Civic patriotism, in other words, promotes a critical constitutional identity. In what follows, I attempt to assess whether the three arguments I have developed to underpin my defence of civic patriotism at the national level would also apply at the European level. They are: political legitimacy; cultural inclusiveness; and social democracy. I ask whether a critical European constitutional identity is indispensable in order to combine diversity and solidarity in Europe, and briefly assess the prospects for its development.

---

52 I owe this formulation to Andy Mason. For his own discussion of patriotic identification, see Mason (2000: 115-147).

4.3. Political Legitimacy in Europe

Interestingly, the closest approximation to constitutional patriotism takes the form of a proposal concerning European institutions. For 'post-nationalist' thinkers, the future of Europe lies in a dissociation between 'rational' legal-political regulation (undertaken at the supra-national level) and 'emotional' cultural identity (cultivated at the national level)[53]. European political institutions should draw their legitimacy, not from an elusive European cultural solidarity, but from European citizens' commitment to abstract principles of democracy and human rights. While the post-national European polity should concern itself with the juridical implementation of universalist principles, nation-states should concentrate on the preservation of the cultural integrity of national identities.

This is in many ways an attractive picture, which captures the liberal intuition of the cultural neutrality of democratic politics, whilst being sensitive to feelings of national belonging. However, although the most perspicacious post-nationalists, following Habermas (1999, 1998b: 151-157, 2001: 5-26), advocate the emergence of a 'European public sphere' shaped by a 'shared political culture' and mediating between 'technical' supranational institutions and 'identificatory' national communities (Ferry 1992b: 141, 147, 188, 197), a radical version of 'neutralist' post-nationalism sees the EU as the embryo of a new type of polity based exclusively on rational 'ethico-political principles' whose legitimacy 'should in no way pertain to a logic of identity or identification' (Tassin 1994: 108).

I think this is both implausible and undesirable. It is implausible because all abstract principles require interpretation in concrete political and legal settings, and the EU cannot avoid, any more than any other political order, engaging in this work of interpretation[54]. It is undesirable because it underestimates the motivational conditions of democratic governance, the most important of which being the continued identification of citizens with their institutions. The development of institutions lacking in civic-cultural significance is likely to aggravate the chief symptoms of democratic malaise, namely, cynicism towards democratic rule, reluctance to share the burden of social justice, resentment towards aloof and acculturated elites, decline of civic dispositions, alienation vis-à-vis an increasingly 'privatized' public sphere. To be fully legitimate, political institutions must be perceived by citizens as democratic forums of self-rule where debate is inclusive and comprehensible, representatives fully accountable, and decisions publicly justified.

A well-functioning public sphere of this sort requires something more than a shared commitment to universal principles, something which motivates citizens to feel that particular institutions are somehow theirs, in a meaningful sense, so that they are in a position to adopt what Habermas calls the 'we-perspective of active self-determination' (Habermas 1999: 263). Attachment to a specific political com-

53   For a lucid exposition and defence, see Lacroix (2004, 2002).
54   On this, see the analyses of Bellamy (1999).

munity provides the sense of trust and solidarity necessary for both the stability of just institutions and their permanent correction by active citizens. Abstract commitments to human rights, justice and equality, although they might justify particular dispositions and actions, do not provide their cause or their motivation.

This is partly connected to the radical indeterminacy of universalistic principles. Agreement by citizens over constitutional essentials, in itself, does not provide a firm common ground for civic solidarity. Such general agreement may in fact paper over deep, reasonable disagreements over the meanings of these principles and over how to apply them in particular cases (think of principles such as equal respect, or free speech, or the right to life). So why would rational and reasonable citizens commit themselves to principles, the meaning of which they deeply disagree upon? Because, I suggest, following Frank Michelman (2001), they are disposed to see those disagreements as strictly tied to struggles over their own constitutional identity without loss of confidence in the invariant content of the principles. In other words, they ascribe their disagreement to uncertainty about exactly who they think they are and want to be as a politically constituted people and not to the validity of the abstract principles themselves. The fixed point of certainty is a certain regulative 'ideal' of the constitution (whose general principles may be immanent to the practice of constitutional argument itself), a regulative ideal in the light of which citizens engage in the ethical, collective interpretation and assessment of *their* institutions and practices. Citizens are attached to their constitutional identity, which is coloured by the 'historical context of a particular community', in Habermas' terms. Such constitutional identities have historically emerged in Europe within nation-states. Think, for example, of the diverse interpretations of such rights as the right to privacy, the right to life and social rights, in countries such as France, Great Britain and Ireland. While the citizens of these countries might see themselves as sharing a commitment to the regulative ideals of the liberal-democratic state, they also see themselves as participants in an on-going dialogue whereby abstract ideals are interpreted and re-interpreted in light of their particular experience.

So where does this leave the prospects for a European constitutional identity? As I have defined it, there is currently little in the way of a genuinely European constitutional identity – an identity which is not shared only by European constitutional judges and bureaucrats but reaches out to the collective self-understandings of European citizens. The risk of dualization of the European body politic is a serious aspect of the much-discussed 'democratic deficit' in the EU. European rights and standards are too often perceived by suspicious national publics as externally and undemocratically imposed constraints.

The British reaction to the Law Lords' reference to the European Convention of Human Rights (ECHR), in order to justify their criticism of the 2001 Act allowing the indefinite detention without trial of foreign terrorism suspects, was very telling in this regard. The Government appealed to the sovereign right of the British Parliament to ignore the European Convention if necessary[55,] while critics prudently retorted to more congenial appeals to the age-old, indigenous, common law tradition of *Habeas Corpus*. Interestingly, both sides largely saw the European Convention as 'foreign' and irrelevant to their national constitutional identities and the political debates surrounding it.

Yet, EU law ultimately only draws on the fundamental rights and principles that are common to the constitutional traditions of European countries. So the ideals of the ECHR are no alien imposition, but the product of the confrontation and interpenetration of a diversity of national 'rights-cultures'. Unless and until the citizens of the *demoï* of Europe can see those processes of constitutional identity-formation as debates about their own constitutional identity, they are unlikely to fully accept the legitimacy of European-wide institutions. European integration, including its legal dimension, should be politicized and not only left to bureaucrats and judges. Thus, what is required at the European level is a version of the deliberative legal and democratic culture of the kind that civic patriotism fosters at national level. Evidently, this is a more stringent pre-requisite for European citizenship than mere assent to general principles and, to that extent, it will take some time for the European polity to duplicate the motivational conditions of democracy.[56]

The legally mediated solidarity between strangers that a constitutional identity provides, has historically been fostered within nation-states, and it is not *logically* bound to stop there. But the emergence of a European civic patriotism will require the reproduction of *at least some* processes of political identity-formation at a European level. Habermas (2001: 15) calls this "the prerequisites for a Union that would assume at least some qualities of a state" (Habermas), namely the emergence of a European civil society, the construction of a deliberative European-wide public sphere, the development of trans-national political parties, intermediary associations and media, and the shaping of a constitutional identity that can be endorsed by all European citizens. National constitutional debates must be brought to bear on one another, and this process of mutual engagement and confrontation of still relatively self-contained political cultures must be complemented by the development of transnational constitutional debates. As Jean-Marc Ferry (2000) puts it, for citizens to feel 'integrated in the "we" of political culture' a European 'culture of citizenship' must be fostered, which requires the 'communisation' of national political cultures in a trans-European public sphere and their critical confrontation through deliberative practices.

What is at stake, is the development of Europe-wide democratic practices and the emergence of supranational constitutional identity at a European level. Such an

55 Yet the European Convention was given domestic effect in Britain by the Human Rights Act of 1998.

56 For sceptical considerations about the likelihood of 'political and affective mobilisation' supplementing 'intellectual adhesion' to Europe, see Schnapper (2004: 352). A slightly different criticism of European constitutional patriotism is offered by Bauböck (1997: 13-17).

identity, in republican and constructivist fashion, does not predate, ground, or found political activity, but is generated by it or, more accurately, it deliberately emerges from the democratic confrontation and interpenetration of existing national political cultures. Whether the ratification of the Constitutional Treaty would have spurred this 'catalytic' process (in Habermas's terms)[57] is doubtful, but what is certain is that some mobilization of a European political community is essential to the legitimacy of the EU polity.

What, then, could the contours of this shared civic or constitutional identity be? Since 2001, Habermas has sought to give substance to this 'thin' European identity as an engaged observer wishing to 'mobilize political debate'. European political identity is essentially imagined as an alternative interpretation of the liberal democratic principles of the Enlightenment to the one prevalent in the United States. Thus Habermas writes about Europeans' commitment to secularisation and the separation between politics and religion, to state redistribution as a counterweight to the blind forces of the market, to a combination of private individualism and public collectivism, and to a principled foreign policy and cosmopolitan order (Habermas 2001a). Such broadly social democratic, left-liberal aspirations are seemingly endorsed by the Preamble of the Constitutional Treaty, which refers to the Union as promoting 'a culture of learning and social progress' for 'the good of all inhabitants including the most deprived', and acting 'for peace and solidarity in the world'. The near-universal opposition throughout Europe to the Anglo-American war on Iraq and the world order it seemed to promise was seen as the first expression of a genuinely Europewide public opinion (Derrida & Habermas 2003). With Habermas, civic patriots welcome such promising signs of the emergence of a European collective self-understanding.

Neutralist post-nationalists object that such a process would amount to replicating the historical process of nation-building, thus disregarding the novel, post-national nature of the European polity and taking the risk of replicating the very nationalist evils that the European community had been designed to fight (e.g. Lacroix 2004: 130-140). This fear strikes me as exaggerated. First, the European Union is so far from being a state that it is implausible to believe that any attempt to boost its civic, republican credentials would usher in an integrated politico-cultural community or European 'nation'. Second, the dangers inherent in nationalism can more easily be kept at bay in a relatively young, reflective polity such as the EU (as we shall see below, European identity can only be a 'post-conventional' critical identity). Third, European civic patriotism does not supplant national and other collective identities; it merely complements them. European citizens should feel a subjective sense of attachment to European institutions, commensurate with the level of co-operation they objectively experience in them. As things stand, it can hardly be doubted that this is not the case. To lament the lack of identification of European citizens with

---

57   For stimulating if cautious reflections on Europe's 'constitutional moment', see Walker (2004: 368-371) and Castiglione, (2004: 393-411).

European institutions is not the same as to aspire to the creation of a full-blown European state.

Neutralist post-nationalists often charge civic republicans with mistakenly applying to the EU polity categories derived from the 19th century experience of state- and nation-building. Yet, post-nationalists themselves are less emancipated from the nation-state paradigm (i.e. the Gellnerian congruence between political and cultural unity) than they claim, as they wrongly equate any process of collective political identification to the creation of a thickly integrated community, a European nation or *demos*. Breaking with the nation-state paradigm, however, requires us to imagine innovative forms of political community whereby citizens recognise each other as being involved in schemes of social co-operation for particular purposes (for example, foreign policy) and whereby they collectively define what it is they want to do (and be) together. Insofar as citizens view themselves as engaged in shared practices of self-rule, this can itself become a source of mutual identification and solidarity (Cronin 2003: 13).

4.4. Cultural Inclusiveness and Critical Identities

In making a case for civic patriotism at a national level, I suggested that it is, perhaps unexpectedly, more inclusive than neutralist constitutional patriotism because it takes seriously the cultural embedding of national constitutions and institutions, and is more sensitive to issues of cultural exclusion. Constitutional patriots would argue that citizens must be loyal to their institutions, provided they respect principles of justice. Civic patriots, instead, are more likely to worry about whether some citizens, such as members of minority groups, might feel alienated even by seemingly neutral legislation and institutions, if the latter are perceived to be culturally biased, embedded as they inevitably are in a particularistic heritage made up of complex ideological traditions, established languages, national symbols, frequent references to a shared – if often mythical – history, particular ways to structure time and space, accepted styles of argument and rhetorical devices, and so forth. As Will Kymlicka (1995: 3-4) has noted, the liberal (and neutralist) attitude of 'benign neglect' in matters of culture is detrimental to a critique of the imbrications between the majority culture and state politics, notably so for members of minority cultures.

In contrast to neutralist constitutional patriots, civic patriots take seriously the importance of cultural mediations between citizens and their institutions and the identificatory role of the latter. In this view, only those democratic institutions that can effectively secure the loyalty of all citizens, including members of cultural minorities, will be legitimate. Civic patriotism does not require that minority groups simply conform to the dominant culture, provided their basic rights are respected. It demands more; namely hat they feel 'at home' with what must be a genuinely shared identity. This puts pressure on the majority group, urging it to open-up the public sphere, to allow widespread contestation of deeply entrenched practices and beliefs, and to trim down its public culture. A strong, republican concept of political equality[58] ensures that inclusiveness is built into the civic patriotic model. It is a condition of the legitimacy of political institutions that all can be listened to and can identify with the decisions reached on the basis of inclusive deliberation. Of course, while every claim will be listened to, not all claims will be accepted. Rather, all groups can expect to have their demands publicly scrutinized and democratically discussed so as to favour the emergence of a shared 'framework of political meaning'[59]. Civic patriots argue that no more can be asked of newcomers than that they become familiar with the country's political culture in such a way as to become 'functioning' citizens. But it also insists that the political culture itself be one of the objects of democratic deliberation. Political culture – or constitutional identity – has an artificial character: it is created and altered by political activity itself. The only thing that can be required of citizens is that they be willing to engage in the conversation, that they see it as their own, and that they learn the skills which allow them to participate in it.

The character of public debate is not a fixed, unchanging property of the conduct of politics in a particular polity, but rather an artificial construct constantly altered by the emergence of new groups and new claims. The political culture of every democratic society bears the marks of the particular struggles of historically excluded groups – workers, the poor, women, immigrants – seeking to appropriate the existing public sphere and make good its abstract democratic promises of emancipation and equality. Even acute class conflicts have been shaped by, and have in turn shaped, national political cultures. Excluded groups have used the radical resources provided by democratic ideals to challenge systematic patterns of exclusion and impose a more expansive, more universalist form of communal self-understanding. They have done so by integrating, and then often subverting, existing particularist institutional and ideological structures.

Hence, civic patriots insist that existing ethnic and civic practices should be scrutinized, and only those that secure the reasoned acceptance of all those affected by it should be upheld. Such critical scrutiny – which assumes the possible destabilization and de-centering of any existing identity – takes place through inclusive processes of deliberative democracy. Civic patriotism believes in the broad malleability of culture and repudiates any essentialist conception of national identity. It takes seriously the importance of invented traditions, imagined histories, and founding myths, as flexible cultural artefacts constituting common (or at least overlapping) worlds of meaning. It draws on critical constitutional patriotism to justify a critical constitutional identity: one which does not pretend to be culturally neutral and based exclusively on allegiance to universalist principles, but which instead recognises its own historical and cultural particularity and seeks to universalise itself. So, the concrete

---

58 "The requirement that all individuals and groups have access to the political process."(Sunstein 1988: 1552)

59 For a sensitive exploration of examples of democratic cross-cultural deliberation, see Parekh (2000).

historical political community remains the object of attachment, even as interpretation of its identity shifts to accommodate the claims to recognition of minorities and newcomers (Cronin 2003: 9). While requiring that all citizens be socialized into a shared political culture, civic patriotism does not take this culture as a fixed legacy but as a 'lived' experience. It urges us collectively to engage in the ongoing project of the universalization of our political culture.

Would civic patriotism, thus conceived, provide an appropriately inclusive understanding of European identity? Civic patriotism is evidently more suited to the deliberative transformation of existing nation-states, characterised by secure boundaries and the co-existence of a dominant historic majority with more recently established immigrant communities and other previously excluded groups. It is *prima facie* less suited to multi-level polities such as the EU, which have a relatively thin common identity and are characterised by deep diversity, including the valued diversity of national constitutional identities. From this incontrovertible fact, neutralist post-nationalists deduce that European citizens should eschew any form of emotional identification and display a purely rational allegiance to abstract liberal and democratic principles. Thus, European identity is supposed to be 'thin', abstract, rational and critically oriented, in contrast to 'thick', warm, concrete, emotional and unreflective national identities.

Neutralist post-nationalists positively embrace abstract values and principles, but only sceptically and critically relate to concrete attachments to particular communities. There are two problems with this account. First, neutralists draw too strong a contrast between post-conventional, post-national identities on the one hand, and conventional, national identities on the other. In fact, there is no reason why European and national identities should not be made of the same 'stuff' – both are a complex mixture of universal and particularist, rational and affective, abstract and concrete concerns. It is true that national identities are still too pervasive, thickly constituted, and relatively uncritical, while European identity is still too rationalist, abstract and thin. Yet, whereas within nation-states civic patriots advocate the destabilisation of existing national identities, at a European level they engage in a more perilous exercise of *simultaneous* identity-shaping and identity-criticising. I argued above that some process of civic identity formation is necessary to ground European political legitimacy. I now want to suggest that it is also essential to the activity of (European) identity-criticising.

For the second flaw of the post-nationalist account is its exclusive focus on the identity-criticising function of the European constitutionalist and legalist order. The collective self-consciousness of Europeans, in the post-nationalist account, can only be negative and critical. It is one that, as Patchen Markell (2000: 57) has put it in his general defence of constitutional patriotism, must 'refuse and resist particular identifications'. Yet, it is incoherent to appeal to a merely negative and critical identity. This is a conceptual and not a normative point. To identify critically with one's polity is still to identify with it, to feel that one's prospects and self-esteem are bound up with it in a particular way, and to take special responsibility for its actions. Of course, we may feel justifiable anger and outrage at the wrongdoings of other countries and rightly protest and criticise them in the name of universal principles of human rights, democracy and so on, but when our *own* community does wrong we feel, *in addition*, a sense of shame and atonement precisely because we experience a feeling of personal involvement and responsibility. Habermas' point during the Historians' Debate was not merely that post-conventional identity should no longer be based on ethnic or cultural traits but on the universal principles of the democratic constitution (the 'neutralists' favoured interpretation). Nor was it merely that wartime atrocities should not be conveniently 'forgotten' (Renan-style[60]) but had to be critically interrogated. His polemical point against neoconservative historians was also that *Germans* had a special responsibility to atone for the evils perpetuated by the Nazis who claimed to speak and act *in their name*. As he strikingly put it:

> "our form of life is connected with that of our parents and grandparents through a web of familial, local, political, and intellectual traditions that is difficult to disentangle – that is, through a historical milieu that made us what and who we are today. None of us can escape this milieu, because our identities, both as individuals and as Germans, are indissolubly interwoven with it" (Habermas 1989: 233).[61]

This unavoidable entanglement generates a special responsibility. If this special responsibility applies to national civic patriots, it should also apply, in my view, to European citizens *qua* Europeans. Things that have been done in the name of 'Europe' should matter to us in a particular way because we, for better or for worse, feel 'European' in some relevant sense. The post-nationalist account would thus benefit from a more Hegelian, dialectical approach to make sense of the ambiguous notion of a 'self-critical identity'. Post-nationalists, in their attempt to de-legitimise any appeal to identity as dangerously bigoted, undercut their own hope that Europeans will actually engage in the process of critical reflection on (and sometimes positive re-appropriation of) their own heritage.[62]

European civic patriots, for their part, demand that European citizens simultaneously and dialectically assert and reflect on the ethical components of the historical identities of 'Europe'. This would involve taking pride in the latter's achievements – the invention of democracy and liberalism, the Renaissance and the Enlightenment, the legacy of wartime Resistance, and so forth – and also assuming responsibility for the darker sides of European history – including wars, genocide, imperialism and colonialism, anti-semitism, racism and Islamophobia. Habermas is confident that

---

60 Ernest Renan in *Qu'est ce qu'une nation?* famously argued that national identity partly had to be based on 'forgetting' painful historical episodes.

61. For a commentary, see Cronin.

62 There is, for example, a slight tension in Lacroix's (2004: 150-166) attempt *both* to defend Habermas and Ferry's historically-grounded, critical conception of constitutional patriotism, *and* to follow Tassin and Markell's suggestion that European citizens should eschew all forms of identity or identification and be open to 'otherness' (Lacroix 2004: 181-187). The latter thinkers lack an account of the special responsibility and identification citizens must feel towards their *own* polity, by contrast to both Habermas and Ferry who, especially in their 're-publican' writings, insist on positive identification (for example, to a common European political culture) as much as on negative dis-identification.

Europeans may have acquired the lucidity and courage to confront their own failings as painful historical experiences on the Continent have acted as "a spur to critical reflection on our own blind spots" and equipped Europeans with a disposition to the "de-centring of selective perspectives" (Habermas 2001a: 20). Only then can a "shared democratic culture in a post-national Europe", based on the ethics of discussion, emerge (Ferry 2000: 72-85, 161-169; Ferry 1992c: 177-188; Ferry 1992a: 80-93).

In what sense is this 'shared democratic culture', which is more historically and culturally self-aware than the abstractly universalist and critical disposition appealed to by many post-nationalists, an inclusive one? Let me take Turkey's membership application to the European Union as an example. Civic patriots do not, and cannot so any more than constitutional patriots, offer a definite answer to the issue of the ultimate territorial boundaries of the Union. Neither liberalism nor republicanism offer convincing theories of where political boundaries should lie and both generally assume some pre-political definition of who belongs to the polity. Yet, the external boundaries of the EU will have to be fixed, for purposes of political stability and legitimacy, although civic patriotism itself does not provide the conceptual and normative resources for doing so. Like post-nationalists, civic patriots eschew direct appeals to the 'objective' historical, cultural 'European-ness' (or lack thereof) of applicants for entry such as Turkey.

Thus, I agree with Lacroix (2004: 188-189) that neither Valéry Giscard d'Estaing's reference to the need to preserve Europe's Christian heritage, nor Bernard Henri Lévy's counter-argument that St Paul was in fact born on Turkish territory are acceptable arguments either for or against Turkey's entry. I also agree with her that the chief debate should revolve around whether Turkey meets broad liberal and democratic criteria, and whether integration is economically and socially viable.

However, I would argue that, in addition, two other important processes should take place, although not necessarily as formal conditions of entry. The first is that Turkey critically and publicly engages with its own past, notably recognizing its responsibility for the 1915 Armenian genocide. The second is that the EU critically engages with its own ambivalent historical attitude towards the Islamic world and Muslims in general. Civic patriots, therefore, do not adopt an attitude of 'benign neglect' vis-à-vis existing shared identities and historical mutual perceptions. While they do not take them as pre-requisites for identity-formation, they take them as the very material out of which future civic identities and a common destiny are deliberately, critically and dialectically forged. Through the integration of Turkey, the Union should elaborate a broader, more expansive understanding of itself. This it can only do if it comes to terms with the ways in which its own particular cultural self-understanding as 'Christian' or 'Western' has shaped and constrained its attitude to other cultures, both outside and within its boundaries. This is both an indispensable and a tricky process, as the heated debates over the meaning of the 'cultural, religious and humanist inheritance of Europe' in the Preamble of the Constitutional Treaty have revealed.

4.5. Social-Democracy in Europe

The last argument that I made for civic patriotism at a national level concerned the preservation of social-democratic practices and ethos in an increasingly globalised world. Criticising the views of some who, like David Miller, argue that social democracy and the extensive redistributive arrangements it requires, can only be sustained by sentiments of national fellow-feeling, I have argued that there is no intrinsic connection between solidaristic feelings and national identity. However, I have developed a prudential argument for the preservation of existing social democratic arrangements in an increasingly globalised world. On balance, economic globalization seems to have had a corrosive impact on the conditions of social democracy. The requirements of global financial discipline have tended to severely constrain the scope for progressive policies and to undermine the social bargain on which the post-Second World War welfare state rested, notably by undermining the power of states to reach democratic consensus on the redistribution of wealth and power (Garret & Lange 1991; Banuri & Schor 1992; Gray 1996; Cox 1997:. 49-71).[63]

In so far as global justice is (regrettably) little more than a distant possibility, and in so far as the only vibrant cosmopolitanism today is that of the free market, there is a case for the defence of local schemes of social justice. Nation-states have thus far proved to be a bulwark against the 'negative cosmopolitanism' (Falk 1996: 53-60) that induces the uneven distribution of social costs, the decline of democratic solidarity, the erosion of social rights, the decay of public services and the widening of inequalities, notably through what has been called the 'secession of the rich' (Lacoste 1997: 300) The intuition here is mainly prudential: as long as market-driven globalization is unable to reproduce the motivational and cultural conditions which have historically underpinned democracy and social solidarity, social democrats have no interest in dismantling existing networks of solidarity.

How could this argument about the 'social-democratic' component of civic patriotism apply to the EU? Any realistic assessment of the current state of 'Social Europe' will lead to a fairly negative conclusion. Not only is the 'social democratic vision' not shared by all European countries (as regular reading of the British press will tell you), and threatened by enlargement and undermined by talk of a division between 'old' and 'new' Europe, but even those countries which publicly endorse the defence of a 'social model' as an alternative to neo-liberal globalisation, increasingly tend to present the EU as epitomizing everything that is bad about economic globalisation.

So, I would be inclined to be less optimistic than Habermas, who argues that Europe should defend its 'own way of life' against the 'predominant global economic regime', which he sees as based upon an anthropological image of 'man' as rational chooser and entrepreneur, a moral view of society that accepts growing

---

63 For alternative views, see the discussion and bibliography in Held, McGrew, Goldblatt & Perraton (1999: 13-4 and passim).

cleavages and exclusions, and a political doctrine that trades a shrinking scope for democracy for the freedoms of the market. Habermas seeks to reformulate social democratic thought in the post-nationalist terms required to redress the negative aspects of globalisation, drawing on a variety of European 'social' traditions such as the workers' movement, Christian doctrine and social liberalism, as a 'formative background for social solidarity' (Habermas 2001a: 10). Europeans should be committed to guaranteeing, not only equal rights and liberties, but also their 'fair value', to use John Rawls' terms (Habermas 2001a: 10). While Habermas recognises that not all advocates of European integration share his substantive social-democratic beliefs, he suggests that social democrats have a tactical interest in promoting greater European economic integration as a stronger Union is a necessary, if not a sufficient condition for the emergence of a social-democratic Europe (Habermas 2001a: 12).

The problem, of course, is that European economic governance has thus far been underpinned more by neo-liberal than social-democratic ideals. Both the independent European Central Bank and the Commission routinely blame the inability of member states to implement structural neo-liberal reforms for the disappointingly poor economic performance of the Euro-zone. Yet, as Keynesian economist Jean-Paul Fitoussi has recently noted, the assumption that weak growth in the Euro-zone is caused by high taxation and expensive social security schemes is not an uncontroversial one and would deserve greater public scrutiny (Fitoussi 2005: 11).

Yet, in the absence of a European public sphere where European economic policy can be democratically elaborated and not left to 'independent' experts, a stronger economic Union seems to have contributed to undermining national social-democratic arrangements. Whether the democratization of economic policy-making at the European level would generate commitment by Europeans to sustain their historically distinctive social-democratic model, remains open to question. I would therefore be less sanguine than Habermas about the likelihood of the emergence of a truly social-democratic Europe. Greater economic integration in practice may undermine rather than support, existing schemes of social democracy. Furthermore, even if European economic governance were to be democratized and open to public scrutiny, there is no guarantee that it will *ipso facto* take a social-democratic turn.

This last sceptical point raises broader issues for civic patriots. Can all the goods that they promote (democratization, social justice, and critical identification) be pursued at the same time? The European Left has tended to gloss over the unavoidable tensions that exist between diversity and integration, between enlargement and solidarity, and even between democratization and social justice. For example, we may wonder how Habermas' defence of a substantive European 'way of life' fits with his commitment to the deliberative democratization and proceduralisation of European identity. It is a moot point whether deliberative democracy and critical constitutional debate at the European level in practice will generate the substantive 'Social Europe' that Habermas, and other social democrats, favour. When Habermas is arguing for constitutional patriotism, he is acting as a philosopher specifying the procedural conditions for the democratic emergence of an inclusive political identity. When advocating a Social Europe, by contrast, he is acting as an intellectual

87

articulating his own vision through a necessarily selective reading of Europe's tradition. This epitomizes the predicament of the Left in Europe. While European integration offers possibilities for the critical, pluralist, democratic universalization of closed and hegemonic identities and traditions, it is also an essentially open-ended process whose substantive outcome – for example, in terms of egalitarian economic and social policies – cannot be pre-empted. If, as philosophers, we should applaud the deliberative opportunities potentially opened up by post-national democracy, as intellectuals we should not be coy about putting forward substantive, principled and often partisan views about what 'Europe' *should* be about. We should do this as European civic patriots, if only as a way to initiate a much-needed public debate about a European constitutional identity.

Part 2 – Arenas: Civil Society and Institutions

5. European Citizenship through Networking?

Stijn Smismans

5.1. Introduction

If European citizenship is about the definition of rights this does not need to imply that the European Union must adopt at all costs uniform European legislation. In the multi-level polity of the European Union, rights are defined at different levels, going from the European, via the national, to the regional level, if the latter has legislative powers. In this multi-level setting, the principle of subsidiarity privileges the lower level, in particular the national, over the European one. Moreover, European legislation tends to be framework legislation, leaving flexible options for implementation at lower levels. Since the 1990s, the EU has also experimented with new policy tools that allow defining rights and formulating policy at the national level, while ensuring a soft coordination or exchange of best practice at the European level. This debate has been particularly stirred by the introduction of the Open Method of Coordination (OMC) in such different areas as macro-economic policy, employment policy, social inclusion, and migration policy. Yet, this soft coordination of national policies is not the only tool for 'networking national policies' in the EU. Already before the creation of the OMC, the EU had created various 'information agencies' that do not define rights at the European level but have the task to encourage the exchange of best practice and information on an already existing normative framework of rights and policies established at the national and partially European level. In the context of these information agencies the idea of 'networking' has sometimes become an explicit normative device; i.e. rather than imposing new European standards from above the encouragement of interaction among all stakeholders in a horizontal network is supposed to lead to more effective and more legitimate policies.

This chapter will first analyse how the concept of policy networks was developed as an analytical tool to be applied to such complex multi-level systems as the EU. It then analyses how the idea of 'networking' has gained also a normative dimension, in particular in the discourse of certain policy actors, as will be shown by means of an analysis of the European Agency for Health and Safety at Work. It concludes that, while it may be justified to reject the exhaustive definition of rights at the European level, European citizenship may be too weak if it is only understood as the definition of rights at the national level accompanied by loose networking at the European level. A minimum set of procedural participatory requirements in European networking, as well as respect of fundamental rights, is needed.

5.2. The Normative Challenge of the 'Policy Networks' Concept

The concept of 'policy networks' has acquired widespread popularity among political scientists,[64] including those analysing EU governance.[65] Recently it has even been introduced into legal scholarship (at least, among those scholars seeking to place 'law in context') (Dehousse 1997; Ladeur 1997, 1999; Armstrong 1998; Vervaele 1999). Generally, policy networks describe "structures of governance involving private and state actors linked together through varying degrees of resource dependencies that determine which actors dominate the network and how decisions are made" (Risse-Kappen 1996: 60). Yet, beyond this general definition, the concept is used in very different ways. Tanja Börzel (1997) distinguishes two 'schools' of policy networks, namely the 'interest intermediation school' and the 'governance school'.

For the first school 'policy networks' is a generic label embracing different types of relationships between interest groups and the State. It is used as an analytical tool for examining institutionalised exchange relations between the State and organisations of civil society. 'Policy networks' is understood as an umbrella concept which integrates the different forms of pluralism and corporatism as specific versions of networks (Rhodes 1997: 32).

However, I agree with those authors who question the added value of policy networks in explaining different forms of interest intermediation.[66] The concept is too general to have much explanatory value and gains more sense only when distinguishing different types of networks. Networks might then turn out to be 'iron triangles' (Lowi 1964; Peters 1986), 'advocacy coalitions' (Sabatier 1988), 'epistemic communities' (Haas 1992) or, indeed, pluralist or neo-corporatist settings that are considered to be a sub-type of policy-network (Rhodes 1997: 32). In these cases, the older theories and concepts tend to have more explanatory value[67] than the generic assumption that the distribution and type of resources within a network explain the

---

64 For the history of the concept in the American and British literature, see Rhodes (1997: 32), and Scharpf (1993). For the French literature, see in particular Le Galès & Thatcher (1995).

65 E.g. J. Peterson (1994), Risse-Kappen (1996), Rhodes (1997: 137). The analyses often deal with sectoral policies, such as structural funds policy (Conzelmann 1995), and environmental policy (Heritier 1993).

66 Dowding (1995); Bennington & Harvey (1994) cited in Rhodes (1997); Hasenteufel (1995: 94). Börzel (1997: 5) also seems to implicitly agree with this opinion. For a more general – sceptical – assessment of the usefulness of the concept of policy networks, see Thatcher (1995).

67 'Iron triangles', and pluralist and neo-corporatist models are actor-centred explanations, whereas 'advocacy coalitions' and 'epistemic communities' search (also) for an explanation in cognitive elements, namely in the role of ideas and belief-systems.

relative power of actors, and consequently the differences between policy networks[68].

The second school identified by Börzel is the 'governance school' of policy-networks. She subdivides the governance school in two groups. The first group of authors uses policy networks only as a metaphor or an analytical concept, merely denoting the fact that policy-making and implementation involves a large number and wide variety of private and public actors from different levels and functional areas of government and society (Börzel 1997: 8). A second group of authors does not merely use policy networks as a framework of interpretation in which different actors are located and linked in their interaction in a policy sector, but stresses that social structures have a greater explanatory power than the personal attributes of individual actors (Börzel 1997: 8). The features of the network itself, rather than the actors within it, become the unit of analysis. Therefore, it is argued that the policy network as a form of governance can overcome the shortcomings of both markets (market failures) and hierarchies ('losers' who have to bear the costs of political decisions). Other authors stress that networks provide abundant possibilities for interaction and communication and consequently provide a basis for common knowledge, experience and beliefs.

While most of the policy-networks literature uses the concept in a descriptive and analytical way, in the latter approach one can find the seeds of a normative use of the network concept as the particular features of the network are said to lead to communicative flows and exchanges of information, which in turn might increase the legitimacy of policy-making processes. According to Ladeur (1997: 46), networks do not merely consist in the identification of stable and pre-existing interests; rather they themselves generate new operating knowledge. Due to this knowledge-generating capacity, networks can better serve the needs of policy-making under conditions of increasing uncertainty than systems based on rational control (Ladeur 1997: 48). Support for such normative claims has been sought in the findings of international relations scholars who, on the basis of analyses of international negotiations, argue that 'the more policy-making processes are characterized by informality and non-hierarchy, the more space there is for communicative action' (Risse-Kappen 1996: 70).

Yet, a comprehensive normative theory of policy-networks remains to be developed, and whereas political scientists may have a natural aversion to such an exercise[69], legal scholars will need to put aside a familiar part of constitutional and administrative law thinking, to reply to the confusing reality of policy networks. Despite the absence of such a comprehensive normative theory, the legitimacy of

---

68 Rhodes (1997: 11), for instance, who does believe in the explanatory value of policy networks, states that 'the different patterns of resource dependence explain differences between policy networks' but adds that 'there must be a theory to explain differences within and between networks'. It is unclear whether the latter is supposed to be an affirmation or a wish.

69 For an exception, see Smith (1995: 119), who invites a more normative use of the network concept, without, however, laying the bases for it.

several EU bodies, namely the network agencies, has implicitly, and even explicitly, been based on the supposed added value of networking.

5.3. The Normative Use of 'Networking' by EU Information Agencies

5.3.1. European Information Agencies

The first two European agencies were established in 1975, namely the European Centre for the Development of Vocational Training in Thessaloniki and the European Foundation for the Improvement of Living and Working Conditions in Dublin. It took another 15 years before other European agencies were set up. Most European agencies were established by the mid-1990s, but the Commission's White Paper on European Governance in 2001 renewed the debate on the role of agencies and led to several proposals for the creation of additional ones[70].

Only a small minority of European agencies (4 out of 15) can be defined as 'executive agencies', i.e. as having a certain executive decision-making power. The Office for Harmonisation in the Internal Market (Alicante) and the Community Plant Variety Office (Angers) implement Community regimes by executing registration procedures and keeping public registers; the European Agency for Reconstruction (Thessaloniki) manages the implementation of assistance programmes to the States of the former Yugoslavia; whereas the Translation Centre (Luxembourg) is in charge of the provision of a particular service. It should be stressed that, even in these cases, the agencies have only limited implementation powers. The Office for Harmonization, and the Community Plant Variety Office, for instance, respect the (parallel) national procedures. Centralised administration or agencies with regulatory power are thus not part of the European spectrum.

Most of the European agencies fall into the category of 'information agencies'. They have no regulatory or executive decision-making power but play a role in various aspects of information policy. Three sub-categories can be distinguished. The first group consists of those agencies that collect, analyse and disseminate information in their respective policy areas by such means as the creation and administration of research teams and projects, the encouragement of exchange of experience and the issuing of various publications. The European Foundation for the Improvement of Living and Working Conditions, the European Centre for the Development of Vocational Training, and the European Training Foundation (Turin) belong to this group.

The second group comprises the European Environment Agency (Copenhagen), the European Centre for Drugs and Drug Addiction (Lisbon), the European Agency

---

70 Current proposals concern a European Railway Agency; a European Centre for Disease Prevention and Control; a European Police College; a European Network and Information Security Agency and a European Chemicals Agency.

for Safety and Health at Work (Bilbao)[71] and the European Monitoring Centre on Racism and Xenophobia (Vienna). In addition to performing the task of the first group, these agencies have a mandate to create and co-ordinate European policy-networks of the actors involved in a particular sector.

A particular sub-category of information agencies is formed by the European Agency for the Evaluation of Medicinal Products (London), the recently established European Food Safety Authority (Parma), the European Maritime Safety Agency (Lisbon) and the European Aviation Safety Agency (Köln). In contrast to the role of most of the other agencies, their information task mainly concerns providing 'independent' scientific expertise, in particular with direct reference to executive or regulatory proposals of the Commission. Although lacking regulatory or executive decision-making power, more so than other information agencies, they have a considerable normative authority since the Commission must take into account the agency's expertise before taking a decision[72].

Our focus here is on those information agencies that have the explicit task to establish a network of all stakeholders in order to improve exchanges of information. The Agency for Health and Safety Protection, based in Bilbao, is used as a case study to show how institutional actors have taken up the discourse on networking as a normative device for legitimate policy-making.

5.3.2. The Example of the Bilbao Agency

The Bilbao Agency's aim is 'to provide the Community bodies, the Member States and those involved in the field, with the technical, scientific and economic information of use in the field of safety and health at work'. The preamble of the Agency Statutes stipulates that "the rules and structure of the Agency must be geared towards the objective nature of the results desired and should be such that it can carry out its work in cooperation with existing national Community and international bodies". Therefore, the Agency is explicitly required to set up a network[73]. The Agency itself stresses its 'decentralised, network philosophy', which implies that "the existing health and safety expertise in the Member States is involved in the

---

71 Council Regulation EC 2062/94, OJ L 216 of 20.08.1994:.1; amended by Council Regulation EC 1643/95, OJ L 156 of 07.07.1995: 1.

72 Craig (1999: 47) has called the Medicinal Products Agency 'quasi-executive' since the Commission is obliged to take into account the Agency's expertise before it can take a decision to permit the access of new medical products to the European market. According to Chalmers (2003: 538) the Food Safety Authority is a 'normative agency'. Although it has no direct regulatory authority, the Regulation 178/2002 EC, providing the new basic food law for the EC, bestows indirect legal effects upon the Authority's opinions by requiring that food regulation should be based on risk analysis.

73 Article 3f and 4 of the Agency Statutes.

Agency's activities in an appropriate way"[74]. Moreover, "in order to act as catalyst for cooperation and information exchange, the Agency must function in an open and transparent way, as an objective and neutral partner, taking into account the viewpoints from all its stakeholders. Furthermore, the decentralised nature of the Agency's organisation has to be taken into consideration both in the planning and in the implementation phase of its work programme"[75]. All Agency activities result from an interaction between the central agency structure and the network components.

The Bilbao Agency respects the principle of a decentralised European administration, in the sense that it does not attribute Occupational Health and Safety (OH&S) decision-making to an independent supranational expert agency. Decision-making remains the competence of the European and national political institutions, whereas implementation should be the task of the national administration. The Agency's aim is merely to perform an information function. Central to the Agency's work are the supposed beneficial effects of 'networking', as transparent exchange of information among various actors is supposed to generate new knowledge and common understanding and thus enhance policy-outputs.

The beneficial nature of networking can be seen to rest on three elements: a) the separation of information exchange and gathering from the normal policy-making process; b) a certain 'pluralist' dimension of the network; and c) transparency of the network.

a) Although the Bilbao Agency is not an 'independent (regulatory/executive) expert agency', its creation is nevertheless based on the supposed benefits of a certain degree of 'independence'. It assumes that decision-making based on political deliberation within the political institutions and the regular administration will profit from a structure situated outside the 'politicised administration' that gathers and exchanges 'objective' information via networking. An agency outside the regular administration can act as a 'neutral gatherer' of information. The Bilbao Agency describes itself as an 'objective and neutral partner,'[76] which not only indicates its independence from the normal decision-making process, but equally its 'neutrality' towards the information gathered. Moreover, the networking established by the Agency is supposed to generate a process of exchange of information among network partners independently of the policy-making process, which will improve policy-outputs by enhanced knowledge and better implementation and application. Networking is thus supposed to generate new knowledge that will not only be to the benefit of European and national decision-makers, but to all 'those involved in the field'[77].

74   Agency Annual Report 1998: 19.
75   Agency Annual Report 1998: 18.
76   Agency Annual Report 1998: 18.
77   Article 2 Agency Statutes.

b) To realise these beneficial effects the network has an alleged *pluralist nature*. It should not be a closed circle of experts but should link 'those involved in the field of OH&S'. It should not only gather scientific expertise but also provide information of a 'technical, scientific and economic' nature[78] and take into account 'the views of the stakeholders'[79]. This does not imply that all network actors have to be equal. Whereas the absence of hierarchical control is a central feature of policy networks, some network partners may well be more important than others. As Renate Mayntz (1991: 11) notes, networks do not require the basic equality of the network actors, but assume only their relative autonomy[80]. In the case of the Bilbao Agency, the National Focal Points (either ministry or agency) are clearly the key actors in the network. This does not prevent the Agency from being seen as providing legitimacy by involving a variety of different concerned actors (Kreher 1997: 240; de Búrca 1999: 78).

c) Networking is most likely to generate new knowledge and common understanding when it occurs in a transparent way. The Bilbao Agency ensures *transparency* via its own visibility, via information on its activities, and via the transparency of the network. Due to its legal personality and permanent structure, an agency is more 'visible' than the myriad of committees. Compared to obscure committees, agencies have been identified as a valid option for increasing the legitimacy of European governance (Dehousse 1997). For the Bilbao Agency the Internet is the central tool to clarify its functioning and to identify the partners in the network. The 'network function' of the Agency includes bringing to light the roles played by various actors. By identifying 'who is who, and who does what', the Agency not only makes policy-making more transparent but may also contribute to enhanced policy-output. Through the information provided on the internet, OH&S policy-actors become more accessible and their information can be more easily exchanged, which in turn will lead to better policy-making at various levels as well as better implementation and application.

The foundational legitimacy of a network agency, such as the Bilbao Agency, thus differs profoundly from the normative assumptions underlying the model of the independent regulatory/executive expert agency. Obviously, one could define every agency as a network agency since they all interact with other institutions and actors and thus may be situated in the centre of a small or big network. However, what I mean here by 'network agency' is an agency whose foundational legitimacy lies in the supposed benefits of 'networking'. Put differently, the agency was created expressly to establish a network since the independence, plurality and transparency of the network is supposed to generate new knowledge and common understanding.

78 Article 2 Agency Statutes.
79 Agency Annual Report 1998:18.
80 According to Ladeur (1997: 50), the inequality of the network components is even a specific feature of the network concept.

Such new knowledge and common understanding might 'vertically' influence policy-makers and 'horizontally' improve implementation and application.

Independent regulatory/executive expert agencies, on the contrary, take the place of the decision-makers and base their legitimacy mainly on independence and expertise. In Majone's 'independent agency' model, networks (called 'issue networks') could be identified, but they are not assumed to ensure the pluralist nature of policy-making. For Majone the 'issue network' is rather supposed to enhance the independence of the agency: 'a regulatory agency which sees itself as part of a trans-national network of institutions pursuing similar objectives and facing analogous problems, rather than as a new and often marginal addition to a huge central bureaucracy is more motivated to resist political pressures'. According to Majone "it is important to notice that a high level of professionalization is crucial to the viability of the network model. Professionals are oriented by goals, standards of conduct, cognitive beliefs and career opportunities that derive from their professional community, giving them strong reasons for resisting interference and directions from political outsiders" (Majone 1996:. 14). The foundational legitimacy of such a 'closed' expert agency is considerably different from that of a network agency aiming at a pluralist, transparent and horizontal exchange of information among stakeholders.

5.3.3. Network Agencies and Other Information Agencies

Most European agencies have been described above as 'information agencies'. All of them will have to develop a certain network to gather 'objective' information ensured through a certain independence from the policy-making process (without taking over decision-making powers). However, only four agencies[81] have an explicit 'networking task' in establishing a transparent pluralist network, independent from the normal administration, which would generate (exchanges of) information among the actors concerned.

For most other information agencies, the focus is more on gathering the scientific knowledge needed by policy-makers, rather than creating a pluralist network that would generate its own dynamics by interconnecting all players concerned in the field. Some of them have a research function, such as the European Foundation for the Improvement of Living and Working Conditions. In contrast to the Bilbao Agency, which focuses on gathering and diffusing information and interconnecting 'those involved in the field', the European Foundation delivers its own studies and co-ordinates research projects, leading to the publication of reports. Its task is not primarily networking based on transparency and plurality[82], but rather providing

---

81 In addition to the Bilbao Agency; the European Environment Agency, the European Centre for Drugs and Drug Addiction, and the European Monitoring Centre on Racism and Xenophobia.

82 In July 1998, the Agency and the Foundation agreed to intensify their collaboration by signing a Memorandum of Understanding. The underlying logic is a division of work that attributes

scientific expertise[83]. It is assumed that such expertise can better be obtained via an agency outside the normal administration.

'Independence' and 'scientific expertise', rather than 'networking' and plurality, are also the key concepts in the recently established agencies in the fields of food safety, maritime safety and aviation safety. The 'raison d'être' of these agencies comes close to the normative arguments of Majone's model, namely insulating the resolution of technical regulatory issues from day-to-day politics and parochial interests. They do not have regulatory decision-making power, as in Majone's model, but they are expressly set up to provide 'independent scientific expertise' in the regulatory process. They are expected to have considerable normative authority since the Community institutions that take the (final) decision will have to take into account the agency's expertise. On the one hand, the 'independence' of the gathered scientific information is the core reason of existence for these agencies, more so than for other information agencies. On the other hand, it should be noted that these agencies are more 'dependent' on the policy-making process than other information agencies because they strongly resemble advisory scientific committees that are (only) consulted on particular regulatory initiatives of the main Community institutions. Although these agencies have legal personality and a more established infrastructure than advisory, scientific committees – and thus more visibility that could strengthen their normative authority – they provide mainly[84] deliberative forums of experts on regulatory initiatives. Put differently, the normative assumptions underlying these agencies can hardly be thought of in the same terms as those of network agencies, i.e. agencies that, outside the governmental and administrative framework, create a pluralist and transparent network of those involved in the field, assuming that horizontal interaction and exchange of information will create its own dynamics leading to improved policy-outputs.

5.4. Problems of the Network Approach

The normative promotion of networking as a policy tool raises several problems, both because the normative ideal shows weaknesses and because reality often is far removed from that ideal.

the 'research function' to the Foundation and the 'information function' to the Agency (interview with Agency Director).

83   The Statutes of the Foundation, therefore, require the creation of a Scientific Committee, as a complement to the Management Board in guiding the objectives and functioning of the Foundation.

84   They have also been given some power to conduct inspections.

5.4.1. Theoretical Problems of the Network Approach

Theoretically, three main elements of criticism can be put forward against the model of 'network agency' in which legitimacy is based on the idea that a body outside of the regular administration could enhance policy-making by linking various actors in a transparent network.

First, just as it is difficult to draw a dividing-line between science and politics, it is equally difficult to separate 'information gathering' from policy-making (Shapiro 1997: 284). Issues on which information is gathered and on which research is done may influence the policy agenda. *Vice versa,* the desired policies will determine the information to be gathered. Moreover, new policy initiatives start mostly from existing ones. Consequently, the information to be gathered often concerns an analysis and appreciation of existing policies. Finally, as soon as information becomes highly relevant to policy outcomes, the information and the information gatherers cease to be seen by the public as neutral and objective and are redefined as part of the political struggle (Shapiro 1997: 284, Chalmers 2003: 547).

Second, the model does not provide clear criteria for organising the network. It seems to assume that networking results spontaneously in exchange of information and better policy-output as long as a certain independence, plurality and transparency of the network is ensured. Various actors are supposed to learn from each other's practices through exchanges of information without establishing structures of deliberation among these various actors. Whereas transparency and the linking of various actors is supposed to generate knowledge and common understanding, it remains unclear which types of actors should be part of the network. Should only public authorities be included? Can private organisations be part of it? Should juridical procedures ensure the strongest possible pluralist character of the network, or should certain interests obtain a privileged position?

Third, neither does the model provide substantial criteria on the content of the information to be gathered within the network. Does exchange of information lead to better policy-making without any steering? Should the information processes be based on scientific credibility? Is information gathered through bargaining among concerned interests or through processes of deliberation?

To answer these questions it may be useful to clarify whether the agency's aim and legitimacy resides primary in its output, in which case elements of expertise would be stressed, or whether its aim is above all to ensure the participation of stakeholders, transparency and publicity.

5.4.2. Ideal and Reality

The example of the Bilbao Agency illustrates how difficult it is to realise better and more legitimate policy through mere horizontal networking. Both the assumed pluralist participatory nature of the Agency network and its added value in terms of output can be questioned.

5.4.2.1. How 'Independent', Plural and Transparent is the Network?

Although the Agency stresses the importance of involving all the stakeholders and its statutes oblige it to provide information to 'all those involved'[85] and to 'the interested parties'[86], they provide few indications as to which organisations should be part of the network and how a certain plurality of the network should be ensured. The Agency and its network do not provide legal guarantees – such as a right to be heard – to ensure a pluralist participation of all those that might have some interest in OH&S issues. Is the network not merely a linking of national administrations? Or, doesn't it risk becoming an auto-referential activity among experts, ignoring the opinions of those interests directly involved in the field? Who participates in the Agency's activities, besides the representatives from national administrations and from the social partners on the Management Board?

The Agency has several tools to realise its information task. One of them is to subcontract to Topic Centres, which are universities or research institutions. Another option is to establish a Thematic Network Group. These are mainly composed of representatives from ministries and/or national OH&S agencies. Only in 1998 did the Agency decide to include representatives from the employers and the trade Unions - appointed by the European confederations - in all these expert groups. In some countries, the contributions of the national experts to the Thematic Network Groups are also discussed with the social partners.

The main method of collecting information is the circulation of surveys through the Agency's network. The core of the Agency's network lies in the national networks set up by the National Focal Points. The decision which organisations or institutions will be part of the national networks, or will become National Focal Points, falls under the competence of the Member States[87]. Consequently, whether the Agency network has a very pluralist character, focuses on social partners' participation, is limited to a 'technocratic circle' of experts, or is a mere linking of national administrations, will depend on the autonomous decisions of the Member States. Which actors become part of the network largely depends on the discretion of the national Focal Points (sometimes in collaboration with the social partners).

The national networks differ considerably, both in the number of participating institutions and in the type of organisations involved. The number of national network partners runs from 8 to 76. In some countries, such as Luxembourg, the network does not contain much more than the public administration and the social partners. In other Member States, such as the UK, the network contains a large variety of organisations of different natures.

85 Article 2 Agency Statutes.
86 Article 3, 1a Agency Statutes.
87 Even Topic Centres, appointed by the Agency Board, will be chosen among the institutions proposed by the National Focal Points. Article 4, 3 Agency Statutes.

In general, the national administration or agency, semi-public prevention institutions, and the peak associations of the social partners are part of the national network. Private consultants in OH&S issues often are also part of the network. Only some national networks also include NGOs, charities, professional organisations and private firms.[88]

One may surmise that national administrative traditions and national traditions of industrial relations may influence the way in which the national network is established. For instance, does the fact that a given national administrative tradition has more experience with 'governance by agencies' influence the network structure? Is the network developed differently according to whether the Focal Point is a division of the labour ministry or an agency? Does a country with a more 'corporatist tradition' involve above all the traditional social partners, whereas a country with a more 'pluralist tradition' seeks the participation of a broader variety of groups?

An assessment of the Agency's network (based on information provided on the Internet and on a questionnaire sent to the Focal Points)[89] makes clear that it is difficult to pin down the structure of the national networks on the basis of these assumed 'national traditions'[90].

First, there is no division between countries in which an independent agency as focal point develops a network of research institutions without 'parochial' interest-based social partners and countries where the national ministry develops concertation-based structures with social partners. There is no sharp duality of 'agency versus ministry' in the choice of Focal Point and the consequences for the national network, but rather a continuum. In France, for instance, the ministry acts as Focal Point but most of its activities are carried out by ANACT, the National Agency for the Improvement of Working Conditions, which has a certain independence of the ministry although being controlled and financed by it. Also in the Netherlands, the Ministry acts formally as Focal Point but the secretariat of that Focal Point is held

---

88 Other than OH&S consultants with a private status. Some national networks, for example, include publishers. (Big) private companies, which are the main addressees of OH&S regulation, are normally not part of the network.

89 Four countries have been analysed more profoundly. They have been chosen on the basis of national administrative tradition (agency tradition or not) and on the basis of a strong or weak corporatist tradition of interest intermediation.

90 Belgium and France have been chosen as examples of countries where a ministry has been appointed as Focal Point; Sweden and UK with an agency as Focal Point. In the latter countries 'government by agency' is more developed. Although Swedish and British agencies are strongly different in nature; and - with the exception of the agency element - British public administration is much closer to the 'standard European system of government' than to the particular Swedish model; see Ziller (2001). For a comparison of administrative traditions in several European countries and the US, see Mény (1993). Regarding traditions of interest intermediation, these countries could be ranked from stronger to weaker corporatist as follows: Sweden, Belgium, UK and France. See P. C Schmitter (1979); G. Lehmbruch (1982) and C. Crouch (1993).

by 'TNO Arbeid', an OH&S consultant[91]. On the other side of the picture, the cases of Sweden and the UK show that countries with agencies as Focal Points also involve social partners in the network, or even provide them a privileged position in the development of Focal Point activities.

Second, national 'corporatist traditions' are not necessarily reflected in the national networks. In all Member States except Luxembourg,[92] social partners account only for a (small) minority of the network partners[93]. Like the other network partners, the social partners can participate in the preparation of the national responses to the requests of the Agency. In a majority of countries, the Focal Point also circulates to all network partners the national reports and final consolidation reports for comment[94]. However, despite their 'numeric minority' in the national networks, social partners play a privileged role in the activities of the Focal Points in a majority of the countries. In particular, the main national confederations of the social partners (normally between 1 and 3 for each partner) often play a role in the development and functioning of the national Focal Point[95]. In two-thirds of the Member States this participation takes place via a tripartite consultation arrangement[96].

Whether such a privileged functional participation in the Focal Point is established does not always correspond with a Member States' tradition of weak or strong corporatism. Sweden and The Netherlands, for instance, do not provide a tripartite concertation on Focal Point activities, despite their traditional reputation for rather strong corporatist interest-intermediation. Yet, these traditional classifications have often focused on macro-economic concertation. This explains, for instance, why France, with its tradition of sectoral tripartite committees but weak macro-economic concertation, generally scores low on the traditional classification of neo-corporatist practice but appears rather 'corporatist' in the organisation of its network as concertation of the traditional social partners is strongly looked for. One may conclude that there are strong differences in the way the national networks are organised (not necessarily corresponding to national administrative traditions or traditions of industrial relations). Two aspects appear problematic.

First, the Agency does not provide clear guidance on how to organise the national networks. As a result, some national networks stress pluralism and/or expertise while others stress functional participation. In one third of the countries information is sent to the Agency only if there is consensus in the tripartite committee assisting the Focal Point. This means that deliberation will 'filter' the 'objectively gathered information'. Deliberation and functional participation dominate over 'the objectivity of the information' gathered through independence, plurality and transparency. In

91 See 'Werkplan 2000 NL-Focal Point', at http://nl.osha.eu.int/content/focalpoint/
92 Five out of eight network partners in Luxembourg are social partners.
93 Annex 5 to Annual Report 1999.
94 European Agency, Report on the Development of the Agency's Network, March 1999:.3.
95 European Agency, Report on the Development of the Agency's Network, March 1999: 3.
96 European Agency, Report on the Development of the Agency's Network, March 1999: 6.

other countries, the Focal Points see their task more as gathering the different elements of information and opinions, which might then be sent to the Agency without prior deliberation or without being summarised in a consensus view[97].

Second, the Agency was created as 'independent from' the Commission and as a supranational body with a certain independence from the national OH&S administrations precisely because the separation from the regular administration is supposed to favour more 'objective information gathering'. However, national administrations have a dominant position in the Agency's network, in particular in controlling the national Focal Points. They have a large discretion in organising the network and may filter the information sent to the Agency. National administrations might be tempted to do so since information provided by other actors might include criticism of the national OH&S administration or might simply increase the workload of that administration. The risk of a lack of 'independence' is real. As the analysis of the Agency's output-legitimacy will show, the first assessments suggest a lack of substantive content in the information provided.

5.4.2.2. The Added Value of the Agency

The Agency's Statutes require that an assessment of its functioning should be made five years after its creation. On this basis, the Commission presented a first evaluation of the functioning of the Agency in March 2001[98], complemented by an assessment study outsourced to a private consultant[99]. The Commission has subsequently consulted the Advisory Committee on Safety and Health at Work (AC)[100] and the Agency on this evaluation report and should[101] produce a reform proposal for the Agency Statutes. Although it is too early to make a judgement on the functioning of the Agency, in particular since the Agency actually started working after some delay, this evaluation, together with the interviews I held, allows us to identify some general aspects of satisfaction and dissatisfaction with the Agency's output.

The creation of the Agency has led to a reshaping and intensification of the OH&S networks. The responses to a questionnaire sent by the Agency to the Member States, show that most national OH&S networks have changed due to the work

---

97 Agency, Report on the Development of the Agency's Network, March 1999: 5.

98 COM (2001) 163 final.

99 R. Arnkil & T. Spangar (2001), 'Does Information Communicate? Evaluation of the European Agency for Safety and Health at Work', available online at http://agency.osha.int/publications/other/20010315/en/index.htm

100 AC, Projet d'avis du Comité Consultatif concernant l'Agence européenne pour la santé et la sécurité au travail, 8 April 2003.

101 Commission draft evaluation report concerning the European Agency for Safety and Health at Work, internal document, Luxembourg 02 April 2003.

of the Agency[102]. The Agency has also formalised existing links between OH&S actors. Network partners will be systematically involved in Agency activities (at least they will be sent systematically requests for information). Moreover, the links among the network partners will be made apparent and visible via the Internet. These 'links' on the Internet are a direct and substantial tool in realising information exchanges. One of the immediate outputs of the Agency is therefore 'transparency', namely it makes visible who is involved in OH&S and provides access to information resources.

Yet, we also must ask whether this has led to increased knowledge, substantial exchange of information, and influence on policy-making and implementation. In particular, we can ask whether the Agency has had any influence on the policy-making of the European Commission[103] and has reached all those concerned in the policy field.

According to the Agency, "the Commission has often used the channel of the Agency to consult the Member States beyond the usual procedures"[104]. However, this optimistic statement does not find support in the interviews held. Except for Agency staff or Board representatives, all interviewed participants in European OH&S policy tend to describe the Agency's influence on the Commission's OH&S measures as very weak. Commission officials interviewed described the Agency's influence on their work diplomatically as 'too early to assess', or bluntly as a 'bad experience'[105]. One AC participant noted that the independence of the Agency from the Commission considerably reduced its added value because the Agency collects information on the issues it deems desirable, whereas the Commission must look elsewhere for information it actually needs for policy-making.

In addition, as a co-ordinating structure of national administrations, there is doubt whether the Agency produces the output it is supposed to deliver. Asked about the Agency's influence on the national administrations, one interviewee described the Agency's working as follows: 'the Member States gather information and make a national report. Their most important concern is that their national report is rightly reflected in the Agency report. Member States representatives (on the Board or from the Focal Points) are hardly interested in the reports of the other Member States or in the coherence of the final Agency report. The Agency cannot do other than compile.'

Yet, the largest dissatisfaction arises where the Agency is supposed to reach all stakeholders and create something like a learning process among a plurality of actors

---

102 European Agency, Report on the Development of the Agency's Network, March 1999: 5.

103 The Agency has the explicit task to provide information to OH&S policy-makers, in particular to the European Commission (Article 3, 1f Agency Statutes).

104 Agency Annual Report 1998, http://fr.osha.eu.int/systems/int_eur_5.stm

105 One can note that in the interviews held with Commission officials, the output of the Dublin Foundation was also not particularly well received; at least as far as OH&S issues were concerned.

leading to improved OH&S application. The path from the Agency information to the OH&S situation in the workplace is long. As a Focal Point representative notes, the Agency desires that its information exists for the benefit of all those concerned, in particular the individual employer and employee, but to date its products remain a concern of the Commission, the Member States and the prominent OH&S experts.[106]

The Agency 'has been reasonably successful in establishing an infrastructure for providing information in the field of OH&S'.[107] but the information provided is read by a very limited group of persons and does surely not reach the workshop level. This is partially because 'the infrastructure' does not provide the information the costumers are looking for. The principal problem of the Agency is identified as the dissatisfaction that customers and users express in relation to the products made available by it[108]. In particular the social partners, both management and labour, have questioned the quality of the information provided by the Agency[109].

Several reasons can be advanced for the 'minimal content' of information provided by the Agency and, therefore, for its limited impact.

First, as emerges from the evaluation and the interviews, most actors complain that the Agency simply compiles information. It is argued that it should also have a research dimension, such as the Dublin Foundation, or at least provide added value to the information through an activity of synthesis or evaluation.

Second, an overly strong independence from the Commission leads to an Agency producing documents that are not useful for the policy-making process.

Third, the Agency has been said to be too ambitious[110], having engaged in too many activities. Yet, a large part of the workload falls on the National Focal Points, which often lack the necessary resources to reply to the Agency's requests. Apparently many Member States do not consider the work of the Agency a priority, or worse, see it as a possible 'intrusion' into their administration. If the National Focal Points do not have the necessary resources to reply to the Agency's requests, the gathered information cannot be of high quality. Moreover, the problem of lacking resources is increasingly also one of the central Agency structure. In particular in relation to future enlargement the objectives of the Agency's activities will have to be restrained. It is generally acknowledged that the information agencies can only reach their objective if they provide the information in the language of their custom-

---

106 Own questionnaires with Focal Points.

107 External evaluation report.

108 Commission draft evaluation report concerning the European Agency for Safety and Health at Work, internal document, Luxembourg 02 April 2003

109 AC opinion 'comment on the Agency's Working Programme 1999' online at http://fr.osha.eu.int/systems/int_eur_5.stm, and comments of the Employer Group and the Trade Union Group in the AC on the External Evaluation report, See: Commission draft evaluation report concerning the European Agency for Safety and Health at Work, internal document, Luxembourg 02 April 2003.

110 AC opinion 'comment on the Agency's Working Programme 1999' online at http://fr.osha.eu.int/systems/ int_eur_5.stm

ers. As a result, further enlargement will heavily weight on the budget of the Agency.

Fourth, it is very difficult to use the Agency as gatherer of information on problems of implementation since the national administrations - which have a dominant position within the functioning of the Agency - appear as both interested party and judge. There are no convincing signs that the Agency to date has contributed to the increased implementation of European OH&S norms. The Agency does not ensure a system of monitoring of the implementation of European legislation in the Member States. Until now, the Agency has issued more general comparative reports, such as on 'national OH&S priorities', and on 'the economic costs and benefits of OH&S measures'. At the request of the trade unions, the Agency established a 'Thematic Network Group on OSH monitoring in 1999' with the aim of periodically organising the preparation of national reports on the state of OSH plus a consolidated report for the EU[111]. However, the 'Thematic Network Group on OSH monitoring' does no longer exist, and the monitoring of the state of OH&S in the Member States has been limited to the organisation of a seminar in 2002 and the drafting of a report on different national monitoring systems. The dominant position of the national administrations within the Agency impedes the Agency from functioning as a (periodical) control on the implementation and application of European OH&S norms.

Fifth, as argued in particular by the social partners, a better involvement of the social partners within the Agency network would contribute to the quality of the information and thus to providing practical solutions to all those concerned in practice.

One can conclude that, except for increased transparency and accessibility of information, it remains to be seen whether the Agency can really lead to exchange of information, influence policy-actors and co-ordinate the national administrations, thus enhancing implementation of OH&S norms. The challenge for the Agency is to ensure that the provided information is read. The first step to ensure this objective is by improving the quality of the information.

5.5. European Citizenship through Networking?

Citizenship implies the creation of rights (and duties). In a multi-level polity, such as the EU with its socio-cultural diversity, there are good democratic arguments to define rights (also) at more decentralised levels and to avoid a centralised definition at the European level. The option to define rights mainly at the national level, and to limit European intervention to networking of policy actors in order to improve exchanges of information and best practice, may thus also be attractive from a citizen perspective.

111 Agency Work Programme 1999: 16.

One should acknowledge, however, that:

a) Networking as such is not a normatively 'good thing'. Networking can include whatever types of actors. To make it correspond with a citizenship approach one has to re-think the participatory features of citizenship beyond the traditional structures of political participation such as election and parliamentary representation.[112] Procedural guarantees for more balanced participation in European networks is an essential element to realise European citizenship in a polity which may not set all standards at the supranational level but in which European networking may nevertheless establish the basic features and the language of many policies.

b) European citizenship defined mainly in terms of economic freedoms and procedural participatory rights – even if enlarged to encompass the reality of European networks - may not be sufficient to satisfy the European citizen. While the creation of a European welfare state may not be desirable, there is an important consensus around fundamental rights which should be respected at all times, independently of the dynamics of markets. The European Union Charter of Fundamental Rights is an important recognition in this sense, despite its unclear legal future given the non-ratification of the Constitutional Treaty. As I have argued elsewhere (Smismans 2005), fundamental (social) rights may interact with horizontal non-binding networked procedures and benchmarking at the European level.

---

112 I have analysed in more detail elsewhere how new modes of governance, such as networking, may contribute to more active European citizenship. However, while new governance may reinvigorate the participatory element of European citizenship, it does not always sit easily with the egalitarian dimension of the two other constitutive elements of citizenship, namely rights and identity. See Smismans 2007.

6. Towards a European Civil Society

Michele Nicoletti

6.1. Introduction

After the fall of the Berlin wall in 1989, the notion of 'civil society' has come back into circulation in the debate about the future of Europe with regard to two different fields.

The first field of application referred to the polities of the countries in Eastern Europe. Here, the term 'civil society' defined what those countries had been deprived of and were struggling to recreate, i.e. a web of autonomous associations, independent of the state, binding citizens together in matters of common concern (Taylor 1995: 204).

The second field of application was the so called 'crisis of politics' in the countries of Western Europe, which refers to citizens' disenchantment with politics; the crisis of representation, referring to issues such as the dominance of executives; and the crisis of the party system as a vehicle for societal representation (Ruzza 2004: 7). In order to face this complex crisis, a strong emphasis has been placed on civil society's contribution to a decentralized, networked exercise of political authority, often referred to as 'governance'. The European Commission's White Paper on Governance gives the following definition of civil society: "Civil society includes the following: trade unions and employers' organizations ('social partners'); non-governmental organisations; professional associations; charities; grass roots organisations; organisations that involve citizens in local and municipal life with a particular contribution from churches and religious communities"[113].

In all these cases, the intention is to invoke something like the concept that developed at the turn of the nineteenth century in contrast to that of 'state'. But, such a definition of civil society in terms of 'non-state sphere' is very unsatisfactory. It does not reflect the history of the concept,[114] nor does it explain why we call this kind of society 'civil'.

To create a European civil society we need a more differentiated concept, which cannot be merely identified either with the political community or with the mere non-state sphere. The aim of my paper is to try to outline a more articulated and

---

113 Commission of the European Communities 2001: 14. For a more articulated definition see the opinion of the European Economic and Social Committee on "The role and contribution of civil society organisations in the building of Europe" (1991: 3-8).

114 On the history of the concept of 'civil society', see: Riedel (1975), Hall (1995), Ehrenberg (1999).

dialectical idea of civil society through an analysis of the roots and the historical development of the concept.

6.2. The Roots of the Concept of Civil Society

A first root of the concept of civil society comes from the ancient Greek and Roman traditions. The term *Civil Society* is a literal Latin translation of the Greek expression *politikè koinonìa*, which defines the community of the *polis*. For the ancient Greeks, the word *polis* originally indicated not so much the physical place where many people lived together as a specific form of human association. *Polis* is more appropriately a form of life, a form of dynamic relationship, than a static reality. More precisely, it is a form of social life in which free and equal individuals discuss and decide in the public sphere about their common destiny. Accordingly, the *civil society* consists of a form of political constitution that implies freedom and equality for all citizens, government under the law, and the consent of the governed. In this case, there is no difference between *civil society* and *political community*. According to this perspective, *civil ethics* identifies itself totally in the ethics of the polis, which demands the absolute priority of the common good over the good of the family or of the single individual and, to a certain extent, over the search for truth itself, as the cases of Antigon and Socrates clearly demonstrate.

A second root of the concept of civil society comes from the Middle Ages. In the early Middle Ages, a new notion of civil society developed in which political authority, unlike the ancient conception, was considered one component among others. According to Charles Taylor (1995: 211), the "idea that society is not identical with its political organization can be seen as a crucial differentiation, one of the origins of the later notion of civil society and one of the roots of western liberalism".

Taylor indicates five factors that shaped the idea of modern civil society during the Middle Ages:
- society is not defined in terms of its political organization;
- political and religious power are different;
- the development of a legal notion of subjective right;
- the existence of relatively independent, self-governing cities;
- the dualism between the monarchy and a body of estates on which the king depends to raise the resources to govern and wage war.

In this context, a much more differentiated model of *civil ethics* developed: citizen's ethics have to conciliate a plurality of duties toward the "city of God" and the "secular city", which itself involves different political levels, i.e. empire, kingdoms, cities.

A third root of the concept of civil society was shaped in the early Modern age. In the 17th century, Hobbes developed a notion of sovereignty that undermined the medieval model of civil society. According to Hobbes, in order to exist at all, a society must be held together by sovereign power, that is, by a power unlimited by any other. Put differently, the identification of society with its political organization marks a return to, and is supported by, the structure of an absolute power. From this perspective, civil society again comes to correspond to a political community fully dependent on the sovereign political power.

Hobbes's contractualist interpretation of the construction of civil society has exerted a strong influence on the history of ideas and has often provided an inspiring model for supranational civil society. Although he considered international relations to be characterized by a sort of state of nature in which the different States live in a condition of *bellum omnia contra omnes*, his view of establishing peace through an act of submission to a unique sovereign power fascinates many people.

Hobbes's interpretation is rather provocative because, in his perspective, it would only be possible to build an international civil society in the presence of a supranational sovereign power. In the absence of such a power, international relations consequently would be subject to the logic of mere force and of the *homo homini lupus* principle.

This model is based on two theoretical premises: (1) Civil society is opposed to the state of nature and is an artificial construction of individuals, whose life is conceived as originally non-social. (2) Civil society is a product of the submission to a unique sovereign power--its life and death depend upon it. According to this perspective, *civil ethics* is a product of instrumental reason, transforming the aggressive individuals into obedient citizens through a taming process.

The first premise contrasts with the famous Aristotelian interpretation of the human being as a social being; an interpretation dominant during Antiquity and the Middle Ages. Such an interpretation – which should not be identified at all with an ingenuous, optimistic vision of human sociability – began to be questioned in the early Modern Age, but it did not disappear from the horizon of political thought. On the contrary, it has maintained its influence in the Aristotelian tradition, which gave rise to some influential theories of international relations developed in the 16th, 17th, and 18th centuries.

Concerning the second premise, we shall see below that the building of a civil society does not necessarily involve the creation of a unique sovereign power. Moreover, in the case of a supranational civil society, it does not necessarily entail the institution of only one legislative political power. An international civil society should rather have the character of a common ethical-juridical framework for respecting and promoting the plurality of social orders and human projects.

6.3. A more Differentiated Meaning of Civil Society

This is why we need a more differentiated meaning of civil society, and for this purpose, Locke's, Montesquieu's and Tocqueville's conceptions can be of help.

According to Locke, society exists before government: the *pactum unionis* precedes the *pactum subjectionis* and takes individuals out of the state of nature. The newly formed body then sets up a government, which may be defined as sovereign, but it stands in fact in a relation of trust to society. Should it violate this trust society regains its freedom of action. Prior to all political society, mankind forms a kind of community in which every individual enjoys his or her natural rights. Any particular political society has to respect this higher law, which is binding on every one. *Civil ethics* includes obedience to civil law and political authority, but also resistance, when the sovereign power becomes tyrannical.

Although Locke employs the term 'civil society' as synonymous with 'political society', he paves the way for the emergence of a new, differentiated sense of the concept in which society is considered an extra-political reality characterized by the economy and public opinion.

"Economics" etymologically corresponds to the art of household management, where the *nomos* was imposed by the manager. The modern economy seems to be an autonomous domain of causal laws with its own organization. The ancient economy reproduced private life whereas the modern economy creates society. This latter obviously has a profound relationship with the domain of politics, but it is not identical with political organization.

A second relevant element of this differentiated sense of society is "public opinion". Public opinion develops entirely outside the channels and public spaces of the political structure. More radically, it develops outside the channels and public spaces of any sort of authority since it is also independent of the church. In brief, public opinion is not elaborated through any official and established, hierarchical organs of definition.

These ideas of economy and public opinion constituted one of the strands in the new notion of "civil society" as distinct from the state. But this notion of civil society, based on both economy and public opinion, and conceived as an independent domain separate from political government, can inspire radical hopes of an anti-political kind. The non-state sphere can degenerate into an anti-state sphere, when civil society wants to swallow up the state in society, in a supposedly common will (Rousseau), or when it wants to marginalize the political as under anarchy. Although both of these tendencies are meant to defend the freedom of society against politics, they can in fact represent a threat to freedom.

To avoid the risks implied by this notion of civil society, it is necessary to resort to another tradition, i.e. that of Montesquieu and Tocqueville. According to Montesquieu, *civil society* is a society ruled by the law and characterized by independent bodies. Although, in his conception, civil society is again identical with the state, his emphasis on its being limited by the law and independent bodies is fundamental also with a view to the development of a differentiated meaning of civil society. It is Tocqueville who applied Montesquieu's categories to an independent civil society.

The result is a concept of civil society as a separate but not self-sufficient sphere. Civil society has to be regulated by law and has to be confronted with political organization. It is within civil society that independent bodies are shaped, which are no longer represented by the old *corps intermédiares*, but by free associations. According to Taylor (1995: 223), these free associations have both social and political importance: "their significance is that they give us the taste and habit of self-rule, and so they are essential for political purposes. But if they are to be real loci of self-

112

rule, they have to be non-gigantic and numerous and exist at many levels of the polity. This itself should be decentralized, so that self-government can be practiced also at the local and not just the national level". If the polity withers away at this level, it is in danger at any level, national and supranational. Quoting Tocqueville, Taylor concludes: "In democratic countries the science of association is the mother of science; the progress of all the rest depends on the progress it has made".

Critics of Tocqueville have objected that the presence of intermediate associations cannot automatically be theorized as constituting a democratic sphere. Local or religious communities, groups of interest and social movements can support authoritarianism as easily as they can advance freedom. However, it must be noted that Tocqueville's concept of civil society does not refer to a generic non-state sphere, but to self-ruled associations constituted by free and equal individuals. In this sense the concept of civil society differs from the one of political community, but it retains its main features (freedom and equality) and has a public dimension. Within civil society, the single individual is not merely the private individual, but the member of free associations of equals who act in the public sphere.

Charles Taylor (1995: 219) has expressed this idea with the following words. The concept of civil society

"comprised a public, but not a politically structured domain. Civil society was not the private sphere. Where Aristotle distinguishes *polis* from *oikos*, and only the first is a public domain, Hegel distinguishes three terms: family, civil society and the state. Civil society is not identical with the third term, the polis, and not with the first term either. That is why I argue that any definition of civil society in this sense, which identifies it simply with the existence of autonomous associations free from state tutelage, fails to do justice to the historical concept. This defines a pattern of public social life, and not just a collection of private enclaves".

A good institutional example of this sort of civil society, even at an international level, is represented by the system of European Universities in the Middle Ages and modern times. This system can be interpreted neither as an expression of the private sphere, nor as a mere part of the national state.

Needless to say, such a concept of civil society implies a re-consideration of the concept of political sovereignty that necessarily goes in a supranational direction. In this regard it is interesting to consider what David Held (1995: 234) wrote about the transformation of sovereignty in the global order:

"the 'artificial person' at the centre of the idea of the modern state must be reconceived in terms of basic cosmopolitan democratic law. In this conception, sovereign authority or sovereignty would derive its legitimacy from this law: a justified power system would be a system bound and circumscribed by this law [...] sovereignty can be stripped away from the idea of fixed borders and territories and thought of as, in principle, malleable time-space clusters. *Sovereignty is an attribute of basic democratic law, but it could be entrenched and drawn upon in diverse self-regulating associations, from states to cities and corporations.* Cosmopolitan law demands the subordination of regional, national, and local 'sovereignties' to an overarching legal framework, but within this framework associations may be self-governing at diverse levels. A new possibility is indicated: the recovery of an intensive and participatory democracy at local levels as a complement to the public assemblies of the wider global order; that is, a political order of democratic associations, cities, and nations as well as of regions and global networks. The cosmopolitan model of democracy is the legal basis of a global and divided authority system – a system of diverse and overlapping power centres, shaped and delimited by democratic law".

6.4. European Civil Society and Public Ethics

In order to create a European civil society, we need to improve this strategy of political and cultural cooperation. According to Habermas (1998c), five factors seem to be relevant:

- A European Charter, which provides the basis of common rights and common recognized institutions;
- A process of democratic legitimation of these institutions, which has to be supported by a European party system that can develop to the degree of existing political parties, at first within in their own domestic arenas, initiating a debate on the future of Europe, and, in the process, articulating interests that cross national borders.
- A pan-European political public sphere that can construct a multivocal communicative context, and which presupposes a European civil society, including interest groups, non-governmental organizations, citizens' movements, and trans-national mass media.
- A common language provided by national educational systems.
- A common political culture, which can create European civil solidarity.

How can we create this *civil ethics* based on solidarity?

The concept of civil society indicates a form of life, which is the product of history, culture and morality. Civil society indicates a civilized society, which differs from barbarism. The concept of civil society is used in this sense by Adam Ferguson, one of the intellectual leaders of the eighteenth-century Scottish Enlightenment. In his *Essay on the History of Civil Society*, Ferguson based civil society on a set of moral sentiments. He located the roots of human sociability in a general capacity to put oneself in someone else's place. This 'fellow-feeling' permits individuals to participate in the lives of others and makes moral judgement possible by reconciling individuality with a civil society constituted by shared ethical relations.

Ferguson articulated a moralist rebellion against the logic of individual interest. He rooted civil society in 'love of mankind', a quality that was dramatically different from the commercial interests some thinkers placed at the centre of human organization. According to Ferguson, civil society, as civilized society, has an ethical basis: the ethics of humanity.

In the history of Europe, the concept of civil society displays a deep connection with the concept of *humanitas*. This concept has represented the meeting point of diverse religious and secular traditions, with meaningful effects on social life and political institutions. My argument is that a pluralistic European civil society can find one possible basis for a shared common public ethics precisely in such concept of *humanity*.

114

6.5. Ethics of Humanity and Responsiveness

In its classical roots, for example in Cicero's writings, the term *humanitas* indicates a typical quality of noble and cultivated people that was reserved to specific social groups of the Roman world and was pointedly denied to the so-called "Barbarians". Some later authors, instead, extend the concept to all human beings. The term *humanitas* began to indicate the human nature. Seneca (1969: 95, 52), for example, asserted:

> "We are members of an immense organism (membra sumus corporis magni). Nature has created us brothers, generating us from the same principles and for the same ends", for if "it is a crime to injure a fellow-citizen since he is a part of the native country [...], it is therefore a crime also to injure every man, since it is your fellow-citizen in the larger city".

The inclusion of all human beings in the unique society of humankind – which is typical of the Jewish, Christian, Stoic and Islamic tradition - is not without effect on the consideration of international relations. According to this perspective, international relations should not be conceived as relations among *separate* entities but as relations *within a common society*. From this common society individuals and peoples derive a common right that also applies to their mutual relations: the universal destination of earthly goods, the right to free circulation and communication, the obligation not to injure others and to respect pacts. As Kant (1912: II, art. 3) observes, this "cosmopolitan right" means that "a violation of rights in one place is felt throughout the world". Therefore the cosmopolitan right should be considered a necessary component of the unwritten code of civil and international law.

When these traditions state that all individuals share a common humanity (*humanitas*), they usually emphasize the common origin of all creatures in God or their common possession of rationality (*ratio*), which imposes on all persons the obligation to recognize others as rational beings. But rationality is not the only distinctive element of this common *humanitas*. According to some authors (E.g. Ricoeur 1990: chap. 7) the affective element plays an important role. It is the faculty of shared individual *suffering*, which has to be recognized as the distinctive element of humanity and of the related rights. This perspective acknowledges the human rights of *all* persons, even though *not all* of them have developed, or can develop, their rational faculties in a complete way, as in the cases of infants or the disabled. "A right exists," Rosmini (1993: § 43, p. 19) wrote, "whenever a person exists capable of at least experiencing pain. If so, other persons have the moral duty not to cause him any suffering."

From this common humanity, every human being, therefore, derives not only rights but also duties, including the duty to treat the other with "humanity". Here the concept of *humanity* is taken in its ethical meaning, i.e. as philanthropy, empathy, and respect. In antiquity, this term referred to the public sphere, rather than to private relations. In the Roman imperial age, *"humanitas"* was above all the duty of the emperor. The holders of public power were primarily subordinated to the obligation to treat the others with humanity.

Also in this case, the influence of the concept on international relations is meaningful. Even in the historical development of the law of war one can find traces of this issue. However hard-fought or cruel a conflict among individuals and nations may be, ethical and juridical laws oblige each side to treat prisoners humanely. But, in order for this obligation to be effective it is essential to acknowledge the humanity (*humanitas*) of the other, i.e. his or her equal dignity. Common humanity (in the sense of humankind) implies human equality, and equality demands humanity of treatment.

On this basis it is possible to draw a connection between international relations and "humanity" in terms of respect and empathy. The recognition that international relations are necessarily inscribed within the horizon of humankind - conceived of as a unique society - is linked to a humanitarian treatment of "other" persons and "other" peoples. The relationship between recognition and respect is present in all the ancient traditions mentioned above, but it becomes increasingly relevant with the onset of the Modern Age when the conquest of new continents raised the question of recognizing the *other* as a human being that belongs to the same humankind and the need to respect her or his rights. How many times did Bartolomé de Las Casas (1999), in his despairing denunciation of the "Destruction of the Indies", use the terms "human beings" or "rational men" speaking of the Indios, and the terms "cruel wild animals" when describing the way the Conquistadores behaved? One can find the same emphasis in eighteenth- and nineteenth-century denunciations of slavery: the "humanity" of slaves was contrasted to the inhumanity of slave-traders. Treating the others in an inhuman way, reducing them to slavery, denies not only the humanity of the victim but also the humanity of the perpetrator. Following Hegel, we can reiterate: "in the slavery of the slave also the master loses his humanity". Slavery is the negation of civil society.

Following this tradition, we can recognize that the concept of an international civil society is because all individuals belong to a unique humanity and have to behave with humanity. Then one could ask whether international civil society is a moral or a political community.

In the cosmopolitan tradition, some authors immediately conceive humanity as a political society, which therefore must have its own laws and authorities. As Wolff (1972: §§ 10-11, p. 8-9) writes:

> "Since the civitas maxima is a civitas, and consequently a societas, and since whichever society must have its laws and the right to make laws on the matters of its own competence, also the civitas maxima must have its laws and the right to make laws on the matters of its own competence. And since the civil law, that is the law established in the civitas, prescribe the means with which the good of the civitas can be obtained, also the laws of the civitas maxima must prescribe the means with which the good of that one can be obtained".

Many critical objections have been raised against this perspective. Here, I want to recall two of them.

i) Humanity can be neither a present nor a future political community, because all political communities are the result of a dialectical process that differentiates one human group from another. A political community, as Habermas (1998c) observes, must always be able to distinguish its members from the others. A political community that includes all human beings could only be a moral community.

ii) Humanity cannot be a political communit, because political communities are always particular and not universal, i.e. they are various and plural. A political community that includes all human beings would represent the end of plurality and difference and could transform itself into an alarming "super-Leviathan". In this regard, some critics recall how the Fathers of the Church asserted that the only temporal power capable of unifying all humanity would be the power of the Antichrist and, therefore, a demonic power. On the basis of these premises—the critics continue—those who employ the concept of "humanity" as a political concept, make an "ideological" use of it, in the sense that they want to cover particular interests behind a universal mask and end up intensifying the violence of the conflicts rather than mitigating it. The war fought in the name of humanity would be a war against the enemies of humanity and therefore a total war. "If one fights its enemy in name of humankind," Carl Schmitt (1963: 55) observes,

> "this is not a war of humankind. It is a war in which a State tries to use a universal concept and to identify with it at the expense of the State's adversary. [...] The term 'humanity' is an instrument particularly adapted to imperialistic expansions and, in its ethical-humanitarian form, is a specific vehicle of economic imperialism. To this purpose, it is worth noting, with one necessary modification, a maxim of Proudhon: 'Wer Menschheit sagt, will betrügen'. [...] All this simply shows the terrible pretension that from the enemy must be removed the quality of man, that he must be declared hors-la loi and hors-l'humanité and therefore that the war must be conducted until the point of extreme inhumanity"

These objections should be taken seriously into account, considering that some recent applications of the doctrine of "humanitarian intervention" seem to confirm these worries. However, on a more theoretical note, such critical remarks seem to be directed against all those who want to build the political community of humankind, following the model that Hobbes used in his description of the genesis of the state political community.

However, the concept of "humanity" serves a useful function as it asserts the existence of a "society" of all people, which is founded on their radical equality as human beings. This idea prevents us from conceiving particular political societies as isolated societies in which human sociality is exhausted and outside of which the disorder of an anarchistic state of nature dominates. The idea of a common origin of all peoples recalls that there are "common" elements which bind all men and women, so that human rights can be conceived not only as rights deriving from the single individual but also from a common membership in this greater society. If the European civil society is based on the concept of humanity, it cannot be a discriminating society.

To put it differently, the concept of "humanity" serves a positive function as it expresses the ethical-juridical injunction to obligate every person to treat the others — whether individuals or peoples – "as persons", and to recognize them as "equals". In this sense, it recalls equality and reciprocity.

Moreover, the concept of "humanity" serves a positive function when it expresses "a regulative" idea for a political action oriented to a common ethical-juridical

117

framework within which to respect and promote the plurality of social orders and human projects. Every individual, people, or nation has a duty in the face of the international civil society of humankind, but nobody has the right to claim to be its only legitimate representative.

A European civil society, finally, requires a broad sense of responsiveness among citizens as well as within institutions. I use the concept of *responsiveness* as it has been elaborated within the constitutional debate on the question of political representation (Böckenförde 1991).

The concept of "representation" is used in two different meanings.

In a *formal* sense, "representation" means the authorization citizens give to their representatives to act on their behalf. It indicates the relationship of legitimacy between the people and the democratic power that enables the government to constrain citizens to abide by its commands.

In a *material* sense, "representation" means the capacity of representatives to make choices that citizens can acknowledge as consistent with what they really think and consider fair. In this case, representation produces identification in spite of differences of opinions and ideology. Besides the power to obligate externally (to command), "representation" has the capacity to generate consent and obedience. In this sense "representation" is a process, sometimes invisible, which has great influence on the life of democracy. It cannot be guaranteed by laws but relies on a capacity of interpretation. This capacity is defined as "responsiveness".

"Responsiveness" denotes the availability and sensibility of the representatives when confronted with the desires and interests of citizens. Neither can responsiveness be reduced to dependency upon the interests of the people represented, nor does it have a simple executive role. Rather, it maintains its own initiative and has the ability to anticipate needs and interests, as well as the ability to take decisions in case of incompatible interests and divergent demands. Responsive decisions are oriented to the idea of a fair balance of interests; moreover, they contribute to generating this balance.

We can better understand the meaning of this theory of responsive representation if we consider how it integrates the two legal conceptions of representation, i.e. that of a free mandate, and that of a strictly binding mandate. Representation is not a mere legal relationship. It presupposes the existence of a specific extralegal relation between the representatives and the represented citizens, which has its foundation and life in a relationship of trust. Consequently, "to represent" no longer means "to be in place of the other", but to give presence and form in the political arena to the interests and values of citizens. This extralegal dimension of representation is of course subordinated to the legal dimension, such that in democratic elections citizens can evaluate to what extent their representatives have this capacity of interpreting their expectations.

From this perspective, responsive representation appears as a dynamic and dialectic process through which the two different moments of political organization and of civil society can find adequate expression.

7. Institutions and Identity Formation: The Case of EU Committees and National Officials

Morten Egeberg

7.1. Introduction

Realist and intergovernmentalist thought claims that the interests and allegiances of national actors are moulded and reshaped at the national level. Thus, when nationals participate in international organisations they bring with them fixed preferences and loyalties. Only their strategies, i.e. the way in which they intend to achieve their goals, might be reformulated in international arenas. Neo-functionalists, new institutionalists and constructivists, on the other hand, assert that international institutions, like all institutions, are capable of transforming the participants' sense of belonging or at least impact significantly on their preference formation. This chapter draws on organisational theory in order to specify more accurately the conditions under which this happens. Political analysis obviously cannot rely extensively on theories that do not accommodate vital aspects of political life such as preference and allegiance formation into their models. Data on national officials who participate on EU committees will be used to shed light on this highly contentious topic in European integration studies. However, the dispute is not peculiar to EU studies; it is indeed one of the great theoretical debates in political science in general.

Our focus will be on national officials who participate in preparatory committees linked to the European Commission and in working parties in the Council of the European Union. The first type of committees assists the EU executive (i.e. the Commission) in developing policy proposals that are subsequently submitted to the EU legislature (i.e. the Council and the European Parliament) for final decision. The Council, which is composed of the constituent Member State governments, has also set up a considerable number of highly specialised groups ("working parties") in order to prepare for and relieve the ministerial meetings. It has been estimated that a clear majority of issues in practice find their solution at this level (Hayes-Renshaw & Wallace 1997). Unresolved conflicts, instead, are referred to the Committee of Permanent Representatives (COREPER) at the next higher level. If the ambassadors in COREPER cannot agree, the final solution will have to be found at the ministerial meetings.

A focus on organisational factors may help us solve puzzles like the following: the extent to which officials from national ministries become socialised in EU committees seems to vary considerably even if their degree of participation is approximately the same. Those who are heavily involved on the European scene do not necessarily adapt more extensively than those who are only moderately engaged. Moreover, socialising people at the EU level is not necessarily conducive to further European integration in the sense of system transformation. On the other hand,

119

rather modest socialisation of national actors in Union bodies, over time, may have entailed a profound restructuring of the once Westphalian state system.

The purpose of this chapter is to discuss the extent to which the organisational setting might account for individual actors' allegiance and preference formation. Those who feel an allegiance to a particular organisation, institution or collective tend to take the interests of this body more or less automatically into account when taking part in decision processes. I proceed from here in the following manner: First, it is necessary to briefly address a few basic organisational themes. One such topic deals with the mechanisms through which formal organisations separate their members' private interests from the interests they are expected to pursue in their organisational roles. Another theme is how the way the organisation is structured impacts on their conceptions of themselves and their perspectives and choices. The theoretical ideas are subsequently placed in an EU context, focusing mainly on Commission and Council committees. Thereafter, sections on data and method and the empirical analysis follow.

7.2. How to Explain the Formation of Allegiances and Preferences Organisationally?

We are dealing with government personnel, i.e. individuals who are embedded in particular formal organisations. Like other persons, these people have their private interests; they want to earn money and obtain prestige, power and a good life. Under certain circumstances, these private interests may affect the preferences they pursue in their capacity as officials. This is more likely to happen in decisions that are tightly linked to their career prospects, like departmental reorganising. It is less likely that officials, even if they wanted, would be able to define and "operationalise" their genuine private interests in any meaningful and coherent way in issue arenas outside the realm of personnel and other public administration policies.

Modern organisations do seem to have a capacity to impose on their personnel the agendas, perspectives and interests that are to be pursued. This does not imply that organisational members give up their private interests from the moment they enter an organisation, but that these interests are of minor importance in explaining their *organisational* behaviour in general. Why is this so? First, modern culture's emphasis on impersonal relationships and rationalised codes of conduct in organisational life helps people separate their private interests from those that should be catered for in their capacity as officials. Second, organisations are normative structures composed of roles and rules. Roles are sets of norm that more or less precisely specify decision premises and appropriateness. Roles oblige people to behave in a certain manner, and to pursue particular goals (Scott 1981). How roles are grouped into divisions, departments or committees expresses how important various tasks are, which considerations should be balanced against each other, and how policies are to be co-ordinated. The division of work also focuses attention on certain lines of cleavage rather than others (March 1994). The relevance criteria embedded in roles guide search processes and bias information exposure. Thus, normative structures forge information networks for the development of common perceptions of agendas and alternatives. Location, physical structure and symbols may strengthen the effects normative and information systems have on decision-makers (Goodsell 1988; March 1994). Organisation is thus a *mobilisation of bias* in preparation for action (Schattschneider 1975: 30). Since a decision-maker is unable to attend to everything at the same time and to consider all possible alternatives and their consequences (cf. "bounded rationality"), it is a perfect match between her/his need for simplification on the one hand, and the selection and filter that organisation provides, on the other (Simon 1965). Finally, organisations are incentive systems. Hierarchies inform people at lower levels of their potential career prospects, thus inducing them to adapt autonomously to role expectations and codes of conduct. And, managers may apply rewards or punishments in order to achieve compliance. Thus, organisational structures embody various mechanisms of compliance.

Two basic organisational dimensions will be outlined in order to understand the allegiances and interests that actors adopt on different occasions. The first dimension is *the principle of specialisation*. Organisation means division of work, and Gulick (1937) found four main cues according to which tasks and resources are distributed among units, namely territory, purpose (sector), function (process) and clientele. If, for example, an institution is internally specialised in relation to the geographical areas served, it is expected to induce spatial identities and encourage policy-makers to pay attention primarily to particular territorial concerns and needs for "intra-local" policy coherence. In this case, the structure reflects the territorial composition of the system and focuses attention along territorial lines of cleavage. Organisations based on a purpose principle, on the other hand, are supposed to foster sectoral horizons among decision-makers and thus policy standardisation across territorial units.

The second dimension deals with whether an individual's affiliation to a particular organisation is of a *primary or a secondary* character. A primary attachment means that a person uses most of her or his time and energy in a particular organisation. The organisation is her or his main employer. Secondary affiliations, on the other hand, engage people only on a part-time basis. The typical setting is a committee structure. Modern systems of governance coordinate policies extensively across levels and sectors through committees. Thus, participants become exposed to new agendas, alternatives, actors and obligations. We therefore expect that committees, like other organisational arrangements, may affect the loyalties and preferences of those who attend. However, the impact will be less profound than in organisations to which persons have a primary affiliation. In cases where the secondary structure's principle of specialisation is the same as in the primary structure (i.e. *compatible* principles) basic interests and allegiances already acquired in the primary organisation (for example sectoral ones) are likely to be sustained by the secondary organisation. However, a wider system allegiance might evolve, provided that the secondary structure (e.g. a committee) spans more than one level of governance or sector. If, on the other hand, the organising principle of the secondary system is *incompatible* with the principle embedded in the primary institution we would expect established mind-sets to be put under a certain pressure, thus eventually resulting in a preference or loyalty change, although probably a rather moderate one. In fact, in a secondary structure it is probably more realistic to expect established worldviews to be *complemented* rather than to be replaced.

To understand a policy-maker's allegiance and identity formation one, accordingly, must first take into account her or his primary institutional affiliation and the prevailing principle of specialisation therein. Secondary affiliations, though, may complement and reshape preferences and loyalties, but only partly. Incompatible organising principles in particular stress entrenched role perceptions and trigger change while compatibility is supposed to sustain crucial elements of established frames of reference.

We now turn to a set of factors that may create variance in the dependent variables *within a given organisational configuration*. First, the *degree of affiliation* to an institution can be seen as a continuum rather than as a dichotomy. Thus, some secondary affiliations may pose more severe claims on their participants' attention than others. Committees may convene weekly and engage members in a lot of preparatory work and informal interaction. Meetings may be separated in time and space from "primary" activities thus making it less likely that allegiances are carried over from one setting to another (March 1994). In addition, seniority in particular committee networks might be positively related to changes in preferences and loyalties. However, this relationship may be contingent upon the kind of lessons they have drawn from the co-operation; are they mainly positive or negative?

Second, in secondary organisations like committees *local cultures*, may have evolved, some of which are more conducive to preference change than others. Such cultural traits could be professionalism, consensus orientation and "thick" trust in key participants (Checkel 1999; Lewis 2000).

Third, the extent to which interests might be substantially reformulated in secondary arenas may depend heavily on *how ingrained and constrained actors' preferences are prior to meetings*. Rationalists often presuppose that agents' mandates are hammered out beforehand in a clear-cut and unambiguous manner. From an organisational point of view, however, the reality may be quite different. Organisations are often better described as loosely coupled systems that may be badly co-ordinated. The ecology of simultaneous decision processes creates shortage of attention, in particular among those who are expected to guide and instruct others, concerning the policy positions they should take in external arenas. The discovery of solutions may precede problems and clearly formulated interests could be the output of a process rather than the input (March and Olsen 1976). Under such circumstances, secondary organisations like collegiate structures could be expected to be more transformative and impinge more thoroughly on participants' preference formation than they normally do.

7.3. Organisational Explanations in an EU Context

At the EU level, we find both primary and secondary organisations. The Commission, for example, is the primary affiliation of the Commissioners as well as of the officials in the services. Thus, we would expect their interests and allegiances to be shaped mainly by the Commission, and more so for officials who hold permanent posts than for the Commissioners. The preparatory committees at the Commission and the Council, on the other hand, represent secondary arenas, in which national officials as well as Commission officials participate. Accordingly, under these scope conditions, preferences and loyalties are supposed to change only partly, although additional concerns and loyalties might emerge. The fact that EU meetings are separated in time and space from the daily activities of most national officials makes the evocation of new perceptions more likely. Particular places, buildings and symbols, like the blue flag with the golden stars, may gradually become associated with a particular code of conduct.

However, since some committees are clearly more active than others, the extent to which socialisation actually takes place may vary significantly. COREPER, for example, meets weekly and is composed of national officials who live in Brussels for several years. The location facilitates extensive informal interaction across nationalities and could be thought to make the COREPER setting particularly conducive to persuasion. A sense of extraordinary collective responsibility and supranational loyalty seem indeed to have complemented national allegiances in this case (Lewis 2000). The working parties at the level below are also comprised of several people from the Permanent Representations in Brussels, although they are supplemented to a considerable extent by officials brought in from national capitals. However, as expected, also among genuine "part-timers" in Council and Commission committees one can observe behavioural and attitudinal traits that may be interpreted as having a supranational flavour (Kerremans 1996; Joerges & Neyer 1997; Beyers & Dierickx 1998; Egeberg 1999; Trondal & Veggeland 2003; Trondal 2001a; Trondal 2001b).

The organising principles underlying EU committees are more or less compatible with the principles embedded in the national institutions from which the committee participants originate. Arguably, the Council's basic principle of specialisation is geography (territory) in the sense that each participant (except the Commission representative) is supposed to represent a particular national government. However, since the Council also divides its work according to sector or function at the ministerial and working party level, an additional specialisation principle is strongly present. Although also at these levels participants are expected to identify themselves with their respective governments, the organisational setting is in fact somewhat ambiguous. The result might well be that sectoral and functional loyalties could also be evoked.

The Commission, however, divides its work primarily according to sector or function, clearly expressed in the existence of directorates general (DGs) for agriculture, energy, transport, budget and so on. At all levels, including the preparatory expert committees, participants, as a main rule, are *not* expected to represent their country of origin. However, this organisational setting is not unambiguous either. Since the participants' primary attachment is to national governments, they may nevertheless feel themselves obliged to take the interests of their masters back home seriously into account. In addition, the Commission itself may be interested in having the views of the Member States presented in order to anticipate more precisely future Council reactions.

As shown in Figure 1, the Council structure can be considered compatible with the organising principle of a Foreign Ministry and its Permanent Representations whose mission is to represent a particular country.

Figure 7.1: *The compatibility of organising principles at the national and EU level*

	Foreign ministries and their representations	Sectoral ministries
EU Council	relative compatibility	relative incompatibility
EU Commission	relative incompatibility	relative compatibility

Although frequent interaction among diplomats in the Council may lead to enhanced collective responsibility and reciprocity, one could argue, therefore, that the territorial allegiances acquired in their primary institutions (i.e. foreign ministries and their delegations) are *sustained* rather than profoundly challenged by the organisational characteristics of the Council. In the Commission setting, on the other hand, the same diplomats would face an incompatible organisational environment, which is expected to *challenge* their established world views, for example by focusing attention along sectoral and functional lines of cleavage rather than territorial ones. Those from national sector ministries are expected to make the opposite experiences. Their loyalties may be further underpinned by the Commission structure while being put under a certain pressure in the Council. Accordingly, Jacobsson (1999) observed that the Swedish accession to the EU entailed an increased demand for *Swedish* policy positions. Through EU participation, sector experts thus became more aware of their *national* identities. At first glance, this observation seems rather paradoxical given the increased level of trans-border interaction. However, it is quite understandable if incompatibility has been at work. In their daily work back home, national sector experts tend to identify themselves with their respective agencies and only seldom with their government as such (Egeberg & Sætren 1999). For the most part, they are, therefore, used to presenting the concerns of their respective administrative units and not those of their government (or nation). The Council setting may thus impose interests and loyalties on them that they are not particularly familiar with, namely their *government's* interests. In order to assess the extent to which preferences and allegiances may be moved, complemented or even reshaped, we accordingly have to take the *organisational characteristics* of the institutional setting into account (Egeberg 2004).

124

Arguably, a territorially based intergovernmental system can only be really transcended if non-territorial principles of organisational specialisation take precedence at the system centre, as is the case in federal and unitary states (Egeberg 2004). Thus, another seeming paradox emerges; resocialisation of national actors at the EU level due to incompatible organisational structures is not necessarily conducive to further system transformation. Although resocialising diplomats in the Commission setting might foster further integration, transforming national sector officials into government representatives in the Council most likely will sustain rather than challenge the intergovernmental pattern. Similarly, established allegiances that are not seriously challenged due to compatible organisational structures might turn out to be highly conducive to further integration. This may be the case for national experts who attend Commission committee meetings since they are supposed to maintain their sectoral loyalties.

This study focuses on the formation of allegiances and preferences among officials from national sector ministries who participate in preparatory (expert) committees in the Commission and working parties in the Council. As genuine "part-timers" in secondary arenas, we expect them to largely retain their acquired interests. However, *additional* and *partly reformulated* loyalties and preferences might evolve as an effect of committee participation. The extent to which this actually happens may depend on the extent to which national mandates and positions really are pre-established; their degree of participation in committees and previous experiences; and their confidence in institutions like the Commission and the Presidency of the Council. Concerning allegiances, national officials, in general, are expected to *complement* their national identities with "thin" supranational loyalties due to committee participation. The extent to which this happens may be contingent upon their degree of participation and previous experiences. Their sectoral or functional allegiances acquired back home are supposed to be sustained in the mainly compatible Commission setting while somewhat challenged in the relatively incompatible Council working party structure. Thus, intergovernmentalist belief systems might be transcended along two paths, first, by adopting more supranational attitudes and, second, by remaining sectorally oriented (Egeberg 1999).

7.4. Data and Method

This study is based on personal interviews with 47 national officials involved in EU level policy-making. The interviews were conducted during the winter and spring of 1998. The interviewees do not make up a representative sample of all national officials engaged in EU affairs. *First*, the respondents are all drawn from a particular policy sector, namely the transport field. Although transport policy from the outset was looked upon as pivotal to European integration, little progress was made until the 1980s. However, the single market programme begun in 1985 provided a ready-made vehicle for encouraging common action in transport (Aspinwall 1998). Within transport, I focus on those working in the road and rail sectors. They are involved in

125

policy-making on road and rail infrastructure and transport, including market liberalisation. As regards road traffic, they are also engaged in social regulation (e.g. driving hours, resting time), vehicle safety and emission control. Most of the interviewees are affiliated with transport ministries or their equivalents, but some also hail from the Department of the Environment and Local Government (Ireland). Due to financial and time constraints, the number of interviews had to be limited. Under these circumstances, I decided to try to cover the two modes of transport in each country instead of selecting officials from several issue areas. The problem with this solution is of course that generalisation of findings across policy fields becomes difficult. However, such generalising would hardly have been possible in any case with so few respondents from each policy sector. On the other hand, concentrating on this particular area makes it possible to utilise the data in a policy study on a later occasion. This limitation of the study was also justified by the fact that the author already had invested considerable time and energy in penetrating the road and rail policy fields in connection with another project. It was considered a clear advantage to have as much substantive policy knowledge as possible even when the interviews largely dealt with generic role perceptions.

Second, the officials included in the study all come from small member states, namely Denmark (10 interviewees), Finland (8), Ireland (10), Portugal (10) and Sweden (9). Given that the number of interviews had to be limited, hard choices had to be made once more. The notion that small countries had not been researched to the same degree as the larger countries was decisive for this choice. One bias that may accompany this selection is that those originating from smaller member states have been known to express somewhat more supranational attitudes than their colleagues from larger countries (Beyers 1998).

Third, the respondents are all affiliated with cabinet level departments. Although we deal with sectoral ministries, their institutional background probably implies an over-representation of people identifying with their national government as such at the expense of more functional orientations often associated with agency personnel (Egeberg & Sætren 1999).

In order to measure "allegiance" we simply asked the officials to which institution they feel an allegiance ("identify with or feel responsible to"). Their perceived allegiance was graded by asking them to locate themselves along a five-point ordinal scale, one scale for each institution. An additional indicator of their allegiances is how committee colleagues from other countries assess their role enactment. Three indicators of preference change were applied: a five-point ordinal scale was used to measure how much consideration the interviewees would give to proposals, statements and arguments from different actors, applying one scale for each actor they were to assess. Another indicator registered how often decisions are reached through consensus formation. Finally, a third scale recorded the extent to which they were prepared to alter their original policy position during or subsequent to committee meetings. (I consider "position" to be an issue-specific preference). The rest of the interview guide, for the most part, is also very standardised in order to obtain quantifiable measures. Due to the small N and the level of measurement there are, however, clear limitations as to what kind of statistical analyses can be performed.

126

Gamma's level of significance is presented, as if we dealt with a representative sample, in order to indicate the robustness of a relationship.

The ideal data set would of course have been without the deficiencies pointed out above. With more resources available, a sample that included officials also from larger countries, from subordinated agencies, and from other policy sectors than transport could have been drawn. Thus, the generaliseability of the findings would probably have increased. My first priority, however, would have been to expand the study to incorporate foreign ministry personnel. By so doing, the compatibility/non-compatibility hypothesis could have been put to a real test.

7.5. Empirical Observations

Table 7.1 shows that officials express a sense of belonging to several bodies at the same time. As expected, their basically sectoral allegiances acquired back home are largely preserved in the Commission setting while somewhat more challenged in the Council in which loyalty to their own government becomes juxtaposed. Obviously, incompatible organisational structures seem to *supplement* rather than *replace* established role conceptions.

Table 7.1: *Percentage of national officials who to a 'great extent'* [1] *feel an allegiance to (identify with or feel responsible to) the following entities when participating in:*

Entities	Commission Expert Committees	Council Working Groups
Own government	66	93
Own ministry	85	93
Own profession	35	17
Own policy sector	55	73
The committee(s)/group(s) in which I participate	24[2]	13[3]
European Union	31[4]	28[5]
N (mean)	(40)	(30)

Notes: [1] *great extent*: Values 1 and 2 combined on a five-point scale. [2] If we also include value 3 on the same five-point scale, 68% feel an allegiance to the committee(s) as such. [3] Values 1-3: 50%. [4] Values 1-3: 74%. [5] Values 1-3: 66%.

We see, however, that allegiance to their own government is strongly present also in Commission committees. This may be because functional role expectations are indeed complemented by national claims on officials' loyalty (Egeberg 1999: 462). On the other hand, sectoral orientations are strongly present even in the Council, quite understandably so given the duality of specialisation principles at work here. When asked to assess the behaviour of their colleagues from other countries, it becomes rather evident, however, that different loyalties do tend to emerge in the two settings (cf. table 7.2).

Table 7.2: *The extent to which national officials feel that their colleagues from other countries behave like experts or government representatives when participating in: (%)*

Behave like:	Commission Expert Committees	Council Working Groups
Mainly experts	32	3
Mixed roles	32	-
Mainly government representative	37	97
	101	100
N	(41)	(30)

The organisational structure of the Council induces officials from national sector ministries to assume roles they are not particularly familiar with back home. Paradoxically then, they become socialised at the EU level, but not in a way that is clearly conducive to further European system transformation. Those in the Commission structure, on the other hand, who are *not* socialised in this respect, carry with them role perceptions that are partly at odds with an intergovernmental logic.

Those participating in Commission committees as well as those on Council groups, however, become socialised at the EU level in another respect. Consistent with our assumptions, table 7.1 shows that "supranational" allegiances develop *to some degree*. Thus, the extent to which they express a sense of belonging to the respective committees or the EU as such, reflects perfectly the organisational structure's *secondary* character for these people. Are there then other factors that may explain the degree to which national civil servants adopt supranational allegiances? Tables 7.3 and 7.4 reveal only two statistically significant relationships.

Officials tend to identify more strongly with expert committees that meet frequently and in which representatives of the Commission behave independently from particular national interests. The integrity of the chairperson also seems to be of some relevance in the Council groups, although this relationship is not statistically significant. Interestingly, individual or institutional seniority does not enhance the sense of belonging to the EU level. Table 7.4 depicts fairly strong positive relationships between EU allegiance and the extent to which the Union is seen as advantageous in one's own policy area. The relationships, however, are not statistically significant.

When national officials identify themselves with their respective EU committees, although relatively weakly (cf. table 7.1), it could be expected that they will at least partly take the interests of other participants into account. Table 7.5 shows that national officials are indeed attentive to arguments advanced by other committee members.

Table 7.3: *The bivariate relationships between 'feel an allegiance to (identify with or feel responsible to) committee(s) or group(s) in which I participate' and the factors listed beneath.*

(Gamma. Those significant at the 0,05 level in italics.)

Independent variables:	Commission Expert Committees	Council Working Groups
Seniority of one's own country in EU	-0,21	-0,05
Personal seniority in EU related work	0,10	-0,36
Number of meetings attended each year	*0,38*	0,08
How advantageous EU has been in own policy area	0,10	-0,06
Consider the Commission to behave independently from particular national interests	*0,44*	-0,25
Consider the Presidency to behave independently from particular national interests	-	0,27
N (mean)	(41)	(29)

Having demonstrated considerable expertise on the subject matter is deemed more important than coming from a large member state per se, especially so in Commission committees. Thus, "the better argument" seems more relevant than an actor's (material) bargaining power (cf. Risse 2000). The chairpersons; the representatives of the Commission in Commission committees and the Presidency in the Council groups also seem to be highly pivotal interlocutors. Table 7.6 reveals that arguments are taken seriously. The officials report that consensus formation is quite usual in both settings. They also consider themselves prepared to modify or alter their original position during or subsequent to meetings rather often. Only a small minority says this should happen seldom (table 7.7).

As expected, the secondary organisational frame, i.e. the committees, seems to impact on their preferences. Do other factors matter as well? Table 7.8 reveals only two statistically significant relationships.

Civil servants from new member states are more inclined to move or reformulate their stances than those emanating from more experienced countries. Representatives of new member states may wish to demonstrate their willingness to co-operate in order to become accepted as good "club members". They may also have more policies that need to be adjusted than those from older member countries.

Table 7.4: *The bivariate relationships between 'feel an allegiance to (identify with or feel responsible to) the European Union'" and the factors listed beneath when participating in:*
(Gamma. None are significant at the 0,05 level.)

Independent variables:	Commission Expert Committees	Council Working Groups
Seniority of one's own country in the EU	-0,04	-0,22
Personal seniority in EU related work	-0,02	0,00
Number of meetings attended each year	0,12	0,10
How advantageous EU has been in own policy area	0,31	0,27
N (mean)	(39)	(29)

Table 7.5: *Percentage of national officials who will give 'much [1] consideration' to proposals, statements and arguments from the following actors when participating in:*

Actors:	Commission Expert Committees	Council Working Groups
Commission	88	63
Presidency of the Council	-	69
Colleagues from other countries who have demonstrated much expertise	88	57
Colleagues from large member states	27	47
Colleagues from member states from own region	63	47
N (mean)	(40)	(29)

Notes: [1] *much*: Values 1 and 2 combined on a five-point scale.

Table 7.6: *Percentage of national officials who report that decisions are reached through consensus formation in:*

	Commission Expert Committees	Council Working Groups
Often	68	54
Sometimes	20	25
Seldom/never	13	21
	(101)	(100)
N	(40)	(28)

Table 7.7: *Percentage of national officials who report that their original position should be modified or altered during or subsequent to meetings*

	Commission Expert Committees	Council Working Groups
Often	45	43
Sometimes	48	37
Seldom	8	20
	(101)	(100)
N	(40)	(30)

Does it matter whether representatives are instructed and co-ordinated in advance or not? First, it should be said that the amount of prior instruction and co-ordination varies considerably across committee types. While 87% of those on Council groups say that they are often instructed about which position to take, this holds true for only 32% of those on expert committees. Preferences thus seem more malleable at the Commission stage than at later occasions. Accordingly, we remember from table 7.7 that expert-committee participants are somewhat more willing to revise their viewpoints as compared to their colleagues in Council working parties. However, table 7.8 depicts no significant relationships in this respect *within* each type of committee. This may be partly due to the way we try to measure the phenomenon. The form of the dependent variable presupposes that a position has in fact been hammered out in advance. We know that this is not always the case, in particular as far as the Commission phase is concerned. As one interviewee said: 'You have an informal instruction, like "you can't agree to that, or that... It's up to you to argue, develop..." ' (interview 42).

The interviews revealed that officials quite often draft their mandates themselves, although they usually try to anticipate the reactions of their superiors. And, when shaping their government's position in the Council, they can not completely ignore what have been said in expert committees (Schaefer 1996: 11).

Are there then alternatives to the primarily organisational explanation, focused on here, that merit attention? It is hard to see how we could come to grips with the phenomena addressed in this chapter without taking the organisational setting within which individual actors interact into account. However, the picture can become more nuanced in some respects by incorporating other factors. For example, the national officials' allegiance to EU committees, in general, is clearly relatively weak compared to their expressed loyalty to various national institutions. Still, their sense of belonging to particular committees seems to vary somewhat, depending on the intensity of the work and the amount of trust they have in the chairperson. Moreover, when it comes to actual preference adjustment and change, the main observation is that the concerns of the other members of a committee are indeed heeded. However, those who present the better argument are particularly heeded. Thus, argumentation and persuasion do seem to have an independent impact on socialisation (Risse 2000, Checkel 2001).

Table 7.8: *The bivariate relationships between "how often position should be modified or altered" and the factors listed beneath.*

(Gamma. Those significant at 0,05 level in italics.)

Independent variables	Commission Expert Committees	Council Working Groups
How often instructed about position to take	0,08	0,37
How often co-ordinated with a central co-ordinating body	0,15	0,27
Seniority of one's country in the EU	*-0,66*	*-0,59*
Personal seniority in EU related work	-0,08	-0,14
Number of meetings attended each year	0,28	0,40
How advantageous EU has been in own policy area	-0,06	-0,28
Consider the Commission to behave independently from particular national interests	0,14	-0,22
Consider the Presidency to behave independently from particular national interests	-	0,01
N (mean)	(40)	(29)

7.6. Conclusion

People have private interests in wages, prestige, power and a good life. By entering formal organisations, these desires may be more or less realised. In exchange, they are expected to pursue the goals of that particular organisation, to behave in a manner that is seen as appropriate and to feel an allegiance to that organisation. Thus, from an organisational perspective, what basically explains socialisation are people's *entries into and exits from* formal organisations. When individuals move from one organisational setting to another, the expectation is that they shift job relevant preferences and their sense of belonging relatively quickly. Like organisations in general, secondary structures such as EU committees provide agendas, alternatives, obligations and colleagues. As expected, secondary attachments are not capable of creating a sense of belonging and allegiance among their members to the same extent as primary structures do, although some changes do occur. It does not seem to matter whether countries or individuals have participated in secondary arenas for a long time or not. Rather, the extent to which participants become loyal to a particular committee seems to depend on the intensity of the work in that particular grou, and on the degree of trust they have in the chairperson. We have seen that the other committee members' arguments are in fact taken seriously into account, and especially those advanced by participants who have demonstrated considerable expertise on the subject matter. Most committee participants express their willingness to modify or revise their positions during or subsequent to meetings. The fact that this willingness is more articulated among those representing relatively new member states may indicate that *entries* into organisational settings affects preference change relatively rapidly.

Important role perceptions are often sustained and further underpinned rather than challenged by taking new roles in secondary arenas like EU committees. This happens to national officials from *sectoral* ministries who face a relatively compatible structure in Commission groups. Interestingly, however, this lack of profound socialisation at the EU level may in fact be seen as highly conducive to further European integration since their allegiances are largely at odds with an intergovernmental logic. In Council working parties, on the other hand, a *partly* incompatible setting seems to challenge established sectoral or functional loyalties more extensively. Somewhat paradoxically, this kind of individual resocialisation at the EU level does probably *not* trigger further system transformation since the newly acquired identities are completely compatible with an intergovernmental system.

The overall conclusion, which might be drawn from this study, is that institutions matter, but one needs to unpack their *organisational characteristics* in order to understand *how* and under what conditions. Although the data material deployed in this study is rather limited, its main conclusions on the impact of the organisational setting within which officials interact are strongly supported by two other studies (Egeberg et al. 2003; Trondal 2001a; 2001b).

8. European Citizenship, Citizens and Civil Society
Riccardo Scartezzini

8.1. Introduction

Since the beginning of the 1990s, the concept of European citizenship has been at the centre of academic and political debate. It has traditionally been amongst the more important concepts in the context of reflections about the meaning and ends of political orders, the definition of a political identity, the development of welfare state provisions, and the definition of membership in the political community. Because of its controversial meaning the concept of citizenship covers a wide range of topics, and is topical in the context of multiple social and political dynamics. This chapter will address the problems and controversies related to the concept of citizenship, paying particular attention to the specific problems of European citizenship.

The chapter is organised as follow: the next section delineates the main questions and problems addressed by scholars dealing with the concept of citizenship and with the relationships between national and European citizenship. It will be argued that it is useful to distinguish reflections on citizenship according to their focus on three broad topics: the problem of definition of fundamental rights at the EU level, the problem of access of European citizens to supranational policy processes and the problem of the political identity linked to the European Union. Sections 3, 4, and 5 address such topics in turn. The final paragraph presents some conclusions.

8.2. The Debate over EU Citizenship: Questions and Problems

Academic and political reflections on the actual and potential characteristics of European citizenship have often made explicit reference to national citizenship. Elements of convergence and divergence with the experience of nation states have been analysed, leading to the conclusions that European citizenship is an insufficient device for strengthening the European polity (Follesdal 2001b), and that it is an unnecessary development of state-based citizenship.

In an intergovernmentalist perspective, the creation of European citizenship is excessive and could be counterproductive because it undermines the sovereignty of the nation-states. For instance Claus Offe (2000) argues that the *acquis communitarie* is eroding the *acquis nationale* based on welfare state and citizenship rights. Similarly, Weale (2005) illustrates how the development of the European Union can be regarded as a threat in analysis focussing on the developmental conquests of national welfare states, like the account of European integration that derives from the premises proposed by Rokkan. In this light, it might be noted that Rokkan's interpretation of the process of nation building in Europe, was sceptical about the advantages of European integration. This view is not shared by those who emphasise the potential of European integration and of the creation of the European citizenship in particular.

In a post-national perspective, European citizenship represents a first step towards an innovative form of relationship between individuals and political authority. In the words of Elizabeth Meehan (1993: 1):

> "a new kind of citizenship is emerging that is neither national nor cosmopolitan but that is multiple in the sense that the identities, rights and obligations, associated with citizenship, are expressed through institutions, states, national and transnational voluntary associations, regions and alliances of regions.".

Similarly, the influential work of Jasmine Soysal (1994) stressed the notion of personhood and the limits of conceptions of citizenship based on territorially bounded nation-states.

In a different theoretical context, the seminal work of Jürgen Habermas contributed to diffuse a supranational conception of citizenship, based on shared political practices and procedures, to be implemented at the supranational level and largely independent of the development of a shared sense of political belonging.

In short, the debate proved clearly that citizenship is a contested concept, and even more so in the context of the EU polity. Two different reasons can be identified. First, notions of citizenship are strongly linked to the notion of stateness, and more specifically to the nation-state. In a very broad sense, citizenship can be understood as an institutionalised relation between citizens and the democratic polity. In the context of nation-states, such a relationship has been institutionalised with reference to civil, political and social rights. In Marshall's (1973, 1992) famous scheme, the development of citizenship' rights follows an incremental path linked to a bounded territory and to membership in a political community.

Nation states are based on the exclusive jurisdiction over a clearly defined territory. Historians have noted that the correspondence among territory, political community and society that characterizes nation-states as political orders is the exception rather than the rule in the history of political institutions, and that such correspondence does not constitute a necessary element for political authority to be exercised. Whatever the relevance of these historical considerations, the composite territorial structure of the Union has been identified as one of its weaknesses. As Wiener (1998: 2) puts it "the Euro-polity is a political arena without fixed boundaries or a centralized political structure, instead it has been characterized as a multilevel polity with a weak core". The European Union consists of different territories: for instance, the Schengen area and the Euro-zone are different and the overall situation is made more complicated by the existence of national opt-out clauses. Overall, the lack of an identifiable demos and of a territory undermines the possibility for making European citizenship fully meaningful to Europeans.

Second, notions of citizenship refer to a sense of belonging to a national political community: fellow citizens and nationals are supposed to overlap. Historians have noted that such overlap is a contingent condition that can be found in the particular political organisation that we call the "nation-state". Balibar (1991) observes that the development of EU citizenship challenges the well-established equation between citizens and nationals. In this sense, EU citizenship can play a constitutive role, contributing to the building of the European polity. In other words, its creation opens up the possibility to develop a common concept of citizenship starting from very different national traditions. The debate has also been connected to the question of European identity, and the meaning of this concept beyond national borders.

These brief notes highlight the potential for controversy and debate embedded in the very concept of EU citizenship. In the following paragraphs, we will analyse in depth these broad questions about the basic characters of EU citizenship and its legal and political relation to national citizenship. Our main questions thus refer to the meaning of citizenship in a supranational context and to what the EU is proposing to its citizens in terms of rights, access and belonging. (Wiener 1998).

8.3. European Citizenship and Fundamental Rights

The inclusion of the notion of EU citizenship in the EU Treaty of 1993 was an important step that made the search for a definition even more compelling. The decision of the Council over the formal creation of European citizenship has been widely debated. On the one hand, scholars have stressed the importance of the inclusion of EU citizenship in the main body of the Treaty, marking its significance as a substantive feature of the Union. On the other hand, it has been noted that from a legal point of view, it is difficult to understand what is new in the notion of European citizenship. In fact, it is based on existing rights and does not add any elements to the previously established set of provisions. More precisely, the text signed at Maastricht, which formally established the notion of European Union citizenship, includes the freedom to move and establish residence anywhere in the EU, the right to vote and stand in local and European elections in the country of residence, the right to diplomatic protection, and the right of petition and appeal to the European Ombudsman.

Scholars have also pointed to a severe limitation as it is impossible to acquire European citizenship by an internal European procedure. European Citizenship, instead, is completely determined by national rules as the status of EU citizen is conferred to "every persons holding the nationality of a Member State" (art. 17). In this light, it is possible to affirm that, as Bauböck (1997: 3) puts it: "for the time being, the dogma of state sovereignty in determining nationality remains unchallenged" (See also Bauböck 1997).

It is because of the complexity of these features that the content of European citizenship is "anaemic" (Follesdal 2001b). In defining EU citizenship as anaemic, Follesdal intended to stress the lack of any active conception of citizenship at the EU level. As noted, the most important goal of EU citizenship rights is to guarantee freedom of movement, and in this light it has been labelled "market citizenship" (Crouch, Eder et al. 2001; Warleigh 2001). A fundamental component of notions and practices of nationally based citizenship refers to social rights. These are intended to support civil and political rights and indeed it has been argued that these three basic types of rights are mutually reinforcing. As Weale (2005:5) puts it: "social rights can be seen as giving substance to political and civil rights. For example, freedom of movement is a hollow right for those who cannot afford housing costs in the place to which they would wish to move". In the context of nation states, social rights are part of democratic citizenship, as they are provided on the basis of membership of the political community, and from this point of view they proved essential in determining consensus and legitimacy of nation-states. Indeed, the proportion of European citizens who express support for social rights, like health care, is still very high.

Following this logic, it could make sense to investigate what social provisions are linked to practices of European citizenship. The establishment of welfare-like social policy at the EU level encountered obstacles and the opposition of "jealous" member states. In particular, UK governments have opposed initiatives for strengthening social policy, as the controversies over the Social Charter in the late 1980s and over the Charter of Fundamental Rights demonstrate.

It has been argued that the difficult development of European social rights is due to their conflicting relationship with the creation of the single market. To enforce social provisions, political authorities need full control over taxation, investment and economic instruments, and it is precisely this sort of control that is undermined by the single market. Consequently, the more economic integration proceeds, the weaker the opportunities for social policy. It has been argued that one of the characteristic traits of "Europe" consists of extended social rights. From this point of view, it might be considered ironic that the process of European integration poses a threat to them.

Moreover, one might note that existing social provisions at the EU level do not necessarily constitute a remedy to market-driven inequalities. In the words of Leibfried & Pierson (2005: 262): "the EU's social dimension is usually discussed as a corrective or counter to market-building, but instead appears to have proceeded largely as part of the market-building process, and was sucked into a free mobility and competition-enhancing process." The point made by Leibfried can be illustrated with reference to anti-discrimination policy. It is among the most relevant initiatives in terms of social rights at the European level, and had its peak at the end of the 1990s with the approval of the Treaty of Amsterdam. Article 13 of the Amsterdam Treaty, the two subsequent directives (Directives 2000/43 June 2000 and 2000/78 November 2000)[115] and the Action Programme against Racism and Xenophobia, are

115 The Council Directive on Equal Treatment on Grounds of Racial or Ethnic Origin adopted in June 2000, prohibits all forms of discrimination on grounds of race and ethnic origin. According to it, equal treatment must be guaranteed in terms of access to employment or self-employment, training, education, working conditions, professional organisations, access to goods and service. It outlaws both direct and indirect discrimination (practices that are apparently neutral but disadvantage a person or group of a particular ethnic origin). It also obliges

part of the so-called "Article 13 package", which outlaws discrimination on the ground of nationality, gender, race, religion, belief, disability, age and sexual orientation. The package is regarded as a milestone in the field, and indeed, its impact on national legislations has been substantial. For countries like Italy and Spain in particular, it represented a policy innovation leading to the creation of new institutional structures.

The point to be made here is that it is plausible to interpret EU anti-discrimination provisions as a tool for enhancing market efficiency and for lowering the barriers to the free movement of workers. Accordingly, the process of EU integration has been primarily driven by the need for building the common market and individual rights have been provided in the context of this logic. In other words, the development of social rights aimed at guaranteeing equal treatment in the market, independently of nationality and all the sources of difference mentioned above. As Moravcsik (1998) noted, the EU polity cannot be understood without reference to the project of integrating national economies.

However, the creation of European citizenship led to important developments in the provisions of social rights. For instance, member states can no longer limit the provision of most social benefits to their citizens, as they have to be granted also to nationals from other member states. Moreover, there are some advantages to the development of the European social citizenship, limited as they may be. Beetham & Lord (1998: 30), for instance, affirm that "one enormous advantage from the citizens' point of view of the two level – European and national – political system is that there is now a degree of competition in rights delivery that breaks the previous monopoly of the state. The citizen has a double guarantee in the event of a failure of state performance in this area."

From this point of view, it would be important to assess how EU citizenship provides citizens with guarantees about fundamental rights. In other words, one should assess the capacity of EU citizenship to bring citizens into the political process and to give them control over collective decisions. In the next paragraph, this second aspect of the concept of citizenship will be addressed.

8.4. European Citizenship and Political Access

Access to the European political community and its policy processes are central aspects of citizenship rights. As Warleight (2000, 2001) noted, after an initial period when citizenship was mainly linked to the development of identity-generating symbols (see next paragraph), recent developments aim at providing EU citizens with

member states to set up independent bodies to monitor implementation of directive and receive complaints. The second Council Directive, adopted in October 2000, on Equal Treatment in Employment and Occupation, aims at guarantee protection against discrimination on basis of religion, sexual orientation, age and disability in employment.

more concrete opportunities for political engagement. In this context it can be argued that citizenship consists of the "right to have rights"(Bellamy, 2001). The expression "right to have rights" refers to the fact that, thanks to civil and political citizenship rights, individuals acquire the possibility to engage in debates on the future of their associative life and about the ends and means of the political community. In this sense, citizenship has an active meaning and is "more than passive acceptance of a pre-constituted package of rights" (Bellamy, 2001: 3). Indeed a definition of citizenship based on an active conception of the citizens is very diffused and has ancient roots in the republican thinking about the ideal link between individuals and the polity (Dahl 1989).

In the sociological literature on the concept of citizenship, the focus on political access and participation is very important. Introducing the notion of practices of citizenship, Wiener (1998) intends to highlight the need to pay attention to the institutionalised relationships between citizens and the political community and consequently to the constitutive role of any definition of citizenship. Bridging the gap between European citizens and European institutions has been regarded as one of the most urgent and ambitious task of European citizenship and one of the most important reasons behind its creation.

There is a broad range of forms of political participation that have to be considered when discussing the potential of European citizenship. The first is voting. It is the main form of political participation in the context of nation states, and on the basis of this deeply-held belief the introduction of EU elections was welcomed as a fundamental step in the process of European integration. Regular elections are at the centre of political life of any country and, from a theoretical point of view, of almost all conceptions of democracy. However, both at the national and European levels, voting seems to be losing its appeal, and indeed the decreasing disaffection of citizens wit electoral practices has been regarded a pathology of contemporary democracy.

Democracy and citizenship rights are highly esteemed all over the world. As Weale (1999:1) puts it: "democracy has ceased to be matter of contention and has become a matter of convention". Yet, the performance of democratic systems is not entirely satisfactory and citizens appear to be more sceptical about the concrete meaning of citizenship rights of participation. For instance, it has been asked whether the declining turn-out in national elections in many European countries, or the exclusion from voting of guest workers in Germany, are symptoms of the reduced relevance of rights of political participation. Similarly, the very low levels of electoral turnout at the local level in the UK sparked a debate about how to motivate citizens to take part in elections and express their preferences. A number of solutions have been proposed and experiments with postal vote and electronic vote have been implemented, with mixed results.

The performance of electoral devices and mechanisms is even more disappointing at the EU level. The electoral turnout in European election is decreasing in all Member states. Furthermore, it is well known that electoral participation has limited significance at the EU level. Elections and basic principles of representative democracy work at the European level in a completely different way as compared to nation-
140

states, because the European Parliament only very indirectly holds European institutions accountable, and because elections affect neither the Council of Ministers nor the European Council and the Commission. In short, voting is a central practice of democratic citizenship that is providing citizens with limited opportunities at the European level.

Overall, it makes sense to examine a broader range of forms of political participation at the EU level and ask whether they have the potential to supplement the weak European electoral mechanism and strengthen the link between European citizens and the European Union. A first basic observation to be made is that new channels that have been enacted to favour public participation are non-binding and largely informal.

Nentwich (1998) lists the available channels for exercising participation at the supranational level, highlighting the potential of direct and indirect forms of participation. He recalls that, from the point of view of EU institutions, EU elections are the most important (although limited) form of direct participation, and that processes such as written consultation, petitions to the European Parliament (EP), committees, public hearings etc., have been added in order to form a structure of opportunities for indirect participation at the EU level. On the whole, such mechanisms provide European citizens with channels for exercising citizenship practices at the supranational level and for the input of public preferences and knowledge in EU policy-making.

The potential and the impact of such direct and indirect channels for participation have been addressed by a growing body of empirical research. Among the results, it is noteworthy that the overall impact of such channels appears to be very limited, and that the capacity for popular control over collective European decisions is still weak. As supplementary tools for exercising democratic citizenship such devices still have to prove their full potential. If, following Weale (1999: 14), we argue that "in a democracy important public decisions on questions of law and policy depend, directly or indirectly, upon public opinion formally expressed by citizens of the community, the vast bulk of whom have equal political rights", then the conclusion is that the EU has a democratic deficit that should be seriously taken into account. Formal channels for public participation are an important step in the direction of overcoming such a gap between EU decision-makers and EU citizens, and the EU institutions seem to be aware of the need to improve them. For instance, in 2002 the EU Commission adopted common guidelines on consultation processes. General standards for consultation processes at the EU level have been set by the Commission in 2002 (European Commission 2002). In so doing, the aim of the Commission was to make different practices for consulting civil society consistent, laying down general principles and practices to be shared by all DGs in their activities. Until 2002, each DG could adopt its own mechanisms and procedures to engage in consultation with relevant sectoral interests. With the aim of guaranteeing transparency, the Commission (2002 Communication 704) proposed a common procedure and stated that "the overall rationale of this document is to ensure that all relevant parties are properly consulted."

Documents like this are becoming more and more frequent and reveal the high level of attention and exchange between EU institutions and organised citizens. However, it should be noted that DGs vary in terms of their willingness to promote processes of written consultation. The Directorate General for agriculture seldom consults the public and generally is interested in gathering opinions on highly technical matters. However, it is undeniable that a dialogue between social and institutional actors is going on in Brussels and that it is actively promoted and supported as a way of ameliorating citizenship practices.

This process dates back to the end of 1990s. The need to improve the overall transparency and accessibility of the EU policy processes led to the publication of the White Paper on Governance in 2001. In this document, the European Commission listed principles that should inform decision-making processes on collective decisions, openness, participation, accountability, effectiveness, and coherence. The White Paper on Governance has been widely debated, highlighting the limits and merits of this important policy document. In this context, it is noteworthy that the document generally equates the idea of participation of citizens with the participation of civil society, i.e. with the participation of associations of citizens. The shift in the actors of participation is an argument for discussion in the debate on the role of civil society. In terms of the debate on citizenship, it can be argued that the White Paper is important for its suggestions about the importance of getting people involved in European policy processes. Paying attention to the opportunities for public participation in policy processes implies giving relevance to the idea that citizenship is also a matter for political struggles.

The argument has been often contrasted with Marshall's famous arguments, which see the development of civil, political and social rights as a relatively straightforward and evolutionary process. The Marshallian perspective is based on the idea that equality is the general end of the development of citizenship rights in the modern era. Consequently, his definition of citizenship refers to the recognition of full membership in the political community.

With reference to the idea of equality, it has been noted that the Marshall's views underestimate the importance of political conflicts in the definition of citizenship rights, and in particular the importance of class dynamics. Marshall expected classes to loose their economic function because the development of social rights would contribute to overcoming inequalities. In the debate on citizenship of the late 1980s, critics of the Marshallian ideas noted that his view on the redistributive potential of social rights and on the opportunities for overcoming inequalities was too optimistic, and that the structure of social relations among classes has not been affected much by the development of citizenship (Barbalet 1992). Overall, the relevance of the approach proposed by Marshall has diminished and a more dynamic view of citizenship and of its development has been advanced.

With reference to this debate, it is important to recall the idea that conflicts over the definition of citizenship and its contents have had a central place in the political life of European states. It is particularly in this context that the importance of political access and participation emerges as a central feature of a definition of citizenship. Even if in contemporary Europe class dynamics are no longer the most relevant

142

form of public mobilization and participation. The idea that citizens' engagement in political struggles is a basic need for any democracy and for any meaningful conception of citizenship constitutes an important argument for discussion.

The need to bring competing visions to the European arena led to the emphasis on civil society organisations and their potential for democratic European citizenship. The attention paid to civil society helps explain the content of social demands about citizenship rights. Welfare state provisions, and more generally social rights, have been the focus of the labour movement, gender equality has been claimed by feminists and minority rights by ethnic groups (Janoski, 1998). All these issues can be at the centre of political attention, and civil society organisations are very active in putting them on the policy agenda of European and national political institutions. In this perspective, a strong guarantee of civil and political rights in the Union is a central concern, and the creation of EU citizenship represents a potentially important step towards the empowerment of EU citizens.

It is mainly in this context that the attention paid to civil society organisations can be understood. As noted above, the European Union strongly emphasises the need to get in touch with organised citizens, and encourages forms of consultation and collaborative governance. Observers agree on the increasingly relevant role played by NGOs in policy-making, particularly in sectors like environmental policy and consumer and anti-discrimination policy. A closer look at the opportunities for civil society to gain influence over policy processes at the EU level reveals the complexity of the European political arena and sector-specific conditions.

For instance, opportunities for gaining influence over the Common Agricultural Policy have been extremely limited for decades. The oldest and most expensive European policy has been beyond public scrutiny and ruled by a closed policy community. The Common Agricultural Policy accounts for 1.6% of European GNP and the agricultural sector for 3% of total workforce. The complexity of the system and its remoteness has made it almost impossible for citizens to understand its dynamics. Reforms have been made possible by external crises, like the BSE crises or the pressures from the international market. Consequently, in recent times the field has been opened to respond to growing consumer and environmental concerns. Overall, however, citizens can hardly exercise any control over it and over the on-going process of reform. In this particular case, the potential for political participation linked to European citizenship proved to be very limited.

From the point of view of the debate on citizenship, a number of questions related to the role of civil society and to the legitimacy of this role, arise. First, the capacity of civil society to represent public concerns has to be investigated. It would be necessary to investigate whether Brussels-based organisations are membership-led or elite-controlled. It might be argued that the complexity of the EU environment necessitates specific skills in order to effectively interact in the European arena. As Warleight (2000: 230) notes, "the function of NGOs may thus more properly be to provide EU actors with expert help rather than enhance EU democracy." In this sense, civil society can only partially assist in the full development of European citizenship.

Indeed, informal channels for public participation have only randomly been accessed by individual citizens. As Richardson (1994: 146) notes, "in that sense, policy making discussions are always conducted with an additional but empty seat at the table – representing the threat of individual citizens who regard something as of high salience."

This observation leads us to the third meaning of European citizenship, namely its potential for fostering a sense of solidarity and belonging among European citizens.

8.5. European Citizenship and Sense of Belonging

It is worth noting that European citizenship is strongly linked with national citizenship because the status of European citizen is conferred on "every person holding the nationality of a Member State".

It is usually stated that the citizens' sense of belonging to the European Union is weak. Since the mid 1980s, the construction of a European identity has been addressed as part of the problem posed by the democratic deficit of the Union, and by the general lack of legitimacy that such a deficit entails. Because there is no European *demos*, it is impossible to achieve the input legitimacy that stems from a diffused sense of solidarity among members of the political community (Scharpf, 1999). A set of common symbols, in particular the EU flag and the hymn, have been proposed in order to provide Europeans with visible and shared resources. The results appear to be modest: Eurobarometer surveys show that European citizens lack basic information about the Union's rules and policies. For instance, in terms of self-identification, Eurobarometer polls show that only 4% of EU citizens see themselves as Europeans. A more positive attitude emerges in relation to the process of integration as such, although it is decreasing even in traditionally pro-European countries such as Italy and France. The attachment to the EU appears to be mainly instrumental, linked to the expected benefits of the common market rather than to a sense of common future among Europeans. The difficulties encountered in the ratification process of the EU Constitution, and in particular the French and Dutch referenda, show the fragility of a common sense of European belonging.

In the context of nation states, belonging has been understood in terms of a common historical, cultural (and in some models ethnic) heritage. Such an understanding of nationality is under pressure and has been weakened in the member states. Multiple sources of affiliation are gaining relevance while undermining primacy of national identity. As Bellamy and Warleight (2001:5) note: "the ties of family, work, ideology, religion and sport, for example, increasingly operate either below or beyond the nation-state, competing with and diluting any sense of a purely national identity". In other words, the primacy of national identity is under question because different loyalties are emerging and because the hierarchies among them are no longer rigid. Walzer (1998) summarizes the argument by noting that it is unlikely that citizenship will be the primary identity of people living in highly complex societies.

144

Scholars of social movements have also highlighted the importance of the new politics of identity for determining political mobilization, signalling the existence of a demand for new affiliations that tend to contradict traditional definitions of belonging and of interests. Current reflections on new social movements, such as pro-environment mobilization, stress their impact on more traditional forms of mobilization. In particular, issue-based concerns are of central importance as they are able to undermine established patterns of mobilization linked to economic issues. The literature agrees in underlining the shifting loyalties that characterize current developments and their changes over time. The lack of temporal fixity is a very important feature of present developments in the field of personal identities; traditional patterns of self-definition are subject to be constant revision. In the context of reflection on the post-modern society, such a situation has been described in a number of different ways. Bauman (2002) proposes the notion of "liquid identity" in order to emphasise the continuous definition and redefinition of roles, beliefs and patterns of behaviour. Similarly, Giddens (1991) argues that individuals in "late modernity" are claiming more autonomy in organising their own lives.

The increasing weakness of national identity also results from the rise of ethnic differentiation, as migration processes contribute to diversify European societies. In this context, it might make sense to ask what answers European citizenship provides to the multicultural character of European societies. Scholars have noted that the derived character of EU citizenship, i.e. the need to become a citizen of a Member state in order to become a citizen of the EU, undermines its integrative potential. Member states retain their power to decide the rules for acquiring national citizenship, and consequently they determine who can become an European citizen. This is a strong limit to the conception of EU citizenship as nation-states have the full power over the rules for acquiring national citizenship, which, however, differ greatly from country to country (Brubaker, 1997). Third country citizens, such as Turks in Germany, have been excluded from the European citizenship. In Italy, one must have been a resident for ten years in order to qualify for Italian citizenship, whereas in France all children born in the country acquire the French citizenship. Although the legal situation is changing very fast at the national level, such examples sketch the puzzling normative situation of national citizenship laws and consequently the highly fragmented condition of EU citizenship. At the same time, EU citizenship confers a limited set of rights to non-nationals, e.g. when welfare provisions are to be provided to all EU citizens. In terms of the academic debate, such fragmentation has given rise to the question about the possibility to develop a common sense of 'Europeaness'. Are different traditions able to converge and to create a shared understanding of the meaning of EU citizenship and identity?

It is debatable whether a common identity is required in order o develop common political institutions. In the perspective of Jürgen Habermas' constitutional patriotism, the most important characteristic to be shared by citizens is the belief in the fairness of the political procedures leading to binding collective decisions. In this case, the content of the self-definitions of individuals is not of particular importance. At the centre of the attention, instead, stands the agreement over a set of rules and procedures that are at the base of the political and associative life of the polity. As we saw in the previous paragraph, procedures for decision-making at the EU level can hardly be regarded as fully controlled by European citizens. From this point of view, the transparency and openness of procedures required by constitutional patriotism is a goal still to be achieved.

A similar point can be made with reference to processes of democratic deliberation at the supranational level. Habermas emphasises the need for the development of the public sphere in order to make deliberative democracy work. Empirical research assessing the existence of debates on European topics among European citizens has produced mixed results, but there is evidence that a number of issues have been discussed in all member states. According to Eder & Giesen (2001), this should be regarded as an initial step for the development of a European public sphere connecting a substantial proportion of European citizens.

Among the topics widely discussed among European citizens, and of particular salience in the context of a discussion about EU citizenship and its meanings, is enlargement. The process of EU enlargement is posing challenging questions to the shared conception of EU citizenship. In particular, the stop and go negotiations with Turkey signal the salience of identity issues in the context of European citizenship.

To conclude, the development of a European identity has been regarded as one of the goals of the creation of European citizenship. Moreover, the development of a sense of solidarity seems to be a necessary step for the enhancement of social rights at the European level, as suggested above. Overall, the process proved controversial and the rejection of the Constitutional Treaty show the partial success of the implementation of practices of EU citizenship in fostering a shared sense of belonging, and in building the European polity.

8.6. Conclusion

This chapter aimed to highlight the problematic features of EU citizenship and its implications for the definition of rights, access and belonging to the EU. This debate questions the nature of political authority in the supranational context and challenges well-established notions of the relationship between individuals and the political community. In particular, the link between 'stateness' and citizenship has come under scrutiny because of its implications for the meaning of democracy and legitimacy. In its efforts to assure EU rights, guarantee access and build a sense of shared identity, EU institutions are not reproducing the characteristics of national citizenship but instead are re-inventing its meanings and practices. The emphasis on civil society as a way of giving citizens control over policy processes, thus fulfilling basic democratic requirements, appears to be an important shift in the general notion of citizens' participation, which traditionally is based on individuals or on participation in elections.

As Magnette noted (1999), EU citizenship has great potential and consequently some of the Member States appear to be worried about future developments. It is also noteworthy that the question of obligations linked to EU citizenship is not topical (Janoski 1998), or has at least received less attention compared to the issue of rights and entitlements.

This chapter has stressed the importance of taking into account three distinct components of citizenship, namely the juridical status and the rights attached to it, the political principle that implies participation in the political life of the community and the identity issue linked to membership. Such dimensions can complement each other, but they can also interact in a rather contradictory way, as we saw with reference to the tension between freedom of movement, social rights and national welfare provisions. Such tensions highlight that EU citizenship represents a puzzle. On the one hand, no other international organisation provides individuals with citizenship status, but, on the other hand, all other political entities that do provide individuals with citizenship status have all the characteristics of stateness. Whatever the problems raised by the existence of the European citizenship, it seems that promising options are left open.

Part 3 – Levels: What Levels of Citizenship? From Local to
    Supranational

9. Memories of Citizenship Founded on the City: Spatialities in Early Urban Europe and Modern Mediterranean Political Cultures

Lila Leontidou

> How would Italy of today, the Italian nation, have come into existence without the formation and development of cities and without the unifying influence of cities? 'Supercountrymanism' in the past would have meant municipalism, as it meant popular disarray and foreign rule. And would Catholicism itself have developed if the Pope, instead of residing in Rome, had taken up residence in Scaricalasino?" (Gramsci 1971: 288).

9.1. Introduction

Gramsci's humorous remark referring to the Italian Risorgimento is the most appropriate way to introduce this chapter. Gramsci, who rendered 'civil society' one of his core concepts and presented deep and innovative analyses of citizenship, refers to Scaricalasino, an imaginary place where the donkeys are loaded, in contradistinction to the city and urbanism. The attraction of the city in Italian culture permeates spatialities of elites as well as popular strata, and reflects a widespread Mediterranean-European geographical imagination. Except in periods of fascism, as we will argue here, Southern Europe shares what in Greece bears the name of *astyfilia*, i.e. 'friendliness to the city'. It also has a long tradition of etymological as well as real cultural connection between citizenship and the city. Urbanism has been the basis for citizenship as, by definition, a Citizen, *Politis*, is the resident of the City, *Polis*, since antiquity. The scope of the *Polis* was wider than a physical spatial unit. It comprised a society, a community, and a State, a fact that actually legitimizes the introduction of 'citizenship' on multiple spatial levels. In antiquity, citizenship was founded on the city, while at present the concept is used from the urban to the national – if not the European – level, despite its etymology based on *the city*.

In contemporary Europe, the question of citizenship founded on the city has re-emerged. Urban studies were stressing "urban performance" in the 1980s and "urban restructuring" in the 1990s. Now, in the first decade of the new millennium, urban governance, culture and citizenship are on the research agenda. Urban governance is broader than government, as it is exercised by more actors than the state itself. Culture does not merely refer to ideas and representations, but also to material culture, institution-building, human association, and social participation. Citizenship is premised upon culture, in the sense of institution building and social capital, in societies based on democracy and public participation. It tends to strengthen civil society as a space in-between the market and the State. Yet, while these spheres are clear, their spatial scale is rather obscure. Citizenship involves social exclusions and territoriality. The latter has been usually founded on the nation state during moder-

151

nity, sometimes on a region, but very rarely on a city. Territoriality used to be 'urban' in the past, but now the city States are only a memory and the city walls just a tourist attraction.

Post-modern cities are open settlements with changing boundaries and sprawling outlines. Their population is mobile and cosmopolitan, with hybrid and shifting spatialities, though "tribes" and "flows" coexist. Castells' (1996) idea of class divisions between cosmopolitan elites and 'tribal' people contrasts affluent mobile individuals with the poor, who are linked up to their narrow spaces of village, neighbourhood, and, rarely, the city. Can we really still agree with Castells' analysis? (Friedmann & Douglass 1998). How often can we find tribal territoriality in the European Union today? Civil societies increasingly consist of cosmopolitan, mobile individuals; citizens interested in international affairs, mobilizing against war or international summits; placeless and multi-placed residents with global spatialities, who mobilize via the Internet and may gather in several cities. These are the new *flaneur* activists (Leontidou 2006).

At the same time, cities are again becoming more important with regard to the question of citizenship. In the past, we have stressed the contrast between Anglo-American anti-urbanism and Mediterranean political cultures, which nurture positive spatialities around the city and the 'urban' (Leontidou 2001). In this paper, we will further analyze and *politicize* this contrast in order to discuss citizenship in the context of political cultures. We will focus especially on antitheses in spatialities of urbanism between democracy and dictatorship and highlight the interplay between citizenship and its contestation in periods of dictatorship, relating it to the urbanism/ anti-urbanism antithesis in the *longue duree*.

9.2. Cultures of 'Polis' and Urbanism in the Mediterranean City States

We will first turn to antiquity as a method to interpret Mediterranean urbanism and citizenship. In a world region embedded in cultures and concepts of the past, spaces of citizenship cannot be understood unless we build the remote past into our theory, this in contrast to American agnosticism about antiquity or its separation into a different realm of research.

> "When the American student did happen to dip into the work of a European theorist he tended to react to it as mere "ancient history"... He rarely saw in it any relevance to his own problems except as a curious contrast" (Martindale's introduction to Weber 1966: 42-43).

The curious contrast is an all-American one. Thomas Jefferson's cities were built in classical and Hellenistic styles, with rhetoric about equality and ancient democracy. Was this just decorative, eclectic or aesthetic? Later on, Plato and Aristotle inspired Simmel, Spengler and Durkheim, who, in turn, inspired Park and Wirth. It is therefore quite impossible to refer only to the present, when the past is so inextricably linked up with today's European culture. Accordingly, we propose to follow the exact opposite route from 'the American student'. Contemporary urban historians must recapture the historical past and should in fact re-insert it into the present, following nineteenth- and early twentieth-century European intellectuals, including Karl Marx, Friedrich Engels, Max Weber and Antonio Gramsci.

In early urban Europe, when the city States were dominant and vibrant, the words *Polis/ Politis*, like City/ Citizenship, had the same roots. The clearest form of the relationship between city and state can be found in ancient Greece during the classical period (around the 5th century BC), and in Renaissance Italy (around the 14th century AD). The linkage dissipated with the decline of city-states, and citizenship has come to be attached to nation-state territoriality. However, we can find urban-based citizenship flickering in Southern Europe, where collective memories of the city and its specific cultures and spatialities have never faded (Leontidou 2001, 2005).

Before the partitioning of the world into Nation-States, city walls rather than national boundaries defined the construction of citizenship. They were consecrated when cities were established, as in the case of Rome where foundations were laid by a ritual involving a couple of bulls (Leontidou 2004). The walls made the difference in territoriality and social exclusion of "the other". Europe's cities have vivid memories of these walls that symbolised their status as states, and have built their identity upon those early ages, restoring ruins and monuments of past epochs. They were mostly urban monuments: civilisations around the Mediterranean have always been distinctively urban. There were few rural monuments, even as far back as the Sumerian civilization, which was also based on a number of separate City States (Toynbee ed. 1967). The same holds for the Minoan, Cycladic and Mycenian civilizations. All Aegean civilisations were based on towns, ports of trade and centres of weaving and other crafts. The first "Europeans" developed imaginations revolving around the sea and the city.

The Greek civilization reinvented the city and gave it a more solid substance and a population of *citizens*. It cultivated a clear urban ideal with advanced political institutions and an in-born spirit of exploration, whether geographical or scientific. The beginnings of "Europe" are associated with urbanism and the sea. The pride and perceived superiority of the City State did not necessarily relate to direct democracy, at least until the 6th century BC. This came later, when Athens rose from a sea of tyranny during classical times, first defeating the Assyrians and then expelling its tyrant, Hippias, in 510 B.C. This short-lived civilization, flowering for just 100 years (510-404 BC), offered many of the ideas and concepts of today's European culture and institutional discourse. *Politis*, citizen, or the person participating in public life, comes from *Polis,* just as Citizen comes from "City". *Polis* is also the etymology of policy, politics, polity, *politismos*, i.e. civilization. Democracy is derived from "Demos" and *Kratos*, the State (Leontidou 2004). The union or community (*koinonia*) of Demi, local communities surrounding the City State, was the full *polis*, according to Aristotle (Demand 1970: 14-15). In addition, colonies (*paroikies*) along the Mediterranean shores were part of it. In the city State, *Polis* and *Kratos*, the State, coincided, and consequently every *Politis* developed his (not her, unfortunately!) spatiality around both of them simultaneously. There was a convergence and a confluence of urban spatialities with those of the *Kratos,* and according to Aristotle's *Politika, Polis* and *Kratos* were the natural extension of the Family.[116] Today we have broadened the scale and talk about national or even European 'citizenship', although Europe is neither a city nor a state.

Direct democracy was practiced in the Athenian *agora*, where ideas and policies were debated in the citizens' assembly without any censorship. The *agora* was a complex space. It literally meant marketplace where commerce centred, but it was actually hybrid space of public encounter, political debate and participation, of communication and leisure, of games and sports. The interpenetration of nature and culture was harmonized in classical architecture by the in-between space of the colonnade, the *stoa*. This was a pathway of columns, open to the outside but covered with the roof of the 'inside'. The *agora* was a place where citizenship was forged, a multiplex spot for leisurely enjoyment of public spaces as well as interaction, commerce, political awareness, participation, discussion and debate. The agora, incidentally, may be considered as an enlargement of another mixed activity in ancient Greece, namely the enclosed *symposium*. People debated, learned and argued philosophy and science while lying on couches and drinking. The Romans turned the *symposium* into a way of life, inspired by the Greeks to indulge in this mixture of activities.

Classical and Roman civilizations considered citizenship and participation in a real, natural city to constitute the precondition for civilisation and the essence of democracy. The city was exalted over and above the countryside. From antiquity until our days, everyday life has been affected profoundly by this Mediterranean orientation toward public space as the place where democracy and citizenship became concrete (*civitas, politeia*) (Leontidou 2005: chap. 1). This is a basic antithesis with the Anglo-American city, where public space is a physical space (*urbs*) with scant enclaves of "speakers' corners" as in Hyde Park. In the *agora,* there were several such corners. In contrast to today's mall, moreover, the *agora*, like the *piazza*, were hybrid spaces where natural and constructed forms merged. The mall instead, is removed from nature, surrounded by parking lots with surface sealing. Other antitheses here are multi-purpose vs shopping spaces, mixed uses vs zoning, and a crucial locational contrast: the Southern piazza is central, while the Northern mall is peripheral. The *agora* and the *piazza* reflect the Southern popularity of the city centre and the inner city more generally, while the mall is based on the car and the suburb in the cities of the North.

The classical Athenian political culture stands in stark contrast to earlier and later periods of city States, which have also witnessed the opposites of democracy, i.e. tyranny, autocracy and dictatorship. Renaissance Venice and Florence, for example,

---

116 In the well-known opening pages from his *Politics*, Aristotle considers the State a creation of nature and ranks it as the highest level of community, in a hierarchy, which, in turn, embraces the pair, the household, the village, and the State (Aristotle 1981: 56-59).

were enlightened tyrannies or paternalistic societies rather than democratic ones. Classical Athens constitutes the clearest instance of citizenship founded on the city. Democracy was direct. Decisions were taken by all eligible "citizens" irrespective of income, property or rank, rather than just their representatives. Leaders were elected to office only in order to carry out the people's will. Pericles was not a ruler, but the city's annually elected leading citizen,. Civil society was interlocked with the City State in antiquity, and men commanded prestige by being *Polites* rather than *Idiotes*.[117] Among the three rights of citizenship found in modern social movements, the city States of antiquity respected two:

- the right to voice, to express (democratisation) and
- the right to human flourishing, but *not*
- the right to difference.

In this, classical Athens was a weak democracy in many ways. Citizenship was based on territoriality and the social exclusion of slaves, women and "barbarians".[118] This exclusion of the "others" actually constituted the main weakness of the Athenian democracy. The social exclusion of non-citizens would soon metamorphose into vulnerability of the city and its citizens. Foreigners were not only excluded from the City State and civil society, but also from the army. This made Athens vulnerable in the Peloponnesian wars. After flowering for a mere century, it surrendered to the Spartans by 404 B.C. In this, the contrast with Rome is very instructive. Rome developed a wise administrative mechanism that fragmented the huge empire into several semi-autonomous cells, while creating a multicultural army to defend them.

Rome was partly based on City States, but also developed the "capital city" idea, an idea that was introduced in the 4th century BC in the Macedonian Empire. In fact, a functional differentiation existed among three Macedonian capital cities: Pella, the birthplace of Alexander the Great, was the political-administrative capital; Vergina was the economic-cultural capital; and Dion was the religious one. The seven Alexandrias (named after Alexander the Great), from the Nile via the Persian Gulf, to the junction of the Acesines and Indus rivers, were also capital cities in their respective regions. The Roman Empire followed with Rome, Constantinople and Cordoba as capitals of large territories (Toynbee ed. 1967). Citizenship was now defined through territory and Empire, rather than cities. One would be an Athenian during the classical period but a Macedonian in the Hellenistic period, not a Pellan

---

117 Note the etymology of 'idiocy'. *Politis* contrasted with *idiotis,* the person in the private sphere: recall Marx's *rural idiocy.*

118 Athenian democracy was weakened by the social exclusion of non-citizens; but compared to earlier despotisms and the subsequent Roman regimes, slaves were few in Athens and Sparta, one slave to two citizens (Toynbee ed. 1967). Female citizens were not allowed to join the debate in the *agora*, but mobilized collective imaginations in art, drama and religion, as goddesses and heroines. It has been argued that this is evidenced in works written by men with women as protagonists (Zeitlin 1996). In any case, women worked while men talked, in a society where work was not valued as in later Europe.

or Verginian. This provides an obvious example of the ephemeral nature of citizenship founded on the city, in multicultural and cosmopolitan societies.

Citizenship always involved exclusions of non-citizens. During Macedonian and Roman periods, however, a major transformation with respect to Athens involved the weakening of the notion of "barbarians" (Leontidou 2004: 599). The dignity of citizenship was not denied to defeated populations. In place of social exclusion or the arrogance of colonialism, which labels foreigners as "others", tolerance and cultural interaction were sought during Macedonian and, to a great extent, Roman times, albeit that slaves cannot be accommodated to this open-ended cultural attitude. Important territorial powers remained after Alexander's death at 32 years of age in 322 BC, such as Egypt under the Ptolemies, where Alexandria was founded in 331 BC, and Syria-Iran under the Seleucids.

9.3. From the Agora to the Piazza in the 'Reborn' Mediterranean City State

Euro-Mediterranean spatialities of urbanism persisted after Rome. A symbolic departure can be found in the prolonged ruralization period after the decline of the Roman Empire. Cities were in ruins by the 4th century AD, but especially so from the 7th until about the 10th century.[119] Cipolla (1980) seems to disassociate 'Europe' from the urbanism of the ancient civilizations, by locating its appearance in this derelict landscape. However, 'Europe' emerged in antiquity and then again as the City State was resurrected in Italy during the Renaissance (Leontidou 2004). In fact, the Middle Ages had a miracle hidden within the modalities of transformation during feudalism: the re-emergence of the City State. The surprise lurked in the North of Italy: radiant City States were 'reborn' – hence, the Renaissance –, cities and urbanism were brought back to life, creative Italian cities re-invented science and the arts. Though this is hardly the place to go into the debate about the causes of the re-emergence of the City State, it is interesting to note four dominant interpretations. It has been attributed to changes in the feudal mode of production by Karl Marx (1961); governance, politics and administration by Max Weber (1966); Henri Pirenne (1927) prioritised commerce; and Fernand Braudel (1975) stressed sea routes for transport.

Italian cities competed, kept alternating in prosperity, power, and influence according to their place in global development. Urban competition was, of course, different from that in today's Europe. Cities competed in trade and wars in a struggle for domination over the Mediterranean shores, colonies and settlements, and in a battle for survival in the face of "barbarian" attacks. Jones (1990) suggests a succes-

---

119 In 387 AD, St Ambrose encountered in Northern Italy *semidirutarum urbium cadavera*, corpses of half-ruined cities (Cipolla 1980; Pounds 1990; Benevolo 1993). Tenth-century Italy and northwestern Europe had sunk back into primitive economies of subsistence agriculture, and consisted of a multitude of feuds (Toynbee ed. 1967).

sion of *metropolitan leaders* in Europe, shifting in significance as the centuries progressed. Amalfi, then Venice and Florence, and later Genoa along with Constantinople (Toynbee ed. 1967; Benevolo 1993) led European development and culture, science and the arts, besides industry and commerce. We can discern their linkage to *globalization*, in the sense of their standing vis-à-vis the centres of the economy of the known world, or to *ecumenism*, linked with the expansion of Christianity and culture more generally.

In general, urban development was dense mostly around the Mediterranean. These new City States displayed a crucial difference though: they were not democratic but exhibited instead several versions of enlightened despotism. Citizenship was linked to the city, but allegiance to the rulers divided populations. City walls were borders, with some notable exceptions of unwalled cities such as Venice. But central public spaces differed. In place of the *agora*, there was the *piazza*, with new functions and a lesser density of political participation. According to Pierro della Francesca, the *piazza*, the town square, was a place to spy on the private lives of others: eavesdropping from *stoa* to *stoa*, strolling and watching rather than participating. From the Roman *forum* to the Renaissance, the *stoa* thus displayed several variations after the *agora*. The basic difference between enclaves for congregation of citizens around the *piazza* and the functions of the ancient *agora*, rested in the former's function as a public space for encounter and communication, in contrast to the participation found in the *agora*, which used to be a central reference point where the whole urban community was centred and citizenship re-confirmed.

Uneven development in European space was marked by an East/ West divide: the prosperity of the Byzantium contrasting with the lands of Charlemagne in the west, which were founded on conflict and movement. Even Charlemagne himself used to relocate among palaces, creating a different current of dynamism (Pounds 1990). Constantinople, the capital of the Byzantium, rose to be the Eastern pole of a unified, though competing, "European" urban network. Until the 14th century, Italian cities were competing with this dominant religious metropolis of the Levant. Constantinople may be considered a unique city, named as *The* Polis, where citizenship was based. "Istanbul" comes from the Greek εις την Πόλιν – to the City. In the collective imagination, the city was identified with civilization – the Greek *polis* and the Latin *urbs* and *civitas*. This Polis somehow protected the ancient legacy of City States, despite the cultural hegemony of Christianity and criticizing pagans. The Polis' notables and Emperors had collected and tenderly kept the treasures from the Athenenian Acropolis, Delphi, and other sacred places (Toynbee ed. 1967). Byzantium was a multicultural achievement, which, however, did not last for long. The Polis fell into Ottoman hands in 1453 and several major ancient works of art were destroyed or lost. The fall of the Polis actually is a story of defeat, not only of Byzantium, but also of the notion of citizenship founded on the city, as well as urban cultures of antiquity and the pagan definitions of Europe (Leontidou 2004). The artefacts looted and burnt with the Ottoman invasion of Constantinople were not just Orthodox Christian: they were also pagan treasures of the ancient City States. After 1453, many of these were lost to the world forever. Long after the burning of the library of Alexandria and 80 years after the destruction of its lighthouse, the Pharos,

157

by an earthquake in 1375, culures and wisdom of antiquity suffered another blow in Constantinople.

This major change in the East took place forty years before the Spanish *reconquista* and Columbus' expeditions. The voyages of discovery were a collective Mediterranean achievement, as well as a balance between cooperation and competition, especially between Portugal and Castile, in conquering the world beyond (Moore ed. 1987: 73). However, the "otherness" of Islam split Europe between East and West. After the Ottoman occupation, the Mediterranean was partitioned in a dynamic western part and the underdeveloped Orient, subjected to Islam, where Christianity was cultivated but subordinate. Contradictory tendencies of tolerance (self-rule) and coercion were developing. The Spanish *reconquista* marked the shift of interest to the West after the Portuguese and Spanish discoveries led to the rise of their own cities, as well as Genoa, and, gradually, Northern ports. During the period of explorations, the 'otherness' of the New Lands emerged in parallel with the 'otherness' of Islam. At the rise of modernism, unbounded 'Europe' was a cultural, not a geographical construct, involving a distance from the 'otherness' of non-Europeans. Citizenship was forged in colonial arrogance combined with Christian morality, to exclude pagans, along with their myths (Leontidou 2004). These became 'the other', outside of the 'superior' Christian faith and outside of European space – not to mention citizenship.

The City State now comes to the foreground and acquires an unexpected relevance for recent developments in the EU. The *polis* and citizenship founded on the city may never be resurrected again, but they lurk and hide within today's Mediterranean heritage of urban monuments. As war and later technological development wounded the South, memories of citizenship founded on City States kept the Mediterranean ports proud and self-confident in their heritage (Leontidou 2001). After the 15th century, Southern cities were surpassed by Northern ports in Belgium and Holland: Bruges, Antwerp, Amsterdam, then London became Europe's metropolitan leaders (Jones 1990: 51-7). The remarkable industrial revolution pushed the Mediterranean from core to peripheral status in the global economy during a slow process of decline from the 17th to the 20th century.

9.4. Modern European Urbanism and Spaces of Citizenship

Most European cities today are cultural milieus with populations who honour memories of citizenship in the context of City States of the past. The ruins of city walls are carefully restored. Ancient monuments are deeply appreciated in today's urban landscape, and city tours circle around the past. In stark contrast to American anti-urbanism, memory plays a key role in Europe; a role that can be investigated and possibly related to citizenship founded on the city.

Elsewhere (Leontidou 2001) we have contrasted two models: Anglo-American anti-urbanism and Mediterranean European urbanism, starting with the proposition of a *geographical* version of Schorske's (1998) perceptive historical model. Schorske

158

traces the process whereby Europe switched from a view of the 'city as virtue' in the Enlightenment, to the 'city as vice' after the industrial revolution. However, the emergence of anti-urbanism is not as fixed in history as Schorske implies, because it often preceded the Industrial Revolution. It was found already in Roman times and later, in feudal Europe, when Paolo da Certaldo (quoted in Cipolla 1980) wrote that *la villa fa buone bestie e cattivi uomini.*[120] Subsequently, the 18th century French Physiocrats and romantic poets represented the city as vice (Schorske 1998: 43-9). The industrial revolution only marked the definitive switch away from urbanism in Northern Europe, when literature and art escaped towards a rural idyll (Williams 1973). In their anti-urban sentiments, the Victorian industrial elite projected an attitude of pessimism, criticism and disappointment against the city, apparently emerging from the squalor associated with urban life during early industrialism in Northern Europe and America.

However, the fact that anti-urbanism preceded industrial squalor in some regions, has led us to draw a *spatial* rather than temporal contrast, exploring the antithesis of anti-urbanism vs urbanism in space rather than through time for the 20th century. In this, we have found representations of cities as spaces of vice or risk in Anglo-American geographical imaginations, contrasting with cities as spaces of virtue, attraction of culture and creativity, in representations of Southern Europeans. We have tried to interpret this antithesis with reference to contrasts in the material reality of the urbanisation process between the two types of cities, exploring in what ways alternative representations of cities, cultural identities and ideas of urbanism, are rooted in different urbanisation dynamics (Leontidou 1990/2006, 2001).

In Southern Europe, where the factory, the railroad and the capitalist economy marginalised the powerful City States of antiquity and the middle ages, the memory of citizenship-founded-on-the-city still mobilises the collective imagination (Leontidou 2001). The Mediterranean fell from the core position in 'Europe', which it occupied for at least three millennia, to its underdeveloped periphery. How could one ever expect its cultures to come to terms with industrialism and industrialisation? Mediterranean civilizations crystallized around the urban-oriented cultures of their former City States and sought dignity in the representation of the city as virtue, as a space for citizenship, in a process of urbanisation triggered by cultural radiance and the memory of the City States.

The attraction of the city in Southern Europe has always been strong in the *longue duree*. From antiquity and the Enlightenment until today, the strongest antithesis to industrial anti-urbanism is to be found in Mediterranean urbanism. Industrialism and Fordism marginalised Southern Europe, but the pride in the heritage and the collective memories of City States have never faded. Urban-oriented identities have been rooted in Mediterranean political systems as diverse as the Athenian democracy, the Venetian enlightened despotism, and others (Leontidou 1990/2006, 2001). In postwar Mediterranean Europe, the city has always represented progress and civilised

120 The town makes good beasts and bad men.

cultural life, whereas the countryside has been considered the domain of material scarcity and ignorant peasants. Moreover, Mediterranean citizens have amplified geographical imaginations of the 'city as virtue', going beyond positive attitudes to the city by creating the 'city as a *magnet*' of people, activities, cultures and development funds. We can find this in several socio-anthropological and geographical accounts, where cultural identities do include the 'urban'.

In Greece, people migrated from the countryside, which for them was a place ravaged by bandits, usurpers or natural disasters, a place of insecurity and flight (Karapostolis 1995) Cities kept attracting migrants in waves of *astyfilia* (Leontidou 1990/2006: 258-61). In Italy, Gramsci was the most fervent urbanist, and so were Calvino and many others. Migrants to every national metropolis have been driving spontaneous urbanisation, creating illegal settlements and congregating in search of formal or informal work. Spanish and Portuguese urban-oriented cultures harmonised with those of the colonies since the period of the Spanish and Portuguese *conquistadores* (Leontidou 2001: 87). Very much later, cities in various regions of Spain have reaffirmed their identities, with a peak in 1992 when three cities simultaneously hosted mayor international events: Barcelona for the Olympics, Madrid as the European city of culture, and Seville for the EXPO 92 (Garcia 1993, Leontidou 1995). There have been many similar instances after that, including the Athens Olympics.

These events belong to the new trend of urban competition in post-cold-war, postmodern Europe, which deconstructs the North/ South dichotomy of anti-urbanism/ urbanism and strengthens the latter through the marketing of places (mostly cities) (Kearns & Philo eds 1993, Jensen-Butler et al. eds 1996, Leontidou 1993, 1995, Couch et al. 2007). Southern cities are excellent in urban competition. Urbanism is turned into an advantage in view of ancient and medieval heritage. In a sense, many Mediterranean towns and cities never lost City State or capital city status in the popular imagination (Giner 1985). As in ancient times, urban identity is reaffirmed, often aggressively, in all corners of Southern Europe. This pride in tradition harmonizes with the tendency for competition and visibility evident throughout Europe. Since these cities underwent constant re-urbanisation, gentrification and the socalled 'urban renaissance' in the context of informality and mixed land use, we have claimed that, not only have they not been 'pre-industrial' or 'pre-capitalist', but they were already post-modern a rather long time ago (Leontidou 1993).

Mediterranean development dynamics have followed the city, rather than industrial capitalism. Urbanisation is based on memories of citizenship and strong cultural identities including the "urban". It has been repeatedly pointed out that urbanisation based on industrialization characterizes the North but not the South of Europe (for a synopsis, Leontidou 1990/2006). In the latter, memories of citizenship founded on the city turned it into a magnet. Instead of the negative statement found in the literature, i.e. urbanisation *without* industrialisation, we propose a positive one: urbanisation triggered by *memories of citizenship founded on the city*, in spaces of hope based on urban-centred spatialities, besides regional or national ones. Now convergence among European cities after the 1990s deconstructs all allusions to evolutionary models. By the re-insertion of memory as heritage and tradition, the North follows the South in spatialities of urbanism. The current 'Mediterraneanisation' of British cities (Leontidou 2001: 95, Couch et al. 2007) points to rising urbanism even among 'New Labour', though still 50% of Britons in 1999 were found to prefer a village.[121] Contrary to the 'development' of the South towards Northern models, posited by evolutionary views, post-modern times have seen Southern urban-oriented cultures explicitly and literally penetrate the North.

9.5. Urbanism in Democracy vs Dictatorship

However, a twist of these antitheses emerges if we politicize the couplet of urbanism/ anti-urbanism, exploring representations and material practices around urban life during various European political regimes, and analysing the different representations of, and attitudes to, the city adopted by the Left and the Right in Europe.

Democratic thinkers and intellectuals of the Left have always been magnetized by the progressive fervour in cities and promises of proletarian uprisings. In his *Mutual Aid*, Kropotkin created hybrid formations and dialectic concepts of the nature/ culture couplet, trying to deconstruct it and to retaliate against social Darwinism by advocating a remaking of 'man' and nature through cooperation rather than competition. Marx and Engels followed a different path to conceptualize urbanity with its various positive and negative aspects. Marx passed from ethical rejection of the modern city as the scene of labour's alienation and exploitation, to a historical affirmation of its liberating potential. As we move away from the Left, however, northern intellectuals would concede that "city air makes man free", but that was about all: the city was painted in black. Oswald Spengler depicted a pessimistic view of the decline of the West, but this is not considered by Schorske (1998) as a clear anti-urban formulation.

Anti-urbanism had a large political spectrum and range in the North; but in Southern Europe it was politically coloured, especially since Gramsci's time. His allegiance to peasants did not avert Gramsci from polemic texts with dynamic urban-oriented narratives. In 1920, he referred to cities as "miraculous engines of life and civil progress" (Gramsci 1994: 136). For him, it was not industry but other forces that created urbanisation, among which memory as embedded in civil society, spontaneity and hegemony, played a leading role (Leontidou 2001: 83).

However, Southern European urbanism has known important discontinuities since Gramsci's time. During periods of fascism and dictatorship, the aversion to big cities by certain classes and groups tended to surface. This has provided interesting instances of ideological convergence across Europe. The countryside would hold a similar place in the political philosophy of Northern and Southern European fascism, from the end of the 19th century, when the neo-rightist French called for a return to

121 Findings in an unpublished paper kindly offered by Tony Champion, IBG-RGS Conference 2005.

the provinces. The most radical proponents of the countryside were Nazi eugenics. They proposed to manipulate nature in order to produce the perfect human being (Kaika 2005: 13). The proto-Nazi writers in Germany "assaulted not the city as vice, but its people as vicious" (Schorske 1998: 48).

> "Although the Nazi movement originated in a *Residenzstadt*, Munich, it chose medieval Nuremberg as the appropriate site for its annual party congress. The demands of the modern industrial state, however, could only be fulfilled in an urban setting. The Nazis, while excoriating the 'pavement literature' of the 1920s, and branding urban art as decadent, brought out in their city-building all the elements which the urban critics had almost strongly condemned." (Schorske 1998: 53).

During periods of contested citizenship in Southern Europe, anti-urbanism emerged. During the Italian fascist regime, the monumentalisation of the capital went hand in hand with the idealization of 'peasant Italy' (Fried 1973, Calabi 1984). Planning (*urbanistica*), received official recognition by Mussolini who built several new towns, the proverbial EUR among them. Ancient Rome was exalted, historical buildings were rehabilitated and even medieval institutions were resurrected (Mariani 1976; Ghirardo 1980). Mussolini also attempted to check migration through anti-urbanisation laws and legislation on forced domicile (Fried 1973: 80; Allum 1973: 27; Gabert 1958; Leontidou 2001). These laws were circumvented at the time, and later, during the 1950s and 1960s, the *Consulte Popolari* in Rome, Milan and Naples struggled for their abrogation (Della Seta 1978: 308).

The case of fascist Italy was not the only one combining anti-urbanist rhetoric for the "masses" with monumentalisation of capital cities. The rest of Mediterranean Europe also witnessed this combination. In Spain, Franco strengthened Madrid (Salcedo 1977), while portraying the city as the centre of vice and evil (Wynn 1984). In Lisbon, a constant tendency of stigmatisation of shantytown residents has resulted in ghettoisation (Beja Horta 2004). In Greece, the clergy has always stigmatised the 'temptations' of the large city. This spread during the dictatorship in 1967-1974, interspersed by threats to control domestic migration to Athens (Carter 1968, Leontidou 1990/2006, 2001). The dictators' aversion toward large urban concentrations is also reflected in exclamations about "parasitic" Athens in several official documents and even research reports at the time (Burgel 1970 & 1972, Doxiadis 1976). They blamed congestion on the migrants, though responsibilities for overbuilding lay elsewhere as the dictators offered speculative opportunities to the middle classes busily erecting multi-storey apartment buildings, clinging stubbornly to the inner city and in fact creating the compact city and the proverbial "*nefos*", the pollution cloud. As this began to darken the Athens skyline in the mid-1960s, the discourse about an "unnatural", "monstrous" city surfaced. Discourses against urbanisation have lasted longer than the dictatorship, but no counter-urbanisation phase is yet in sight in Athens, or other Mediterranean cities, for that matter (Leontidou 1990/2006: 212-5).

During fascism and dictatorship, Southern anti-urbanism created urban competition, but also tended to stir regional rivalries. Mussolini's pro-Roman discourse reinforced anti-Roman sentiments among other cities (Fried 1973: 71), and so did Franco's policies in favour of Madrid (Salcedo 1977). Urban rivalries appeared especially fierce before and during political consolidation in the Iberian Peninsula and Greece, and during and after the fascist regime in Italy. The bipolar urban networks, but also urban primacy and relevant spatial practices, have long created a tension between the two largest cities. "Milan and Barcelona, Rome and Madrid, epitomized industry and bourgeois society on the one hand, political and administrative power on the other" (Giner 1986). Piraeus also competed with Athens in the past, and now Thessaloniki occasionally voices a rivalry against the capital city. Greece, like Spain, saw regional, town and island rivalries, but without the Spanish linguistic diversity or autonomist movements. However, these were long-established urban rivalries, which peaked during the military junta and facilitated the policies of the dictatorship for the control of spontaneous urban growth and industrial decentralisation, as well as policies in favour of the capital city, though to the exclusion of migrants.

Political parties as antithetical as the extreme right and the 'greens', have exalted the countryside and proposed or pursued anti-urban spatial practices in the recent past. Now, neo-liberalism and the advent of the entrepreneurial city have created new party mixtures and deconstructed many of the above dualities, creating a sort of convergence between North and South, between anti-urbanism and urbanism (Leontidou 2001). Oddly and unexpectedly for the standard convergence theories, this took place on the terrain of the South and of democracy. The combination of urban competition, gentrification and 'Mediterraneanisation' with neo-liberal political cultures, leads to several unexpected hybrids, as well as the reversal of evolutionist and convergence models (Couch et al. 2007). Northern cities tend to follow the culture, the topologies, land use and landscapes of urbanism. Southern cities are *not* developing towards Northern models. On the contrary, anti-urbanism is moderated by urban competition and reversed by gentrification.

9.6. Citizenship Founded on the City: Conclusion

From antiquity and the Enlightenment through the industrial revolution and on to the present days of urban competition, urbanism has been contested, debated and transforming. Several space-time articulations of urban types emerge from the above analysis. Citizenship has been founded culturally on the city during the era of City States, and the lasting memory of that period sometimes led to the recurrence of city-based citizenship in Europe. Though the industrial revolution and the consolidation of modern nation-states were based on cities and urbanisation, Anglo-American cultural-spatial stereotypes cultivated anti-urbanism - the 'city as vice' squalor and misery – and painted the city with a dark shade while nurturing spatialities of rural nostalgia. By contrast, in this paper we have claimed that the urbanisation model of Mediterranean Europe must be considered within an alternative narrative.

Mediterranean urban restructuring has not been based on any industrial revolution and economically motivated urban growth. This fact destroys the definitional linkage between urbanisation and industrialisation. In Southern Europe, urbanization,

163

urban landscapes and life patterns have been rooted in cultural traditions as well as economic restructuring, and have been related to memory and representations of urbanism. It is possible that the 'cultural turn' in Geography is suited to the ways of thinking, seeing, and remembering of Southern European citizens, while the "political-economy approach" is more appropriate for Anglo-American development models. What is reclaimed here has been illustrated in post-war American Human Ecology as sentiment and symbolism, or affective and moral sentiments ascribed to neighbourhoods; today's cultural geographical discourse will rather speak of identities and their urban anchorage.

As the 'cultural turn' now expands, urbanism surfaces throughout Europe. It emerges in post-modern Anglo-Saxon cities with their gentrifying neighbourhoods. Conversely, the flight from the city has seized the congested cities of Southern Europe, evident in massive waves of holiday and weekend travellers outward from the dense agglomerations. Despite our effort to contrast and stress antitheses, we always encounter their deconstruction through change, contradictions and ambivalence. Urbanism and anti-urbanism have been *embedded* into representations of the city and cultural identities varying in time and space, as two faces of the same coin.

Citizenship has been affected by these variations. The collective imaginary of urbanism and the grass-roots spatialities which affect material realities of urbanization, have been further unpacked in this paper by addressing governance, urban politics and institution-building in a North/ South comparison. Totalitarian governments saw urban spatialities differently from democratic ones. On the level of urban governance, there is an interesting paradox along the axis of planning vs spontaneity. Urban planning, which emerged in the context of British anti-urbanism, has sustained strong metropolitan governments, organized development and citizens' movements. By contrast, Mediterranean urbanism has often reproduced the informal city-building processes, illegal building, and citizens' movements oriented to squatting (Leontidou 1990/2006).

In essence, this is not a paradox. The attraction of the city has created an important grass-roots culture for the "right to the city" (Leontidou 2006). The drive for land colonisation and social movements for shelter made popular strata skilful in contravening planning regulations in the Mediterranean (Leontidou 1990/2006). Urban governance varies from utter weakness in Greece, to rising sophistication in Spain. In the former, devolution is blocked by clientelist relationships, which require centralism in order to be effective. In the latter, social movements formulate demands for different spatial scales. Research in post-modernity is moving away from the dominance of the Nation State concept, and turns again toward cities as well as regions. Regionalism and Federalism clash throughout the E.U. Regionalism counteracts federal governance and poses questions of citizenship, not to nation states, but to regions on the one hand and larger units, such as the European Union, on the other (European citizenship, "Fortress Europe"). The Committee of the Regions has been unsuccessful, but probably only in this conjuncture.

Different spatialities thus crystallize along varying spatial scales in Europe, raising several questions. How has the issue of citizenship been posed in different societies? Is citizenship less and less founded on the city that once was its synonym?

164

What questions of exclusion, territorial as well as cultural, are posed in different space-time instances? For example, what was the relationship between "barbarians" and Macedonians during Hellenistic times? How did foreigners become Londoners during the massive migrations from the Empire, whereby British cities were transformed? And in the 19th century, when Athens became the capital of Greece after the liberation from Ottoman rule, how would the '*epilydes*' of the massive city-ward migration become Athenians? How would they defend their citizenship against the emerging elite of the diaspora Greeks returning from Europe and Africa (Leontidou 1989/2001)? How would all these different kinds of people obtain a work permit, compete as candidates for public office, and claim citizenship or leadership of the city and the nation?

We can only pose these questions here, in connection with the argument of this paper, linking the city with citizenship. Their investigation must revolve around the contemporary debate between assimilation (the melting pot) and multiculturalism, which has informed research on citizenship, migration, racism and social exclusion. Spatialities have been constantly changing and now, in the context of gentrification and re-urbanisation, questions of citizenship in post-modern cities have deconstructed antitheses and couplets of the past: North and South often converge (Leontidou 2001, 2005). Cultural dimensions of citizenship based on the city, as distinct from the nation and beyond, re-emerge in the context of today's hybrid spaces. Are we really urban citizens in the post-modern city? Or are we citizens of the world as markets and the public sphere become global, but also as we change place of residence, jobs, identities, or when we rally on city streets "abroad"? The digital revolution widens spatialities and it becomes a question, how relevant place-bound identity is for *flaneur* activists, multi-cultural subjects, and hybrid social formations.

10. Governance Citizenship or Multi-Level Political Representation?
Simona Piattoni

10.1. The Notion of Citizenship in Governance Structures

There is general agreement that the complexity of decision-making in European societies is increasing, not so much because the problems themselves are getting more complex, but because their effective solution requires the involvement of increasing numbers of actors, each contributing specific resources or holding veto power. Complexity, in other words, is more a consequence of the increasing interaction among previously separated entities (globalization) and of the effective distribution of material resources and rights to access to decision-making (social and political citizenship), than of the escalation of the sheer organizational complexity of the problems themselves. The knowledge and resources required to solve today's problems are held by a large number of actors who cannot be simply compelled to contribute them but must be enticed to do so. As these actors belong to different territorial tiers (states, regions, cities, etc.) and to different non-territorial entities (firms, associations, movements, etc.), their participation requires the activation of complex governance arrangements that include, but are not limited to, conventional structures of government. Simply put: the greater complexity of today's governance problems is the outcome of the growing interaction among European societies and of the never-ending process of social and political democratization in today's advanced industrial societies. The involvement of increasingly larger sets of actors in the process of decision-making is becoming the distinctive feature of rule in advanced industrial societies, and in European societies in particular. Regardless of the level of government one begins with when studying European decision-making processes, one necessarily ends up analyzing also the involvement of other levels of government and non-governmental organizations. *Government* has therefore given way to *governance*: the loose combination of continuously shifting sets of (individual and collective) actors, each contributing specific resources to flexible decision-making networks (cf. Kohler-Koch & Eising 1999).

Yet, the shift from government to governance takes place also at each territorial level. At the *international level*, governance indicates the agreements voluntarily entered into by formally sovereign states, which, however, realize that their sovereignty is severely circumscribed by mutual interdependence. International regimes and institutions are created this way. In order to deal with the externalities of each other's sovereign decisions and actions, several such states decided to move one step further and create supra-national institutions for the management of such externalities (and much more) – the European Union. At the *national level*, governance denotes the increasing need of democratically elected legislatures and governments to delegate much decision-making to social groups, to lower levels of government, or to non-elected agencies as a way of easing the policy-making overload while retaining ultimate responsibility (i.e. political accountability) for its implementation. At the *sub-national level*, governance is a useful term, which signals the effort of sub-national governments, bureaucracies and agencies to master the intelligence and the energies that ensure the successful management of the territory. In all of these cases, governance is used to indicate the more or less spontaneous contribution of independently controlled resources by a set of mutually independent actors towards a common goal.

In the *European Union*, governance is essential as all of the above factors, plus some additional ones, apply simultaneously. The European Union implies sustained coordination among formally sovereign states, which acknowledge mutual interdependence more so than the members of any other international organization. It also requires the mobilization of the compliance enforcing structures (read, bureaucracies and agencies) of the national states, which retain formal responsibility for policy outcomes. Yet, it is crucially dependent upon the collaboration of lower-level communities and social groups for the implementation of a host of EU-level policies and for bridging that distance between EU institutions and EU citizens known as the "democratic deficit" (Bache & Flinders 2004)

10.2. EU Governance

Governance has been particularly theorized at the EU level, not only because the complexity, which needs to be managed is particularly high here, but also because the EU lacks any conventionally defined government. The Commission is a "distinctive institution", which is, at the same time, more (but also less) than a bureaucracy and less than a government:

> "The lack of a clearly identifiable elected government at the EU level means that the Commission is more powerful than a traditional civil service, less powerful than an elected executive, and also more exposed to political attack from both national governments and the public than are public administrations in traditional states" (Sbragia 2002: 4).

So, while at the national level governance can be conceived of as *governance plus*, that is government plus networks of experts, non-governmental organizations, business associations, trade unions, interest groups, etc., at the European level governance is *governance minus*.

> "The EU, in fact, has a governance system which simultaneously incorporates traditional national governments and the decision-making process of the EU. ... History provides few guideposts as to how (peacefully and through the use of law) to address the dilemma of having two modes of governance co-existing while not sharing in equal measure the 'legitimacy space'" (Sbragia 2002: 6)

Whereas Sbragia underlines the difficulty of eliciting allegiance and creating legitimacy for an institution *sui generis* like the Commission while the national blueprints still exist and operate, others (Christiansen & Piattoni 2004) have underscored the ambiguous nature of the governance that ensues from it. The attempt to seek legitimacy by extending participation in policy-making through involving, at least in a consultative role, many diverse non-governmental organizations, fails because the list of invitees to the policy-making arena remains fundamentally haphazard and smacks of technocracy and elitism. It is again Sbragia (2002) who suggest that the Commission tries to compensate for its lack of backing from a directly elected government and for the impossibility to draw legitimacy from feelings of (European) identity by "seeking ... linkages below the level of national governments" (Sbragia 2002: 7). And this naturally leads to the properly territorial dimension of governance.

Liesbet Hooghe and Gary Marks (2001) make some progress towards a theorization of territorial governance by distinguishing two types of *multi-level governance*, which they minimally define as "as binding decision making in the public sphere" (Hooghe and Marks 2003: 233, fn 1) and which implies the reallocation of authority and the spilling-over of decision-making beyond core representative institutions. *Type I governance* is characterized by *dispersion of authority to a limited number of non-overlapping jurisdictions at a limited number of levels.* Jurisdictions tend to bundle authority in large packages, which remain stable over time. *Type II governance* is characterized by *many fluid, patchwork-like, overlapping jurisdictions with flexible, fungible, fluid competencies.* These two governance types configure different ways of balancing the coexistence between traditional governmental structures and unconventional governance structures within the EU.

The first type of governance resembles the traditional theory of federalism. Many scholars of Europe understand the relations among different levels within the EU and whatever reallocation of tasks occurs as an effect of the EU in this way. While levels of jurisdictions may be added or existing levels may acquire new powers, such changes are understood mainly as an occasional reallocation of tasks among mutually exclusive, limited-number, multi-purpose jurisdictions. They dub the second type of governance "multi-level" and suggest that in this case jurisdictions are numerous, operate on diverse, overlapping territorial scales, are task-specific and are constantly being made and unmade. The second type is more difficult to picture: multiple, overlapping, task-specific jurisdictions operating at different territorial levels which can be constantly redefined and whose membership can continuously vary. We do not have a word to describe such an arrangement although we have plentiful examples of this type of jurisdictions coexisting with jurisdictions of the first type (Skelcher 2005). As the notion of multi-level governance, which is being proposed by this literature, approximates this second (ideal)-type, we are confronted with the task of figuring out how it can function and whether it can command legitimacy.

10.3. The Legitimacy of Multi-Level Governance Structures

Legitimacy has at least two components. Decisions are legitimate if they solve widely felt problems (output legitimacy), or if they are taken at the end of a process of consultation that ensures that everyone with a legitimate stake is heard (input legitimacy). Output legitimacy is what most scholars of the European Union focus on (references). Here I will concentrate on input legitimacy: who has a legitimate claim to be heard in any given decision-making process?

There are two main representation problems with governance. The first problem has to do with the coexistence of multiple bases of *legitimacy* of the various actors involved in governance arrangements. While each type of actor may be legitimate in its own right, the composite legitimacy creates a problem. Some citizens may be satisfied upon knowing that decisions are shaped by technical knowledge, while others may be alarmed at the possibility that knowledge held by few may determine the fate of many. Some may consider groups of concerned citizens (pressure groups) or organized associations for the promotion of functional interests (interest groups) as legitimated to speak in the name of the general public, while others may feel that neither type of group is sufficiently legitimate. And so on. The decisions flowing from this composite collection of individual and collective, institutional and non-institutional actors may thus appear legitimate to some, but illegitimate to others. Hence, they may not be broadly received and obeyed. Enforcement of decisions made in such a way may be problematic; their efficiency may be questionable. Efficiency is obviously assessed differently by different publics and cannot be considered as a ground for legitimacy. For these reasons, political legitimation – the process of certifying some individuals as legitimated to speak for others when making decisions –still appears to be crucial and the involvement of democratically elected governments still lends a fundamental boost to governance legitimacy.

A second problem concerns the internal *representativeness* of the actors involved in the governance process. Representativeness has two aspects, an internal and an external one. The actors involved in the governance process may not be representative of the wider category to which they belong. A specific company expert may not adequately represent mainstream scientific opinion or even scientific corporate knowledge and therefore may fail to command wide acceptance. A given trade union may not represent the panoply of positions about certain labour issues and therefore may lack the necessary consensus. The process through which pressure groups rally their members may leave specific classes or strata systematically unrepresented. These are all internal representativeness problems, which weaken the legitimacy of each individual governance partner.

There are, in addition, external representativeness problems linked to the number and diversity of the actors and interests involved in the decision-making process. If technical experts were involved, while consumers were left out of the governance arrangement that regulates, e.g., some utility provision, the decision-making process would be severely skewed. If industrial interests were heard but environmental groups were left out, the developmental choices that would ensue would result severely thwarted. In other words, the decisions that eventually are made depend heavily on the specific composition of the governance structure and may display a systematic bias, and thus command little legitimacy. Also on external representativeness grounds, the involvement of democratically elected governments must be a fundamental component of governance arrangements. Multi-level governance reproduces the familiar problems of electoral versus functional representation, only with a heightened intensity since governance arrangements have a serendipitous flavour and appear contingent upon many non-controllable (unpredictable, informal, personal) factors.

Given the above legitimacy and representativeness problems, might governance decisions be more legitimate and more representative if taken at a particularly low level of aggregation, or if taken only when such a level, let's say the region, is crucially involved in the decision-making process, as the principle of subsidiarity may seem to suggest? May scale alleviate legitimacy and representativeness problems?

First, legitimation problems may be alleviated when descending governance levels because the different stake-holders, although carriers of diverse knowledge, resources, interests and rationalities, may be more willing to acknowledge each other's entitlement to participate in the governance arrangement if it is clear that all can contribute some crucial element to the solution of the shared problem. Awareness of being in a small boat rocked by powerful waves may induce the occupants towards reciprocal legitimation and willingness to cooperate (a fundamentally similar impulse is said to lie behind the willingness of widely fragmented but small societies towards consociational arrangements).

Second, representativeness may also be significantly increased, both internally and externally, when the territorial scale at which governance takes place is smaller. Consultation may approximate the "ideal" of direct democracy or, in any event, barriers to the activation of concerned citizens may be considerably lower at a regional level than they would be at the national of supra-national level. More actors could then participate, each speaking (more accurately) for a smaller proportion of the populace.

Third, the identity of the actors involved would clearly still matter, but it would contribute to the legitimacy of the governance process rather than detract from it. At a smaller scale, there is a real possibility of meeting and talking personally with the people directly involved in given governance decisions, observing their actions and thus formulating a fairly precise opinion of them (and eventually even soliciting their removal if proved ineffective). Dialogue could really be bi-directional rather than the mono-directional "dialogue" that the Commission often entertains with non-governmental groups and organizations.

For all these reasons, it appears that the regional level might be particularly apt to experiment with legitimate and representative governance arrangements. Regional citizenship would imply participation in a wide array of governance structures. And this seems precisely the direction in which a number of European states are moving by implementing various types of devolutionary processes. Summarizing a broad literature on European regional development policies, one may say that those regions in which the political and administrative elites pin their political careers on the successful management of territorial governance processes enjoy higher levels of effectiveness and legitimacy (cf. Bukowski, Piattoni & Smyrl 2003). But what about the electoral channel of representation? Do the different tiers simply co-exist; do they form a complex pattern of multi-level representation, or do they rather cancel each other out? Does regional citizenship work best when it is understood only in

171

terms of participation in policy-making processes (functional citizenship) or when it is also expressed through electoral participation (political citizenship)?

10.4. Political Citizenship in Europe: Which Level?

The empirical study of political representation in Europe is handicapped by the disproportionality between the data available at the level of individual member states and those available at the European Union level. Apart from studies of European elections (e.g. Reif & Schmidt 1980, Reif 1997), the European Parliament and Euro-parties (Bardi 1987, Hix & Lord 1997), and mass opinion polls on European integration issues (the various Eurobarometer publications), focused but comprehensive studies on mass and elite orientations, issue positioning, and political participation are rare (for Italy, see Cotta, Isernia, Verzichelli 2005). The study of the cross effects between these two levels is still in its infancy, even though several works have tried to fill the gap (Bogdanor 1996, Norton 1996, van der Eijk & Franklin 1996, Marsh & Norris 1997, Katz & Wessels 1999, Schmitt & Thomassen 1999, Hix & Goetz 2001).

At the national level, a substantive literature has developed on the themes of political disenchantment and party decline. Increased electoral volatility, decline in party membership, decrease in electoral and political participation, creation of extremist parties, and fluctuating levels of interest in politics are often invoked to document a generalized disenchantment with, and detachment from, politics in Western Europe (Dalton & Wattenberg 2000, Dalton 2004, 2006). Yet, these phenomena do not occur with the same intensity in all West European polities (Katz & Mair 1992) and their import for democracy is therefore the object of dispute (Hayward 1996).

While most authors agree that these trends have changed the role of political parties, the general conclusion is that the parties as organizations are in no danger of being eliminated (Katz & Mair 1995). While they may no longer perform many of their once characteristic functions, they still are a constitutive element of democracy, as they have been since the transformation of parliamentary parties into electoral parties. According to Andeweg (1996), political parties no longer:

- 1) socialize members to citizenship;
- 2) provide education and training for their cadres;
- 3) diffuse political information for their members;
- 4) provide services (from housing to jobs) to their members;
- 5) aggregate citizens' demands into more or less coherent manifestos and agendas;
- 6) mobilize large segments of the population on a relatively permanent basis.

However, they retain the crucial functions of selecting candidates for office and of staging political elections, which, in turn, give citizens the feeling of belonging to the polity.

While some of the tasks unattended to by parties have been taken up by other agencies – the educational system does most of the socializing and educating, mass media diffuse information, the welfare state takes care of most services – other functions, such as the aggregation of demands and the permanent mobilization of the population, have been genuinely neglected. Mobilization, for example, is now mostly a question of self-activation or is sporadically spurred by ad-hoc movements. These changes may even be good for democracy: the liberal ideal of autonomous and informed citizens expressing their preferences through the political system may finally be attained! Yet, if democracy itself may not be in any immediate and serious danger because of these changes, worrying about the state of health of political parties is not the same as worrying about what may have happened to political representation.

From the statement that political parties are an essential ingredient for liberal democracy, and the observation that current trends have not, all changes notwithstanding, undermined their role - particularly when it comes to selecting candidates for office and integrating citizens into the political system - may follow the fallacious conclusion that nothing serious is really happening to democratic representation. I rather believe that the failed discharge of the last two functions listed above – aggregation of citizens' demands into more or less coherent manifestos and agendas, and mobilization of large segments of the population on a relatively permanent basis – has impressed a rather significant change onto political representation.

The general picture that emerges from these studies is that the relationship between represented and representatives is changing, both domestically and at the European Union level. At a minimum, the link between represented and representative is "loosening". The elites no longer know (or think that they can know) how to take their cues from the masses, as they supposedly did during the heydays of mass political parties (for a sceptical view, see Lane 1996; for an optimistic view, see Charlot 1996). Political leaders do not act on the basis of the preferences expressed by their followers, but rather follow the mood of the electorate (as detected by opinion polls and consensus ratings) or their own intuition and preferences (political entrepreneurs).

In reality, this phenomenon might not be that novel. After all, the literature on "catch-all parties" – which connected political parties' increasing tendency to target voters at the centre of the ideological spectrum through increased use of non-divisive electoral themes with the decline of opposition in West European democracies – dates from the late fifties and sixties (various essays by Otto Kirchheimer in Burin & Shell 1969). As a precursor of the contemporary "mass" party, the rise of the "catch-all party" marked the same mutually contradicting tendencies in political representation that we observe more clearly today. On the one hand, party leaders seem to be less constrained by grass-roots control and freer to set their own political agenda (within the growing limits imposed by international trends). On the other hand, they take greater pains to utter the right sound bites and not to alienate the masses by touching unpopular themes. The paradox is that of party leaders who, while they are theoretically freer to set their own agenda, are practically more timid to do so. We will see that this is not a paradox at all, but rather an intrinsic dilemma in representational democracy, which, however, may have intensified recently.

The represented-representative relationship will be analyzed below in greater detail. Here we shall provisionally conclude that this relationship has become looser: political representatives increasingly act on their beliefs and on the imperatives of the global market and European integration, occasionally seizing the "windows of opportunities" that may suddenly open before them, in the hope of not being demoted by their own electorates. The represented have fairly clear general ideological orientations, which still guide them in their voting choices, but these are of little guidance in the many detailed issues that modern governance needs to tackle and in the often fairly arcane (and ideologically non clear-cut) integration issues. Both represented and representatives have readjusted to this lack of clarity in their reciprocal relationship. The represented grant greater room of manoeuvre to leaders, only to sanction them heavily (by replacing them) in case of misjudgement. The representatives, in turn, anticipate the wishes of the masses barring international constraints.

10.5. Multi-Level Political Representation?

The nature of political representation is changing within member states because general social trends reduce the number of functions once performed by political parties, and because the solution of governance problems requires the activation of larger numbers of individual and collective actors that do not operate in political arenas but rather in functional and direct arenas (Piattoni 2000a). These trends are taking place irrespective of the process of European integration. However, such a process is certainly the second most important factor of change within European member-states.

Studies of European-level political representation are hampered by the fact that the conceptual apparatus with which we normally study political representation was developed with the nation-state in mind (see, in particular, Jachtenfuchs 1997, Kohler-Koch 1999 and the introductory essay in Katz &Wessels 1999). Treating the European parliament "as if" it were a national parliament and European parties "as if" they were national parties is wrong (Marsh & Norris 1997). Instead, I find it useful to try to extract from the existing conceptual apparatus those concepts which can not only "travel" (Sartori 1970) across different levels but can also be applied to different levels simultaneously. I have no particular interest in measuring to what degree the European parliament can afford European citizens direct representation "as if" we could apply to it the (minimal) requirement of the "responsible party government" model, which we normally consider relevant for national parliaments (Marsh &d Norris 1997: 154). I am rather more interested in highlighting two issues. First, what kinds of *distortions* the existence of a European parliament introduces into political representation, both at the European and at the national level. Second, that political representation is not only affected by European and national electoral arenas but also by the other arenas in which different types of representation can be expressed.

The European Parliament is not a national parliament. The constitutional limitations of the European Parliament render it a largely imperfect representative assembly, very different from any such national assembly. These limitations are too well known to be discussed at length here (Wessels &Diedrichs 1999, Kreppel 2002, Corbett, Jacobs & Shackelton 2005, Rittberger 2005): they concern the procedures for electing the parliament (still highly uneven across member states hence resulting in highly uneven "mandates"); the absence of a European public discourse; the absence (or only just budding existence, cf. Hix 1999, Marks & Wilson 1999) of Europe-wide cleavages and hence of Euro-parties worthy of the name (which leads to lukewarm responsiveness of members of the European Parliament to Europarties and European voters, and to a much stronger responsiveness to national parties and voters); and the still severely limited powers of the elective assembly (particularly its non-existent constitutional powers).

The type of political representation afforded to European citizens by regional elections, where they are held, is also limited. Studies show that regional representatives either do not mention European-level problems at all, or do so in order to mobilize against some decisions that are felt as damaging to the region – much like what happens in national-level elections. Even when the elections strike a real "multi-level" chord, they normally engage the regional and the national levels and rarely venture as far as the European one. In regional elections, citizens either express the tension between regional and national social citizenship (Jeffery & Hough 2001), or "they express territorial distinctiveness while affirming a commitment to common, statewide values as a recipe for maximising influence and benefits from common statehood" (Jeffery n.d).

What about the representation afforded to citizens through European quasi-institutions such as the Committee of the Regions and the Economic and Social Committee? The representation afforded by these institutions is even more mediated. Elected and non-elected representatives of regional and local governments meet in the Committee of the Regions, while the representatives of workers' and employers' associations meet in the Economic and Social Committee. Each citizen, then, is represented only to the extent that these lower-level governments act as mouthpieces for the entire territory and those associations promote the functional interests of a given category of workers or entrepreneurs. It is rather the direct involvement of these institutional tiers and associations in decision-making and policy implementation which give greater leverage to citizens to influence the policy-making process. Research on civil society participation in European decision-making presents an equally mixed picture. Civil society organizations do not seem capable of channelling "the voice of the people", but rather take position on issues and values, which are shared by the population to unknown degrees and with unknown intensity.

The political channel of participation, therefore, appears to be particularly fragmented across the European, national and sub-national levels and across functional and issue lines. Regional citizenship is far from accomplished and multi-level political participation is still marginal and fragmented.

11. Cosmopolitanism and European Post-National Citizenship: Rethinking the European Political Tradition

Gerard Delanty

11.1. Introduction

The Maastricht Treaty, which codified a European citizenship, is often held to be an indication of a trend in the direction of a Europeanization of citizenship, which can also be seen as leading in the direction of a post-national citizenship. Is there a European post-national citizenship as a new kind of citizenship, or is there simply an Europeanization of citizenship? What does it mean to speak of a European citizenship?

One view is that residence rather than birth is an increasingly important factor in determining citizenship rights. A legally codified European citizenship now exists as a post-national citizenship, albeit one that is based on prior national citizenship (Lehning & Weale 1997, Wiener 1998, Hansen & Weil 2001). It is certainly the case that, in present-day European societies, many civic and social rights are now determined by residence rather than birth. In this respect, nationality is not the decisive feature of many rights. Yet, the question remains as to the form of citizenship and whether a new post-national citizenship is emerging out of the disparate national traditions.

According to Habermas (1992; see also 1994, 1996b, 1998d, 2001b) and others, nationality and citizenship have become separated. With the emergence of a European constitutional order, it is possible to speak of a trans-national polity based on citizenship as opposed to nationality. Where nationality is exclusive, citizenship is inclusive. One theory is that the very idea of citizenship is becoming blurred as new kinds of rights become more salient. This is especially so with regard to the distinction between citizens and non-citizens. According to Yasmin Soysal (1994), it is no longer possible to distinguish between the rights of citizenship and human rights. In many countries, minorities, migrant groups and refugees can claim various kinds of rights on the basis of appeals to human rights, which now form part of the legal framework of most European nation-states (see also Jacobsen 1997, Cesarani & Fuller 1996). Other approaches claim that a European citizenship is emerging, along with wider societal transformation, as a result of the various processes of Europeanization (Balibar 2002; Eder & Giesen 2001). Eder & Giesen argue that citizenship could be the basis of a new kind of social integration in a post-national Europe. Others see the emergence of a European kind of citizenship as an expression of a global move in the direction of world governance. In this view, European citizenship is a step in the direction of world citizenship (Heather 1990, Held 1995). Other accounts are less optimistic about a new age of trans-national citizenship but broadly confirm the emergence of a unique kind of European citizenship on the trans-national level, which interlinks with the national (Weiler 1999).

In these accounts, post-national citizenship is invariably seen as a process that has emerged out of national citizenship traditions and has taken on an enhanced significance as a result of EU-led developments. The question addressed here is whether it is meaningful to speak of cosmopolitan citizenship and whether such a kind of citizenship is relevant to the current European context. Cosmopolitan citizenship is increasingly coming to the fore in political philosophy and its relevance for Europeanization has not gone unnoticed, as is evident from the literature (Delanty 2000, Hutchings & Dannreuther 1999, Archibugi et al 1998, Beck & Grande 2004). However, it remains a marginal influence on current debates, especially with respect to issues of Europeanization.

Briefly put, the central argument advanced here is that cosmopolitan citizenship is not an essentially new kind of citizenship that can be identified exclusively with a trans-national constitutional order based on rights, but rather refers to modes of inclusion that go beyond the traditional ties that bind the individual to the polity. In this view, cosmopolitan citizenship is neither national nor supranational citizenship. Rather, cosmopolitan citizenship is related to issues of membership pertaining to new cultural spaces that have been opened up as a result of transnational processes, including those related to Europeanization, but also more generally to globalization. It differs from other traditions of citizenship in not being underpinned by a notion of sovereignty based on a unitary conception of 'the people.'

The argument proposed in this chapter is that cosmopolitanism is a European tradition itself, and while not a rival tradition as such to other traditions, it should be seen, as is the case with all citizenship traditions, as expressing a particular dimension of the multileveled context of citizenship today. In short, there is no single European tradition of citizenship but a plurality of which cosmopolitanism is one. This chapter, therefore, constitutes an attempt to locate cosmopolitanism as a part of the European political heritage and to suggest that its place in that tradition may be more central than that of republicanism, which currently tends to be the favoured narrative of citizenship (Friese & Wagner 2002).

11.2. Traditions of Citizenship in Europe

As with many contested concepts in the social sciences, citizenship is not easy to define. The problem is due to the fact that the idea of citizenship has come to us from three different political traditions, namely the liberal, republican, and communitarian ones. According to a commonly held view, republicanism is the characteristic European tradition of citizenship and can be seen as the political and philosophical basis for European citizenship. Another view states that European post-national citizenship is the expression of a variety of national traditions, all of which are leading in the direction of a trans-national citizenship. These are all questionable assumptions. Taking the three main European traditions of citizenship - liberalism, republicanism and communitarianism – it can be shown that there is no clear cut distinction between these as far as particular national contexts are concerned. Republicanism is itself a mixture of several components and it is difficult, if not impossible, to specify exactly what European republicanism might consist of. Moreover, all these traditions are based on a notion of 'peoplehood' that is not easily applied to the trans-national European context.

The liberal idea sees citizenship largely as a legal condition. In this understanding of citizenship, which had its origins in English seventeenth-century political theory, citizenship concerns the rights of the citizen. The liberal heritage imparted to the idea of citizenship a strong association with law and a view of the citizen as the bearer of rights. In this view, citizenship is a legal status that defines the relation of the individual to the polity. Although it does entail duties, it is largely seen as one of rights. The traditional rights in liberal theory are the negative ones that specify the rights of the individual to be free of arbitrary violence and the positive rights to exercise political participation by voting. In the liberal tradition, citizenship participation, overall, has been limited to voting. This is because for liberal theory citizenship is just one dimension of democracy, the others being constitutionalism (or liberal democracy) and the representation of social interests (or parliamentary democracy).

In modern democracies liberal theory has mostly been modified by social democracy, at least as far as the theory of citizenship is concerned. T.H. Marshall (1992) reflected this tendency when he wrote his influential work on social citizenship. In this account social rights compliment the traditional liberal rights and, in Marshall's evolutionary theory, represent the end of the historical narrative of citizenship as a discourse. Social rights not only complement civic and political rights, but they are also enabling rights in that they compensate for some of the social disadvantages brought about by capitalism. It will suffice to mention here that this theory reduced citizenship to a passive condition whereby the citizen was a recipient of rights, and neglected the active dimension, ignoring for instance that many of these rights were the product of social struggles. Its evolutionary model cannot be so easily applied to many countries with different historical trajectories of rights. Finally, it failed to address other kinds of rights, such as cultural rights (Mann 1987).

In republican political theory – from classical thought to the Renaissance and the Enlightenment – citizenship has been largely associated with the participation of the public in the political life of the community. This has given rise to a strong association of citizenship with civil society and, in general, with a definition of citizenship that stresses 'virtue' and the active membership of a political community. Classical and modern republican theory differs from the rights discourse in stressing much more strongly the relation of citizenship to democracy. Where the rights discourse reduced this to a minimum, the republican tradition maximizes the democratic nature of citizenship by seeing it as a form of political participation in public life. With its origins in the classical Greek *polis*, the Roman *civitas* and the renaissance City State, the modern idea of republican citizenship was born with the Enlightenment and the ideas of the American and French Revolutions. In this tradition the very idea of the republic is inextricably connected with citizenship (Pettit 1997). However,

179

modern or civic republicanism has been a very backward looking doctrine, seeing citizenship in decline in modern times. Hannah Arendt, one of the most famous proponents of republican theory, went so far as to see the republican ideal undermined by the social question. According to Robert Putnam (1999), modern individualism has eroded the ability of contemporary American society to generate social capital. Civic engagement, voluntarism and associational membership – epitomized in declining membership of bowling clubs, the quintessential feature of white Anglo-Saxon America – are in decline due to a nascent individualism, he argued, and consequently democracy is undermined. What makes democracy flourish according to Putnam, whether in Europe or America, is the stable core of a cultural tradition based on common values.

The communitarian conception of citizenship emphasizes duties and identity. In return for rights, the citizen had to perform certain duties, such as the duty to take up arms, to pay taxes, mandatory education, and the general duty to be a good citizen. In general, the communitarian tradition of citizenship has been tied to an organic notion of the people as an ethnic group based on blood ties and a shared cultural community. The people are defined less by civic and legal ties than by a common community of destiny. The communitarian tradition is one that is very difficult to disentangle from the liberal and republican models in that it is mostly presupposed in these traditions as the cultural basis of a civic or political community. One modern expression of it is in constitutional conservatism, which is closely linked to liberalism, giving a constitutional role to certain cultural traditions – a state church for instance – while anchoring the political culture in a principle of tolerance. The principle of tolerance is what marks it off from the more staunchly secular underpinning of republicanism, which demands a stronger separation of church and state. In this case, it is less a question of tolerance than of equality.

While it is possible to find examples of national traditions that are based on one citizenship tradition, according to a recent study, there is no single trajectory for the development of citizenship (Bellamy Castiglione & Santoro 2004). The specific national forms that citizenship took have varied greatly as a result of the structure of the state, the nature of class relations, cultural and ideological divisions, contingent events such as war, and so on. It is out of the interaction of such factors that the different national citizenship traditions emerged. The implication of this approach is that some of the standard categories of citizenship regimes do not quite fit into most of the national traditions. Most countries exhibit instances of liberal, republican and communitarian forms of citizenship. Moreover, what counts as republicanism or liberalism also varies from country to country. Liberal principles are often indistinguishable from republican ones. What emerges out of this is a view of citizenship as highly mixed, instead of uniform or evolutionary. In Germany, France and Britain the respective models of communitarian, republican and liberal traditions do not quite hold. For example, as Ulrich Preuss (2004) argues with respect to Germany, contrary to many preconceptions, nationality and citizenship were differentiated in the German tradition. In the case of France, Cécile Laborde (2004) has argued that citizenship cannot be understood simply in terms of republican nationality as a *ius soli,* in that it also contains liberal and communitarian components. It has been noted by Jose Harris (2004) that, in the case of Britain, contrary to Marshall's famous trajectory of citizenship culminating in social citizenship, social rights predated citizenship, which was a relatively recent innovation. In many countries, most notably Portugal where, as Rui Ramos (2004) shows, the *ius soli* was established relatively early, the appeal to the principle of nationality had no connection with democratization. In Scandinavian countries, as argued by Birte Sim and Hege Skjeie (2004), women's political integration led to a model of citizenship that did not correspond to the three dominant models.

In contrast, Italy may be an example of a country where the republican tradition has been more influential than other traditions. However, when we look more specifically at the republican tradition, what emerges is not a distinctive European political tradition but a variety of historical forms, all of which do not constitute a model of citizenship that can be claimed for the European heritage. Three problems emerge that can briefly commented on.

First, as already indicated, republicanism took numerous forms in Europe, not all of which can be easily related to what today is called republicanism. Republicanism was primarily an early modern phenomenon. Italian City States of the Renaissance period constitute one kind of, essentially, city government before the age of the nation-state. However, republicanism was not antithetical to nationalism. There is the early modern Protestant form of republicanism associated with the Puritan movement in England of the mid-1640s, when a republican commonwealth government was established by Cromwell in opposition to Catholic Royalists. This movement, despite its opposition to monarchy, was important in establishing the foundations of the modern nation-state in Britain. A different and more tolerant variant of republicanism emerged in the Netherlands where a commercial bourgeoisie was more central to politics (Blum 2002). There is a clear connection between Protestantism and republicanism. While the extreme example of this was the Puritan republic of Geneva in the seventeenth century, early modern republicanism was the political form in which non-conformist Protestantism developed. The tie with religion was broken with the rise of republicanism in revolutionary France where it was a far from democratic movement. Revolutionary republicanism was led by new elites whose pursuit of political power required state-based forms of violence. Republicanism in France, in any case, led to the establishment of a central nation-state based on republican principles.

The second problem with republicanism as the European political heritage thus is the fact that its connection with democracy, which we are led to believe must be integral to citizenship, is at best tenuous, if not entirely absent. One of the many criticisms made of Robert Putnam's attempt to rescue republicanism for the present day is that it is nostalgic for a bygone world of traditional cultural values. In his case it is a world associated with the bowling clubs of Jeffersonian agrarian republicanism. Moreover, it was a view of culture that accepted the exclusion of large segments of the population – women and minorities – from a polity whose values were narrow, gendered and closed to the reality of diversity. Putnam's version of republicanism may be communitarian in inspiration, but the limits of the model also apply to Europe. It is certainly the case that republican ideas have been hugely influential

181

in Europe, but these have not been inherently democratic and, what is more, have often been decidedly exclusionary. One only has to think of the controversy over the headscarf and veil in present-day France to recognise the limits of republican political values for multicultural societies. In this context, an interesting contrast can be found in different traditions of republicanism. Siep Stuurman (2004) has shown how the different conceptions of space play out in different models of citizenship in France and the Netherlands, in terms of different views of rights pertaining to the private and public domains. This is ultimately a question of where the limits of the state lie. In the latter, a curious mixture of liberal and communitarian models lead to a marked different from France where the state has a far greater presence in people's lives.

Finally, perhaps one of the major limits of republicanism is the assumption that it makes about peoplehood. Republican thought emerged at a time when the polity in question was a relatively small one or, rather, when the polity was conceived as being based on a single conception of 'the people'. Thus, the French Revolution invoked a unitary notion of the people as a political entity. The subsequent republican state set about the goal of constituting the people as a national citizenry, defined in total by the state. As noted above, it entailed a view of the public realm under the jurisdiction of the state. Today, political thought and practice has moved beyond this conception of politics that requires a strict separation of private and public. Yet, the problem of how peoplehood should be conceived remains.

The contention of this chapter is that cosmopolitanism is more relevant than republicanism to the European context and may be seen as the most salient European heritage.

11.3. The Idea of Cosmopolitanism

Cosmopolitanism can be contrasted to a narrow patriotism, or nationalism, and to internationalism. In ancient Greek thought it stood for the global responsibility of the citizen and has come down to modern times as the belief that states must also have responsibilities that go beyond their own territories. In claiming 'I am a citizen of the world', Diogenes the Cynic articulated one of the first notions of cosmopolitanism as an act of individual freedom, but it was the Stoics who explicitly advocated the idea and established the political tradition of cosmopolitanism that we now associate with the term. The idea of being a citizen of the world, *kosmou politês*, challenged the narrow view of the Greek polis as the exclusive measure of human community. The Stoics were critical of the tendency in Greek thought to reduce political community to a narrowly defined polis. Zeno advocated the notion of an ideal cosmopolitan city based on membership of a wider human society and argued that political obligation derives from deeper subjective feelings. The idea that the citizen belongs to a universal order - a cosmopolis - formed the basis of the universalistic worldview of Roman and Christian thought and gave to the modern age a vision of human community extending beyond the community into which one is born or lives.

While being integral to the universalistic religions of the world, it nevertheless is more of a modern than a classical idea. The modern cosmopolitan citizen exercises freedom in determining the extent of his or her obligations to others. This is not something that is the result of indoctrination or rule learning. The cosmopolitan attitude requires a conscious effort to transcend the narrow confines of one's immediate existence.

The modern ideal of cosmopolitanism is a product of the European eighteenth-century Enlightenment and is generally associated with Immanuel Kant, who in *Towards Perpetual Peace* (1795) introduced a clear legal dimension and inaugurated cosmopolitan political philosophy. The basic idea underlying the Kantian approach is the need to complement international law with cosmopolitan law. Where the former recognizes only states as sovereign actors, cosmopolitan law sees international law as more basic and constituting a higher form of sovereignty. Cosmopolitan law transcends both national and international law in setting normative standards for what states can do, both within their domestic jurisdiction and beyond. In this sense, cosmopolitanism goes beyond the limits of internationalism to a view of the world as fundamentally connected. Cosmopolitanism is not the same as universalism in that the latter is opposed to fixed systems of thought. Cosmopolitanism could be described as the capacity to relativise one's own culture.

With the rise of globalization theory in the early 1980s has come new interest in cosmopolitanism in the Kantian tradition, which has moved increasingly from an ideal to a reality (Bohman & Lutz-Bachmann 1997). The new cosmopolitanism goes beyond the limits of both ancient moral cosmopolitanism and the legal cosmopolitanism inaugurated by Kant; it is primarily a political cosmopolitanism. The end of the Cold War, the collapse of Apartheid in South Africa, the rapid development of global information technologies, the consolidation of the European Union, plus new human rights laws and international criminal tribunals, have clearly given some substance to the cosmopolitan vision. States, while being the major political actors, are no longer exclusively in control of the international arena, which increasingly involves global civil society. Although it is doubtful that this emerging global civil society constitutes a new political order along the lines of a world polity, it certainly forms the basis of a new kind of cosmopolitanism that is neither purely moral nor legal. In it, citizenship plays a leading role.

Cosmopolitanism expresses the universalistic dimension of the nation and is at odds with particularistic tendencies. Cosmopolitanism can be seen as a movement towards openness that resists the drive to closure characteristic of the nation-state.

This does not mean that cosmopolitanism is antithetical to the nation-state. Postcolonial theories of nationhood have drawn attention to the hybrid and multi-vocal category of the nation as already cosmopolitan (see also Cheah & Robbins 1998). Aihwa Ong (1997) thus sees a new cosmopolitanism in transnational migration and diasporic movements. This is a kind of cosmopolitanism represented by movements from the periphery whose carriers are diasporic nations.

11.4. From Idea to Reality: Cosmopolitan Citizenship

Citizenship theory has undergone major changes in the past few decades that can be understood in terms of cosmopolitanism. Central to the new conception is a growing awareness that citizenship must address the question of culture and, related to this, the challenges of globalization. The introduction of a cultural and global dimension into the debate on citizenship was reflected in some of the following developments, which all point to a fundamental rethinking of the very concept of citizenship. [122]

The equation of citizenship and nationality, as for example in T.H. Marshall's theory, can no longer be taken for granted. Citizenship refers to something wider than nationality, which denotes formal membership of a state. This separation of citizenship from nationality can be related to a corresponding shift in Europe from birth to residence as a criterion of many rights of citizenship. While this does not extend to all rights of citizenship, such as political rights, and is based on a prior national citizenship, it is a significant move in the direction of post-national membership. Citizenship is no longer exclusively a bundle of rights underpinned by a passport. As noted earlier, accompanying the separation of citizenship and nationality is a blurring of the distinction between the rights of citizenship and human rights. The internationalization of national law has led to a situation in which it is more difficult for states to separate insiders from outsiders (Soysal 1994). According to Joppke (2005), the national state has now embarked on an irreversible path towards a new age of individual human rights.

While some critics see the very concept of citizenship as necessarily entailing exclusion (Mann 1987; Hindess 1998; Wimmer 2003), others see it as essential to multiculturalism (Parekh 2000). A new challenge for citizenship is in reconciling group rights with the rights of the individual (Kylimka & Norman 2000). The general position appears to be that some degree of group rights, within a broadly based liberal conception of rights, is a necessary dimension of democracy. The rise of group or cultural rights replaced the previous concern with social citizenship and, as a result, citizenship is no longer exclusively about the pursuit of equality, it is also about the preservation of group differences (Touraine 2000). The important point in this is the confluence of culture and citizenship (Lurry 1993, Stevenson 2000,; Cowan Dembour & Wilson 2001). Until recently, the concerns of most approaches to citizenship were quite indifferent to cultural issues and conflicts over identity. As is well known, citizenship has been historically formed around civic, political and social rights. Even if T.H. Marshall's account of the formation of modern citizenship reflected a very one-sided view of what was at best the British experience, it is certainly true that his omission of the sphere of culture was characteristic of most conceptions of citizenship.

---

122 Some of the following points of definition are based on my entry on citizenship in *Encyclopaedia of Social Theory*, 2 vols General Editor, G. Ritzer. London: Sage, 2005.

Citizenship was held to be based on formal rights and had relatively little to do with substantive issues of cultural belonging. It was a fairly static concept that reflected the durability of the existing national state. Although Marshall acknowledged a relation between rights on the one side and, on the other side, duties and loyalties, the substantive dimension was never central to his conception of citizenship. In the civic republican tradition, which emphasized more strongly participation and an active, as opposed to passive, view of the citizen, the cultural dimension of citizenship did not receive much more attention. Until about the late 1980s, multiculturalism and citizenship performed quite different functions. Citizenship, on the whole, pertained to the national citizenship of an established polity and was generally defined by birth, or in some cases by descent, while multicultural policies served to manage in-coming migrant groups. Today, this distinction has virtually collapsed. Migrant groups have increasingly become a part of the mainstream population and cannot be so easily contained by multicultural policies. At the same time, the 'native' population itself has become more and more culturally plural, due in part to the impact of some four decades of ethnic mixing, but also due to the general pluralization brought about by post-industrial and post-modern culture. In Britain, for example, there is a greater awareness of the constituent nations of the Union as well as of regionalisation. The focus on production and social class, which informed Marshall's account of citizenship, has given way to greater interest in subcultures based around leisure pursuits and consumption. In addition, new and more radical ideas of democracy have arisen as a result of the rise of new social movements. The social is now becoming more cultural and with this come new kinds of participation.

In such considerations, the question of technology and citizenship has become important (Frankenfeld 1992; Zimmerman 1995). New technologies - such as communication and information technologies, new reproductive technologies, the new genetics, biotechnologies, surveillance technologies, and new military technologies aimed at populations rather than states - have transformed the very meaning of citizenship, which can no longer be defined as a relation to the state. The new technologies differ from the old ones in that they have major implications for citizenship, given their capacity to refine the very nature of society, and in many cases, personhood. Citizens, in private and in public roles and as consumers, patients and university students, are encountering the new technologies increasingly through the market. In the area of rights, we find issues of privacy, rights to information, victimization and new concerns, such as for instance global responsibility, responsibility to nature, to future generations, concerns that go beyond the traditional conceptions of the dutiful citizen. Social inclusion is now extended to technology, which is affecting citizenship, opening up more and more possibilities for personal life styles, consumption and culture.

One of the most discussed new faces of citizenship today is its extension beyond the nation-state. This conception of citizenship takes two broad forms, which are often conflated. On the one side, there is the idea of global citizenship in the more specific sense of a form of citizenship that is located in a trans-national space. On the other side, there is the essentially cultural question of cosmopolitan citizenship, viewed as a particular consciousness towards the wider world.

Global citizenship is clearly related to globalization and the growing recognition that citizenship extends beyond the horizons of the nation-state to encompass global forms. One school of thought rejects the very notion of citizenship beyond the nation-state as neither possible nor desirable. Others see new opportunities for citizenship in areas of governance and new social spaces beyond the level of the nation-state.

But, rather than seeing global citizenship and national citizenship as exclusive, it makes more sense to see them as embodying different levels of citizenship. It is possible to identify at least three such levels: the subnational (that is, local or regional) level, the national level, and the global level. No account of citizenship can ignore the global dimension, although this does not mean that more local forms of citizenship have become redundant. This indicates a view of citizenship as multi-level, rather than spatially confined to national societies. It also points to a flexible citizenship whereby citizens, especially those affected by trans-national processes, negotiate more and more the different levels of governance (Ong 1999). This indicates a cultural dimension to global citizenship, best viewed as constituting a different aspect of citizenship.

Cosmopolitan citizenship is a term that is best applied to the process by which critical and reflexive forms of belonging enter into discourses of belonging. As societies become more and more interpenetrated, due not in the least to processes of globalization, new expressions of citizenship emerge such as those discussed in the foregoing analysis. The existing literature does not distinguish adequately between cosmopolitanism and globalization. Cosmopolitanism is not found exclusively on the global level, but is also to be located on the local and national level. It can also entail resistance to globalization. Central to cosmopolitan citizenship are forms of inclusion that are not exclusively rights-based and which cannot be reduced to a constitutional order. In the foregoing, new cultural challenges have been referred to as constituting the space of cosmopolitan citizenship.

11.5. Defending Cosmopolitanism

Cosmopolitanism has not been without its critics. Communitarians argue that community must be rooted in a cultural form of life. Cosmopolitanism is dismissed as the desire to have no commitments to one's local community, for to belong to the world is in effect to belong nowhere, it is often argued. Thus, Michael Walzer (1983) claims that there are no cosmopolitan values of any substance, for community is necessarily 'thick' whereas cosmopolitanism cannot be thick because it is by definition not rooted in a common way of life. A counterargument to this view is that:

- (A) Walzer reduces consciousness of global issues and concerns to trivial concerns;
- (B) he conflates culture with an underlying consensus;

186

- (C) does not see that even a 'thin' morality can be sufficiently 'thick' to be significant, and
- (D) he fails to consider that global 'thin' ethics might be 'thicker' than many allegedly thick moralities.

Another school of thought rejects the very notion of citizenship beyond the nation-state as neither possible nor desirable (e.g. Zolo 1997). Cosmopolitanism is equated in this respect with the desire to create a cosmopolis, which is generally equated with either a world state or an unrealistic notion of global civil society and is accordingly dismissed as dangerous or undesirable.

The defenders of cosmopolitanism, on the other hand, see opportunities for citizenship in areas of governance and new trans-national spaces beyond the level of the nation-state (Archibugi 1995). For cosmopolitans it is a mistake to see cosmopolitan citizenship as an alternative to other kinds of citizenship such as a national and local citizenship. It should instead be conceived of as an additional dimension of citizenship that has come into existence today along with new forms of democratization. To the extent to which cosmopolitanism is underpinned by a cosmopolis, it is a multileveled cosmopolis rather than a world state. Moreover, it can be argued that cosmopolitanism is evident in the growing volume of trans-national debates, movements, and politics. It is not then just idle speculation or a hopelessly utopian project but a real force in the world (Cheah & Robbins 1998). To ignore the reality of cosmopolitanism is to ignore the proliferation of new discourses beyond the nation-state.

Martha Nussbaum (1996) has given a strong defence of cosmopolitanism as the opposite of narrow patriotism. Far from rejecting responsibilities, cosmopolitanism is an expression of dialogue with others and of a fundamental allegiance based on justice and reason to people, wherever they may be. In this sense, it is possible to conceive of cosmopolitanism as having a civic dimension and being compatible with community and, above all, with morality. However, it is not necessary to dismiss patriotism as the opposite of cosmopolitanism. There is a concept of the nation that is not entirely the opposite of cosmopolitanism; indeed some of the most influential programmes in modern nationalism, for instance Giuseppe Mazzini's Young Europe movement, founded in Berne in 1834 to promote republican nationalism and outlined in *The Duties of Man*, was based precisely on the cosmopolitanism of nationalism.

It is evident, however, that whatever form cosmopolitanism is taking, it is very different from the one Kant envisaged. It is no longer a question of 'perpetual peace' confronting a Hobbesian order of perpetual violence. It is unlikely that the emerging global civil society and its diverse modes of organization, which range from local urban protest movements to globally organized anti-capitalist demonstrations, constitutes a cosmopolis in the Kantian sense. Cosmopolitanism is best seen as a current tendency to counteract the narrow vision of politics associated with doctrines based on class or nation (Fine 2003). The cosmopolitan perspective, in this looser and more critical sense, is part of the social sciences in a way that it was not in the past (Beck 2000; Beck & Grande 2004). The way in which we think about cosmopolitanism today is very different from the Enlightenment discourses, largely because of the increasing speed of globalization, which has opened multiple orders of governance beyond the state and within the state and which has established the need for a universal global ethics (Apel 2000; Singer 2003).

11.6. Conclusion: Cosmopolitanism and Europeanization

We have now reached a point at which the connection of cosmopolitanism with European post-national developments can be established. A cosmopolitan perspective brings an additional dimension to bear on European citizenship. It suggests a model of citizenship beyond a purely constitutional order based on formal rights, such as those acknowledged in the Maastricht Treaty. Instead, cosmopolitan citizenship entails a greater emphasis on a substantive kind of citizenship based on solidarity and recognition of cultural differences. Cosmopolitanism, more broadly, can be related to the transformation of European societies in terms of the encounter of the local or the national with the global. This can be related to a form of post-national self-understanding that expresses itself within, as much as beyond, national identities. Cosmopolitan currents are evident within national identities. The local global nexus is often the site of major social transformation. This is the significance of Europeanization, which can be understood as a reflexive relation of the national and global levels.

The idea of cosmopolitanism invoked here is more than the simple co-existence of difference in the sense of neo-functionalism or of multiculturalism. The relation is not merely one of co-existence because the various levels co-evolve, and as they do so an emergent reality is produced. The obvious convergence of European societies does not mean some overall cohesion or uniformity but a transformative process. It is undoubtedly for this reason that Europeanization is ultimately difficult to democratize, since the cosmopolitan currents that accompany it tend to produce difference and with this come more and more points of view and contentious demands (see Trenz & Eder 2004).

This view of cosmopolitan citizenship is thus different from a notion of supranational or transnational citizenship. It is not primarily a question of membership of a supranational polity that distinguishes it from traditional kinds of national citizenship. While it should not be viewed as an alternative to national forms of citizenship, cosmopolitan citizenship gives expression to aspects of belonging and membership that tend be excluded from national citizenship policies. To the extent to which the EU embarks on a project of supra-nationalism and attempts to create its own version of a national citizenship, albeit on a larger scale, the danger will be that the cosmopolitan moment will be lost in a liberal conception of formal rights within a constitutional order. This chapter has attempted to show that the republican tradition of citizenship is not an alternative. Although this tradition does highlight a number of different and quite important aspects of citizenship that tend to be neglected in the dominant liberal tradition, which appears to have found a new form in the EU today, the cosmopolitan tradition offers an additional perspective, and one that is not rooted in the notion of a sovereign people within national boundaries. Cosmopolitan citizenship shifts citizenship from exclusivist paradigms towards more open ones of inclusion. While resisting the tendency towards closure in national polities, it also resists global forces. As Europeanization is increasingly coming to be articulated in relation to globalization, cosmopolitanism will play an ever-greater role.

12. European Citizens in Arms: the EU's International Identity and the Militarization of a 'Civilian Power'

Paolo Foradori

12.1. Introduction

This chapter explores the international dimensions of the process of constructing a common EU identity. The deepening integration of the Common Foreign and Security Policy (CFSP) and the recent progress in the European Security and Defence Policy (ESDP) − culminating in the first EU military operations abroad in 2003 − are crucial developments that have significant consequences beyond the specific politico-military sphere on the creation of a sense of belonging to a common polity. Indeed, it is precisely at the critical level of *high politics* − i.e. the realm of defence, survival and external projection of power − that processes of self-definition and self-identification become stronger and more clearly defined.

Exploring the international identity of the EU means examining the EU's role as a global actor; its ability to make an impact on the international stage by exerting influence over the big issues which define the international environment. Put differently, the study of the Europe's international identity must analyse the extent to which the EU is able to provide answers to the major questions at the root of international politics, which in essence means issues of war and peace.

Thence derives the interest in the development of a common defence and security policy, which the EU has decided to purse in order to attain an autonomous military capability that will 'increase its ability to contribute to international peace and security' and thus play 'its full role on the international stage.[123]

The inclusion of the military option in the EU's 'tool box' for international action constitutes a historical moment in the European integration process. However, this development is not devoid of problems as far as the process of identity construction is concerned. To what extent, has the militarization of the EU altered the civilian character of the Union? Does it still make sense to speak of Europe as a 'civilian power'? Does the EU increasingly resemble a traditional power? These complex issues require thorough examination for at stake is the very nature and identity of the EU as an international actor.

This chapter is organised in three sections. The first section reviews the debate about the EU's international identity and presents the 'civilian power model'. The second section is devoted to a brief overview of the ESDP and the recent developments of the EU as a 'conflict manager'. The third section discusses the transforma-

---

123 European Council, Cologne, 3-4 June 1999, in Rutten (2001: 41).

tion of the civilian power model as a result of integration in the field of defence, arguing that despite important changes, the EU is likely to retain its distinctive features as a *sui generis* international actor.

12.2. The EU's International Identity and the 'Civilian Power' Model

The construction of a common European citizenship presupposes the development of a collective identity. Only the latter can, as a sort of social glue, facilitate the emergence of a sense of belonging to a common socio-political project in which the individuals of a polity become 'citizens', i.e. holders of rights and duties who share the essence of common values, interests and norms of social life.[124]

The notion of citizenship, therefore, is not separable from the one of identity. Identities, however, are not innate, natural phenomena. They are social constructions, which develop and mature through dynamic processes of continuous interactions that induce the re-elaboration and re-discussion of existing models of identification in favour of new and re-imagined syntheses. Over time, this process leads to the formation of well defined, although fluid, role-specific understandings and expectations about self (Wendt 1999).

The process of EU identity construction has a crucial international dimension. This is to be understood not as a synonym for 'foreign policy' or 'external relations', but rather as a 'position from which to commence conceptualizing the global role of the European Union as being greater than the sum of its parts' (Manners & Whitman 1998: 246).

An accurate analysis of the EU's international identity requires a thorough examination of both its material elements (actual power, capabilities, effective impact on global affairs), and the more ideational aspects, which relate to the image of itself as a collective international actor that the EU has developed over time. Crucial is also how this image is perceived by the other actors in the international system. Without neglecting the determinant weight of power politics, every actor acts *also* on the basis of its *self-image*[125]. In the words of Manners & Whitman (2003: 383), the notion of international identity is 'an attempt to think about how the EU is constituted, constructed, and represented internationally', where by constitution is meant the constitutive history and principles of the EU; by construction the way in

---

124 The CFSP is replete with references to 'identity'. The Preamble of the Treaty on European Union declares that the implementation of CFSP will help reinforce 'the European identity and independence in order to promote peace, security and progress in Europe and in the world'. Article 2 states that one of the main objective of the CFSP is 'to assert its identity on the international scene'.

125 For Mitzen (2006: 271) *habits* are even more important than capabilities in determining identity. Building on the notion of 'ontological security' developed by Anthony Giddens, the author maintains that the 'EU's civilising identity is supported by healthy basic trust, which guards against the securitization of subjectivity that "great power Europe" implies'.

which the EU has been, and is, understood; and by representation the ways in which the EU represents itself, and is represented in the minds of those interacting with it.

Contrary to rationalist approaches to foreign policy, which are limited to materialist assumptions about the actors' underlying interests and objectives, it is crucial to attribute a causal role to social factors such as identities, norms and roles that affect actors' behaviour, not only by shaping their strategies, but also their interests and preferences. The very nature of these interests and preferences largely depends on the actors' self-perception, i.e. the appropriate line of conduct they should follow given the role they ascribe to themselves, as well as the external image they want to diffuse.[126] The CFSP and the ESDP accordingly are *significantly* shaped by the way the EU looks at its common history, by the values which inspire its foreign policy and by the distinctive elements which define its security stance, in a constant interaction between elements which refer to identity, interests and policy (Jepperson, Wendt & Katzenstein 1996: 33-75).

As Sedelmeier " (2004: 125) puts it:

"EU policy makers do not simply calculate which strategy is most likely to advance their given interests in a certain situation, but they ask what their particular role in a certain situation is and which obligations that role prescribes in this situation. The formation of preferences – which actors might well pursue strategically – is endogenous to the process of identity and social role formation.

The literature describes the EU's international identity largely in terms of a 'civil power'. This apt concept was formulated first by François Duchêne (1972, 1973) who, writing at the beginning of the 1970s, ascertained the substantial irrelevance of military force as an instrument for resolving security disputes. In that context, the EU appeared to be a novel type of actor, capable of exerting an impact on international affairs without conducting a traditional state-like foreign policy and, above all, without resorting to coercive means. The EU asserted itself as 'the exemplar of a new stage of political *civilization*' (1973: 19), whose power consisted in the ability to promote and encourage international order and stability through diplomatic, political, cultural and economic instruments. Duchêne's notion refers to the EC/EU's achievements in domesticating relations between states, i.e. in promoting structures of peaceful conflict resolution in the larger European region and not only amongst its member states. In his words:

'the European Community's interest as a civilian group of countries long on economic power and relatively short on armed force is as far as possible to domesticate relations between states, including those of its own members and those with states outside its frontiers. This means trying to bring to international problems the sense of common responsibility and structures of contractual politics which have been in the past associated exclusively with "home" and not foreign, that is alien, affairs' (Duchêne 1973: 19-20).

---

126 This follows a 'logic of appropriateness' according to which actors determine 'what the situation is, what role is being fulfilled and what the obligations of that role in that situation are' (March & Olsen 1989: 160).

Duchêne's view quite naturally provoked an immediate reaction and a lively debate. Hedley Bull's (1983) response was particularly incisive. For Bull the notion of a 'civil power' quite simply is a 'contradiction in terms'. The relatively peaceful international environment of the early 1960s, could not possibly justify the conclusion that military might and *power politics* had lost their relevance in international relations. If Europe had ambitions of being a player on the global scene, Bull argued, it would have to attain military self-sufficiency, equipping itself with conventional as well as nuclear arms.

However, the idea of the EU as a civil power found, and continues to find, many advocates. The argument that, also in the current international scenario, the security threats facing the EU are not necessarily addressed best by military means was further developed by Karen Smith (2000). According to Smith, a possible militarisation of the EU would rather risk to aggravate the threats to European security, giving rise to a 'security dilemma' in case the deepening of the European security and defence policy were to be perceived as threatening by other countries. Jan Zielonka (1998: 229) instead, pointing to the essentially civilian character of the entire process of European integration, deems the acquisition of military capabilities inopportune as it would compromise the 'distinct profile' of the Union. Nor would a militarization of the EU be necessary. NATO and national forces are adequate for the defence of Europe and its interests, while the effectiveness of an EU force would be uncertain in a clear north Atlantic divisions of tasks, in which the 'quiet superpower' Europe should rather concentrate on what it does best – the use of *soft power* – leaving the recourse to force to the USA (Moravcsik 2003).

The debate over the EU's international identity has been further enriched by the introduction of the concept of 'normative power'. The concept aspires to go beyond the simplistic dichotomy of civilian versus military, which is too rigidly anchored to the old question of whether the EU resembles a traditional nation-state, as well as being limited to the discussion over capabilities (Rosecrance 1998; Manners 2002; Manners & Whitman 2003). The concept of normative power, in contrast, constitutes an attempt to redirect the focus of the analysis from the simple practical aspects of the capabilities of EU institutions and policies towards a cognitive approach, which includes both substantive and symbolic elements. According to this approach, the strength of the EU as an international actor resides not so much in the size of its tangible forces as in the power of its defining ideas and norms, which have a real impact on global politics.[127]

The EU is different from pre-existing political forms: 'the most important factor shaping the international role of the EU is not what it does or what is says, but what it is' (Manners 2002: 252). The peculiar historical context in which the process of European integration takes shape, the hybrid nature of the Union hovering between

---

127 The idea, implicit in the notion of normative power, that alongside military and economic power, there exists 'ideological power' and thus a 'ideological impact' has a long tradition. Regarding the EC/EU see, for example, Galtung (1973).

intergovernmentalism and supranationalism, the post-national pooling of sovereignty and its constitutional and politico-legal nature make the EU a polity ontologically different from the other actors operating in the international system.[128]

Being constructed on a normative basis, the EU is predisposed to act in a normative way. On the global scene, the EU aims to redefine the international norms in the image of the shared principles of its members, thus redefining what is considered 'normal' in international relations. Given these distinctive features, a normative power is much more than a power that does not employ military instruments; it is indeed a 'civilising power', striving to civilise the anarchic state of international relations along the lines of its own, democratic, domestic politics (Maull 2000).

12.3. Common Defence and the Process of EU militarization

After having clarified the concept of a 'European civil power', the developments of European integration in the field of security and defence need to be considered. After the failure to create a European Defence Community (EDC) in the early 1950s, security issues for half a century were taboo in Brussels and the policy area strenuously resisted every move towards integration.[129]

It was only towards the late 1990s that such *issues* suddenly reappeared on the agenda of the EU. Three main sets of factors explain this re-emergence. The first one is of a systemic nature and relates to the change of the international context after the Cold War. Due to the disappearance of the Soviet threat, Europe progressively lost its strategic relevance. This ended Europe's dependence on its US ally, but at the same time it marked a re-orientation of US military priorities away from the Old Continent. In an international environment no longer characterised by a monolithic threat from the East but by a host of diverse new threats (de Wijk 2003: 205) the diminished American interest in European security, plus the. marked divergence in strategic visions between the US and Europe, meant that the EU urgently had to assume its own responsibilities.

The second factor derives from the internal dynamics of European integration. After the extraordinary progress made in the economic and monetary field during the 1990s, deepening of the political dimension had become the logical next step in the programme of an *ever-closer Union*.

---

128 For an interesting and constructive critique of the concept of 'normative power' see Sjursen (2006: 249). After having highlighted the lack of precision and problematized the concept, also in a interesting comparison with the US, the author maintains that a true 'normative power' would be 'one that seeks to overcome power politics through a strengthening of not only international but cosmopolitan law, emphasizing the rights of individuals and not only the rights of states to sovereign equality'. If this were so, the author would find it difficult to conclude that the EU is a normative power.

129 For a precise reconstruction of the process that led to the birth of the ESDP see Gnesotto (2004).

Above all, the international constellation of the mid 1990s imparted a strong dynamism to the developments in the field of collective security. The utter irrelevance of the EU in the wars of the former Yugoslavia impressed upon the European leaders the weakness of a Union unable to assert itself in a conflict unfolding in the heart of Europe. 'It seemed absurd, if not scandalous, to keep multiplying EU directives on all aspects of economic and social life while ignoring the atrocities committed in Sarajevo' (Haine 2004: 38). The EU's scanty weight in international affairs was demonstrated even more clearly in the Kosovo war of 1999, as a result of internal differences that precluded the formulation of a common position and technical and operative shortcomings of its armed forces when engaging in military operations according to the new canon of modern *warfare*. Moreover, the tragedy of the Balkans highlighted the internal problems of a transatlantic alliance ever more skewed in favour of the US and the ineffectiveness of diplomatic negotiations not backed by credible military instruments with people like Milosevic.

Once British fears of weakening NATO had been assayed and an acceptable compromise between the extremis of the French Europeanist position and the Atlanticism of the United Kingdom had been found with the agreement of Saint-Malo (1998), the ESDP was officially established at the Councils of Cologne and Helsinki in June and December of 1999. The member states were 'resolved that the European Union shall play its full role on the international stage.

> "To that end, we intend to give the European Union the necessary means and capabilities to assume its responsibilities regarding a common European policy on security and defence [...] The Union must have the capacity for autonomous action, backed up by credible military forces, the means to decide to use them, and a readiness to do so, in order to respond to international crises without prejudice to actions by NATO." (European Council, Cologne, 3-4 June 1999, in Rutten 2001: 41)

To give substance and content to this political choice, the so-called *Headline Goal* was established, which committed the member states to create a Rapid Reaction Force of about 50-60.000 men, fully deployable within 60 days and able to operate in the field for at least one year. By 2003, those forces would need to be militarily autonomous and thus equipped with appropriate command, control and information capabilities, logistical, supporting units and, if so required, also with air and naval support (about 400 combat airplanes and 100 naval units including five aircraft carriers).[130].

It is not possible to retrace here the sometimes non-linear and frequently bumpy history of the ESDP from Cologne onwards. In sum, it can be said though that – notwithstanding the initial difficulties, the extreme sensitivity of the *policy* area, and the many shortcomings which continue to characterise the ESDP – after the monetary field, this is the area in which the EU has achieved, in the words of the High Representative for the Common Foreign and Security Policy, 'the most rapid and spectacular progress' (Solana 2004: 5). These development become even more sig-

---

130 See the Conclusions of the Presidency of the Helsinki Council in Rutten (2001: 82-91).

nificant when one realises that they took place in an extremely adverse international context, which was subjected to serious transatlantic tensions at its most critical moment due to the US led war in Iraq and the resulting internal differences in the EU over whether or not to support this intervention.

In little more than eight years, the military competences of the EU have been formally included in the treaties, decision-making structures and permanent military institutions have been created[131], the Headline Goal has been reached, a *European Defence Agency* has been established[132] and in 2003 a European Security Strategy was elaborated and approved.[133]

Even more important, in 2003 the process of EU militarization culminated in the first-ever ESDP missions conducted entirely under the EU's aegis. These are missions undertaken under the command and control of the EU and aimed at achieving the so-called Petersberg Tasks, defined in article 17 of the EU Treaties as 'humanitarian and rescue tasks, peacekeeping tasks and tasks of combat forces in crisis management, including peacemaking'.[134]

As of today, the EU has conducted some fifteen operations, covering the entire spectrum of options available to the ESDP, from police missions (EUPM, Proxima, EUPOL Kinshasa), and civilian missions as envisaged by the Council of Feira (EUJUST Themis), to expressly military missions (Concordia, Artemis, Altea).

Although these important missions doubtlessly represent a significant step forward in the formulation and implementation of an EU defence policy, the ESDP still displays many weaknesses, both of a quantitative and qualitative nature. These weaknesses concern some sectors of crucial importance for the exigencies of modern warfare, and in particular[135] the limited 'usability' and 'deployability' of the EU forces. No more than 10-15 per cent of the 1,8 million persons under arms in Europe can be used for combat missions abroad. The mobility of the European forces is

---

131 These are the Political Security Committee (COPS), the EU Military Committee (EUMC) and the EU Military Staff, with its seat in Brussels.

132 Its full name being 'European Agency for Armaments, Research and Military Capabilities'. Operative since 2004, the Agency seeks to promote the integration of the operative aspects of military capabilities with aspects of acquisition and planning, thus creating a link between military planning and the armaments sector (above all in the areas of research and procurement).

133 The document entitled 'A secure Europe in a Better World' is available at: http://www.consilium.europa.eu/uedocs/cmsUpload/78367.pdf

134 It is interesting to note that, had the European Constitutional Treaty been approved, the ESDP would have been significantly extended, including an extension of the definitions of the mission providing for the use of force on the part of the EU. Moreover, the Constitutional Treaty allowed for structured cooperation in the defence sector, and it contained a collective assistance clause in case of an armed attack against the territory of the members states, thus clearing the way towards collective defence, which hitherto is the prerogative of the member states and NATO.

135 This section is based on Schmitt 2004: 104-106 and Biscop 2004: 514.

limited due to a lack of sufficient means for transporting troops and their equipment to distant locations (strategic transport).[136] There are weaknesses concerning the effective engagement in high-intensity operations in hostile environments, because of shortcomings in the main sectors of the so-called C4ISTAR (command, control, communications, computer, intelligence, surveillance, target acquisition and reconnaissance), which encompass the fundamental elements of modern warfare according to the new doctrine of the 'Revolution of Military Affairs (RAM)'. Those shortcomings, in turn, make inter-operability between European forces problematical, and even more so the ability to engage in joint action between ESDP and NATO forces, in particular American forces.

Irrespective of the actual achievements of what were limited missions[137], the most important result, without a doubt, is the political and symbolic one of a united Europe responding to international crises and proving able to act on the ground, sending common forces to crisis areas for the first time in its history. The missions demonstrate the will and determination of the EU to proceed with integration in the delicate sector of security and defence and to strengthen the EU as an international actor. These are important developments, 'if not for the simple fact that their mere existence would have been unimaginable only five years ago' (Howorth 2003: 30).

Secondly, even if the military capabilities of the EU have not yet been tested against the more demanding of the Petersberg Tasks, nevertheless, the missions undertaken have allowed the EU to gain an initial, albeit limited, experience in the field, something which is an indispensable basis for any further steps that might be taken in the future. Additionally, the missions undertaken have allowed the EU to test the military procedures of command, control and communications; the logistical and legal aspects related to cooperation in the field with non-member states and, above all, with the host nation and the complex modes of implementation of the 'Berlin plus' accords between the EU and NATO.

At present and in the near future, the ESDP clearly will not be able to engage in high-tech and high-intensity operations and will need to rely on NATO assets for the more exacting missions. Nevertheless, at least at the political and symbolic level, the taboo of European defence has been broken and the road ahead has been irreversibly marked, as confirmed by the intention of the EU to equip itself by the year 2010 with highly operative and rapidly deployable troops to be employed in high-intensity operations. With the elaboration of the Headline Goal 2010, the EU has shown its irreversible determination to contribute to peace and international security, committing itself to the whole spectrum of military operations as defined in the Petersberg Tasks, including the more robust ones.

---

136 This lack has a negative effect on reaction times and the deployment of the European forces and makes it extremely difficult to maintain the deployed forces in the field for longer periods and to support them logistically, particularly in the case of large-scale ESDP operations of high intensity in remote theatres of operation.

137 In total they involved a few thousand men, with very restricted mandates, weak rules of engagement and still largely dependent on the assets of NATO.

12.4. But Still a Sui Generis International Power

The deepening of ESDP, outlined above, and the EU's determination to equip itself with real military capabilities, raises the question whether the traditional image of the EU as a civil power still makes sense. Isn't there an apparent contradiction between the ongoing militarization of the EU and its alleged civil character?

The risks are evident. 'Incorporating military capabilities into a civilian identity is difficult on many levels, and finding a way to reconcile the use of force in particular instances with the identity as a civilizing power will be an ongoing challenge." (Mitzen 2006: 283) Manners himself (2006: 183) has partially reconsidered his previous position, claiming that the "militarizing processes beyond the crossroads provided by the European Security Strategy are already weakening the normative claims of the EU in a post-11 September world characterized by the drive towards "martial potency" and the growth of a Brussels-based "military-industrial simplex."' This slippery trend is manifest also in the recent misdirection of the traditional civilian European security culture away from the people-centred normative concerns for, freedom from fear and want, human security and sustainable peace, towards more conventional security concerns that prioritize military intervention over non-military conciliation. Manners (2006: 189-194) is concerned that the unreflexive militarization of the ESDP since 2003 may tempt the EU to use short-term military responses instead of its traditional reliance on long-term structural conflict prevention and transformation.

However, the view that it is still possible to describe the international identity of the EU with the concept of 'gentle power', notwithstanding the progress of ESDP, is also convincing, at least in part. These arguments hold that such a power is defined not only through the means it employs, but also, and maybe primarily, by the ends it seeks to achieve. If force is used in specific circumstances only and within clearly defined limits in order to promote *civil goals,*[138] the use of the term 'civil power' would remain legitimate. [139]

According to Stelios Stavridis (2001), the attainment of a military capability increased the international credibility of the EU, thus finally enabling it to act as a real civil power committed to the diffusion of principles of justice and democracy. Military means might be essential to realise effective civilian power. The issue then would rather be one of the gradual transformation of the EU from a civil power 'by default' to a civil power 'by design', which is to say, from a simple unarmed pres-

---

138 Examples of civil ends are: international cooperation and solidarity; promotion of democratic principles; respect for human rights; diffusion of equality justice and tolerance; sustainable development and environmental protection. These ends transcend national interests and have a universal importance.

139 In embryonic form, the point is made in Duchêne (1972, 1973) and further developed by Maull (2000) with reference to Germany as a civil power notwithstanding its participation in the military operations of the Kosovo conflict of 1999. A similar argument with explicit reference to the EU is advanced by Whitman (2002).

ence on the international scene, to a power which disposes of credible military instruments to be used parsimoniously and as *ultima ratio* in the pursuit of civil objectives of international politics.[140]

It would seem reasonable to maintain that the development of the ESDP has significantly distanced the EU from the ideal-type of a 'civilian power'. Irrespective of whether they are to be employed or not and for what exact ends, the strengthening of the its military capabilities doubtlessly served to signal the clear intention of the EU to move beyond the traditional civilian power model, which had characterised it at least until the end of the Cold War.

This certainly does not mean that the EU is transforming itself into a traditional military power, or should aspire to become a 'superpower' in the classical meaning of the word.[141] The development of the ESDP and the militarisation of the EU notwithstanding, the Union retains its peculiar international identity, characterised by the conformity of its actions with the values and principles embedded in the communitarian ethos[142]. This clearly sets it apart from other international actors.

As argued in the first section, reflections on the role of the EU in international affairs cannot be limited to the issue of instruments of action and material capabilities but must involve also the ideas and norms that give shape and substance to this role (Manners 2002). If by norms we mean 'collective expectations about proper behaviour for a given identity' (Jepperson, Wendt & Katzenstein 1996: 54), we can presume that the EU will continue to be predisposed to act internationally according to its particular self-image and its normative and identity-related commitments. The idea again refers to the concept of Europe as a 'normative power' guided by the 'core norms' that are comprised in the EU's *acquis* (Manners 2002)[143] and by the EU's main foreign policy objectives.

---

140 The emphasis these authors place on the ends rather than the means does not convince Karen Smith (2005). According to her, to assign a privileged role to the ends makes it difficult to establish a clear and unequivocal demarcation line with respect to means and thus to distinguish between 'civil' means and 'military' means. Moreover, to argue that a civil power is one that uses military might only when all other means have failed is vague and entails a conceptual confusion, making it no longer possible to discern a clear dividing line in the use of force. How to define in an unequivocal way what is a 'civil end'? Which exactly are the human rights one wants to promote? What is to be understood by promotion of democratic principles? What type of democracy are we talking about?

141 A radically different opinion is expressed by Gnesotto (2004: 1), for whom: 'the idea of Europe as a purely civil power is outdated. "The great debate of the 1980s over Europe as a civil power or a military power definitely seems to be a thing of the past."

142 Moreover, from a study by Henrik Larsen (2002) on the discourse and terminology of self-description of the EU clearly emerges that it continues to perceive and describe itself as an essentially civil power.

143 According to Manners (2002: 242-244), the normative foundation of the EU, as it has developed over the last fifty years through a series of declarations, treaties, policies, criteria and conditionality, allows us to identify five fundamental norms: peace, liberty, democracy, rule of law and respect for human rights. In addition four 'minor' norms are said to exist, i.e. social

As has been correctly observed: 'although the EU is no longer a "civilian" power, it will never become a full "military" power or *Machtstaat,* in the sense of having a "European army" capable of engaging in the full spectrum of military operations. Rather, the EU is developing the capabilities to conduct Petersberg-type missions, including military crisis management. All the Petersberg tasks, it is argued, involve the exercise of coercion rather than what Thomas Schelling called *brute force'.* (Hyde-Price 2004: 3). Moreover, it should be noted that issues of territorial defence and of nuclear capability remain strictly within the competence of NATO (Jørgensen 1997).

In short, it is very unlikely that the EU will behave as a traditional actor despite rapid integration in the defence sector and growing common capabilities because of its role-specific and principled, contra-Westphalian and multiple international identity building on the communitarian values of pluralism, solidarity and international tolerance. As Manners & Whitman (2003: 400) have convincingly argued: 'pacifism rather than aggression; principles rather than pragmatism; slow, consensual and structural rather than rapid, conflictual action; networking rather than hierarchical; open rather than closed; and contra-normal rather than conventional, all are identity traits which contribute to ensuring that the EU's international identity is constructed through unconventional socio-cultural differences'. These elements provide an 'institutional environment' for EU actions in global affairs (Sedelmeier 2004: 131), limiting the realm of practicable policy options at the EU's disposal – and in particular the resort to the use of force – giving greater legitimacy to those options which better reflect the general European civilian identity.

The specific character of the Europe's international identity is also reflected in the *crisis management* activities the EU has engaged in. The EU favours a broad, comprehensive and holistic vision of conflict management that addresses all dimensions of security: socio-economic, political, demographic, cultural, ecological as well as military. This integrated policy transcends the borders between the pillars of the Union, encompassing external trade and development cooperation, as well as the CFSP and the ESDP. The rich 'tool box' at the EU's disposal includes both structural long-term and direct short-term preventive actions, consisting of *inter alia* development aid, trade, arms control, human rights policies, environmental policies, political dialogue, diplomacy and capabilities for crisis management, military as well as civil (Biscop 2002).

The point is clearly expressed in the European Security Strategy (2003: 7), adopted in 2003 which states that:

> "In contrast to the massive visible threat in the Cold War, none of the new threats is purely military; nor can any be tackled by purely military means. Each requires a mixture of instruments. Proliferation may be contained through export controls and attacked through political, economic and other pressures while the underlying political causes are also tackled. Dealing

solidarity, anti-discrimination, sustainable development and good governance. EU norm diffusion is shaped by six factors: contagion, informational diffusion, procedural diffusion, transference, overt diffusion and the cultural filter (ibid.: 244-5).

with terrorism may require a mixture of intelligence, police, judicial, military and other means. In failed states, military instruments may be needed to restore order, humanitarian means to tackle the immediate crisis. Regional conflicts need political solutions but military assets and effective policing may be needed in the post conflict phase. Economic instruments serve reconstruction, and civilian crisis management helps restore civil government. The European Union is particularly well equipped to respond to such multi-faceted situations "

The EU still clearly prefers positive civilian to coercive military measures and the military instrument is an ultimate instrument, to be used only when other means have failed. When the EU is constrained to intervene militarily in the affairs of third countries, it does so according to precise ways and procedures: minimal and proportional use of armed intervention, adequate legal basis, moral authority, respect of the Geneva Convention, conformity with the EU's commitments in the field of arms control, transparency and democratic control of the intervention (Bailes 2000).

This comprehensive 'peace-management' doctrine constitutes the specificity of the EU security policy, as compared to NATO for example, and also its potential strength. It commits the EU to international rules and norms, emphasising the notion of 'effective multilateralism' and its 'diplomacy first' attitude. It induces the EU to promote human rights and pursue representative democracy, the rule of law, social justice and development, as the key objectives of its foreign policy.

Again, this is not simply the result of the EU's lack of military capabilities and Kagan's psychology of 'power and weakness'. Rather, it is largely due to the 'uniqueness' and 'post-modern' nature of the EU as an experiment in reconciliation, to its reliance on a method of political coordination based on the search for consensus and problem-solving strategies, and to the fact that its foreign and security policies are based on a process of 'institutionalisation of cooperation' (Bono 2004: 396).

12.5. Conclusion

Europe's aura of a 'civilian power' was certainly compromised by the deepening of the ESDP and the acquisition of greater military capabilities. However, the distinctive feature of the EU's international civilising identity will prevent any sudden, involuntary and drastic transformation of the EU into a traditional great power. The EU can be seen as an international actor *sui generis*: no longer a civil power in the narrow sense, but neither a classic military power. To paraphrase Robert Kagan (2003), the EU locates itself halfway between Mars and Venus, between Hobbes' bellicose world and the post-modern dream of Kant, though maintaining a certain preference for the pacific vision of the philosopher from Kaliningrad.

The EU's decision to equip itself with military capabilities not only seems justified but in some ways also inevitable, given that the EU avowedly aspires to become a credible international actor. Only when having at its disposition the entire range of instruments of coercion and international action can the EU acquire the necessary credibility to effectively exert influence over global affairs. The EU will have acquired full international legitimacy only when it will be able to play a *non-marginal* role in the effective management of emergencies and acute international military crises (Telò 2005: 207).

The developments of the ESDP testify to the great potentials of a European security and defence policy. The road taken leads in the right direction, but it is necessary to proceed with conviction and a stronger commitment in order to avoid the paradoxical risk, highlighted by Reinhardt Rummel (2002: 454), that the EU, by having compromised its image as a civil power while remaining weak militarily, may actually weaken instead of strengthen its position and international credibility.

List of References

Ackerman, B. (1980), Social *Justice in the Liberal State*. New Haven: Yale University Press.

Allum, P. (1973), *Politics and* Society *in Post-War Naples*. Cambridge: Cambridge University Press

Andersen, S. & K. A. Eliassen, eds. (1996), *The European Union: How Democratic Is It?* London: Sage.

Andeweg, R. (1996), "Elite-Mass Linkages in Europe: Legitimacy Crisis or Party Crisis?" In: Jack Hayward ed., *Elitism, Populism and European Politics*. Oxford: Clarendon Press.

Andeweg, R. (1999), "Towards Representation Ex Alto-Ex Post? Political Representation Between Individualisation and Europeanisation". Paper presented at the workshop on "Multi-level Party Systems: Europeanisation and the Reshaping of National Political Representation", *European University Institute, Florence*, December 16-18.

Apel, K.O. (2000), "Globalization and the Need for Universal Ethics: The Problem in Light of Discourse Ethics", *European Journal of Social Theory*, 3 (2), 137-55.

Archibugi, D. (1995), *Cosmopolitan Democracy: An Agenda for a New World Order*. Cambridge: Polity Press.

Archibugi, D., D. Held and M. Köhler, eds. (1998), *Re-imagining Political Community*. Cambridge: Polity Press.

Aristotle (1981), *The Politics (Revised Edition)*. Harmondsworth: Penguin Classics.

Armstrong, K.A. (1998), "Legal Integration: Theorizing the Legal Dimension of European Integration", *Journal of Common Market Studies*, 36: 155-174.

Aspinwall, M. (1998), "Planes,Ttrains, and Automobiles: Transport Governance in the European Union", in B. Kohler-Koch, ed, *The Transformation of Governance in the European Union*. London: Routledge.

Axelrod, R. (1984), *The Evolution of Cooperation*, New York: Basic Books.

Bache, I. & M. Flinders eds. (2004), *Multi-Level Governance*. Oxford: Oxford University Press.

Bader, V. (1997), "The Cultural Conditions of Transnational Citizenship. On the Interpenetration of Political and Ethnic Cultures", *Political Theory* 25 (6): 771-813.

Baier, K. (1989), "Justice and the Aims of Political Philosophy." *Ethics* 99: 771-90.

Bailes, A. J. K. (2000), "European Defence: Another Set of Questions", *The RUSI Journal*, 145 (1): 1-40.

Balibar, E. (1991). "Is there a Neo-Racism?", in: I Wallerstein, ed., *Race, Nation, Class: Ambiguous Identities*. London: Verso.

Balibar, E. (2004), *We the People of Europe: Reflections on Transnational Citizenship*. Princeton: Princeton University Press.

Banchoff, T. & M. P. Smith, eds. (1996), *Legitimacy and the European Union*. London: Routledge.

Banuri, T. & J.B. Schor, eds. (1992), *Financial Openness and National Autonomy*, Oxford: Oxford University Press.

Barbalet, J. M. (1992), *Cittadinanza: Diritti Conflitto e Disuguaglianza Sociale*. Padova: Liviana.

Barber, B. (1984), *Strong Democracy. Participatory Politics for a New Age*. New York: basic Books.

Bardi, L. (1987), *Representation in the European Parliament*. Baltimore: Johns Hopkins University.

Barry, B. (1989), *Theories of Justice. A Treatise on Social Justice, 1*. Berkeley: University of California Press.

Barry, B. (1991), "Is Democracy Special?", in: B. Barry, *Essays in Political Theory 1*. Oxford: Oxford University Press.

Bartholomew, A. (2000), "Constitutional Patriotism and Social Inclusiveness: Justice for Immigrants?", paper presented to the *Exeter Colloquium on Constitutionalism and Democracy*, 24-25 November 2000.

Bauböck, R. (1994a), "Changing the Boundaries of Citizenship", in: R. Baubock, ed., *From Aliens to Citizens*. Avebury: Aldershot.

Bauböck, R. (1994b). *Transnational Citizenship: Membership and Rights in International Migration*. Aldershot, Elgar.

Bauböck, R. (1997), "Citizenship and National Identities in the European Union", *Harvard Jean Monnet Chair Working Papers* , 4.

Bauböck, R. (1999), "National Community, Citizenship and Cultural Diversity", *Institute for Advanced Studies, Vienna. Political Science Series*, 62.

Bauman, Z. (2002), *Modernità Liquida*. Roma- Bari: Laterza.

Beck, U (2000), "The Cosmopolitan Perspective: Sociology of the Second Age of Modernity", *British Journal of Sociology*, 51 (1), 79-105.

Beck, U. & E. Grande (2004), *Das kosmopolitische Europa*. Frankfurt: Suhrkamp.

Becker, L. C. (1996), Trust as Noncognitive Security about Motives", *Ethics* 107: 43-61.

Beetham, D. & C. Lord (1998), *Legitimacy in the European Union*. London: Longman.

Beja Horta, A.P. (2004), *Contested Citizenship: Immigration Politics and Grassroots Migrants' Organizations in Post-Colonial Portugal.*. New York: Center for Migration Studies.

Bellamy, R. & A. Warleigh, (1998), "From and Ethics of Integration to an Ethics of Participation: Citizenship and the Future of the European Union." *Millennium* 27(3): 447-470.

Bellamy, R. (1999), *Liberalism and Pluralism. Towards a Politics of Compromise*. London: Routledge.

Bellamy, R. (2001), "The `Right to have Rights': Citizenship Practice and the Political Constitution of the European Union." *ESRC "One Europe or Several?" Programme Working Paper* 25/01.

Bellamy, R., D. Castiglione & E. Santoro, eds. (2004), *Lineages of European Citizenship: Rights, Belonging and Participation in Eleven Nation-States*. London: Palgrave.

Benevolo, L. (1993), *The European City*. Blackwell, Oxford

Bennington, J. & J. Harvey (1994), "Spheres or Tiers? The Significance of Transnational Local Authority Networks", Conference paper, *PSA Annual Conference*, University of Swansea, March 29-31, 1994.

Beyers, J. & G. Dierickx (1998), "The Working Groups of the Council of the European Union: Supranational or Intergovernmental Negotiations?", *Journal of Common Market Studies* 36, 289-317.

Beyers, J. (1998), "Where Does Supra-Nationalism Come From? Ideas Floating Through the Working Groups of the Council of the European Union", *European Integration online Papers*, 2:http://eiop.or.at/eiop/texte/1998-009a.htm.

206

Biscop, S. (2002), "In Search of a Strategic Concept for the ESDP", *European Foreign Affairs Review*, 7 (4), 473-90.

Biscop, S. (2004), "Able and Willing? Assessing the EU's Capacity for Military Action", *European Foreign Affairs Review*, 9(4), 509-27.

Blum, H. (2002), "The Republican Mirror: The Dutch Idea of Europe" in A. Pagden, ed., *The Idea of Europe: From Antiquity to the European Union*, Cambridge: Cambridge University Press.

Böckenförde, E. W. (1991), *Demokratie und Repräsentation in Staat, Verfassung, Demokratie.* Frankfurt a.M.: Suhrkamp.

Bogdanor, V. (1996), "The European Union, The Political Class and the People." In: Jack Hayward ed. *Elitism, Populism and European Politics*. Oxford: Clarendon Press.

Bohman, J. & M. Lutz-Bachmann, eds. (1997), *Perpetual Peace: Essays on Kant's Cosmopolitan Ideal*, Cambridge, MA: MIT Press.

Bono, G. (2004), "Introduction: The Role of the EU in External Crisis Management", in: G. Bono & S. Ulriksen, eds., "The EU, Crisis Management and Peace Support Operations", *International Peacekeeping* 11 (3), (special issue, Autumn 2004), 395-404.

Börzel, T.A. (1997), "Policy Networks – A New Paradigm for European Governance?", *Working Paper EUI*, RSC 97/19.

Braithwaite, V. & M. Levi, eds. (1998), *Trust and Governance*. New York: Russell Sage.

Braudel, F. (1975), *The Mediterranean and the Mediterranean World in the Age of Philip II.* London: Fontana/Collins.

Breckenridge, C.A. et al, eds. (2002), *Cosmopolitanism*, Durham, NJ: Duke University Press.

Brennan, T. (1997), *At Home in the World: Cosmopolitanism Now*, Cambridge, MA: Harvard University Press.

Bresser-Pereira, J.C. (2002), "Citizenship and Res Publica: The Emergence of Republican Rights", *Citizenship Studies*, 6(2): 145-164.

Breton, R. (1995), "Identification in Transnational Political Communities", in: K. Knop, S. Ostry, R. Simeon & K. Swinton, eds., *Rethinking Federalism: Citizens, Markets, and Governments in a Changing World*. Vancouver: British Columbia Press.

Brodie, J. (2004), "Globalization and Citizenship Beyond the National State", *Citizenship Studies* 8(4): 323-332.

Brubaker, W. R. (1997), *Cittadinanza e Nazionalità in Francia e Germania*. Bologna: Il Mulino.

Bukowski, J., S. Piattoni & M. Smyrl, eds. (2003), *Between Europeanization and Local Societies. The Space for Territorial Governance*. Lanham, MD: Rowman and Littlefield.

Bull, H. (1982), "Civilian Power Europe: A Contradiction in Terms", *Journal of Common Market Studies*, 21 (2): 149-64.

Bullman, U. ed. (1996), "The Politics of the Third Level." Special edited issue of *Regional and Federal Studies*, 6(3), 3-219.

Burgel, G. (1970 & 1972), *La conditionIindustrielle a Athenes*, vol. I & II. Athens: EKKE.

Burin, F. S. & K. L. Shell, eds. (1969), *Politics, Law and Social Change: Selected Essays of Otto Kirchheimer*. New York: Columbia University Press.

Butler, D. & A. Ranney, eds. (1994), *Referendums around the World: The Growing Use of Direct Democracy*. London: Macmillan.

Calabi, D. (1984), "Italy". in: M. Wynn, M., ed., *Planning and Urban growth in Southern Europe*. London: Mansell.

Callow, A.N. Jr., ed. (1973), *American Urban History: an Interpretative Reader with Commentaries,* 2nd edn., New York: Oxford University Press.

Canovan, M. (2000), "Patriotism is Not Enough", *British Journal of Political Science*, 30: 413-432.

Carens, J. (2000), *Culture, Citizenship and Community. A Contextual Exploration of Justice as Evenhandedness*. Oxford: Oxford University Press.

Carter, F. W. (1968), "Population Migration to Greater Athens", *Tijdschrift voor Economische en Sociale Geografie*, 59(2): 100-5.

Castells, M. (1996), *The Rise of the Network Society*. Blackwell: Oxford.

Castiglione, D. (2004), "Reflections on Europe's Constitutional Future", *Constellations*, 11 (3): 393-411.

Castiglione, D., & R. Bellamy (1998), "Between Cosmopolis and Community: Three Models of Rights and Democracy within the European Union", in: D. Archibugi, D. Held & M. Köhler, eds., *Re-Imagining Political Community: Studies in Cosmopolitan Democracy*. Cambridge: Polity Press.

Cesarani, D. & M. Fulbrook, eds. (1996), *Citizenship, Nationality and Migration in Europe*, London: Routledge.

Chalmers, D. (2003), "'Food for Thought": Reconciling European Risks and Traditional Ways of Life", *Modern Law Review*, 66 (4): 532-562.

Charlot, J. (1996), "From Representative to Responsive Government?", in: J. Hayward, ed., *Elitism, Populism and European Politics*. Oxford: Clarendon Press.

Cheah, P. & B. Robbins, eds. (1996), *Cosmopolitics: Thinking and Feeling Beyond the Nation*, Minneapolis: Minnesota University Press.

Checkel, J. (1999), "Social Construction and Integration", *Journal of European Public Policy*, 6, 545-60.

Checkel, J. (2001), "Why Comply? Social Learning and European Identity Change", *International Organization* 55: 553-588.

Choudhry, S. (2001), "Citizenship and Federations: Some Preliminary Reflections", in: K. Nicolaidis & R. Howse, eds., *The Federal Vision: Legitimacy and Levels of Governance in the US and the EU*. Oxford: Oxford University Press.

Christiansen, T. & S. Piattoni, eds. (2004), *Informal Governance in the European Union*. Cheltenham: Edward Elgar.

Cipolla, C. M. (1980), *Before the Industrial Revolution: European Society and Economy, 1000-1700*. London: W. W. Norton & Co.

Closa, C. (1992), "The Concept of Citizenship in the Treaty on European Union", *Common Market Law Review* 29: 1137-69.

Closa, C. (1998), "Supranational Citizenship and Democracy: Normative and Empirical Dimensions.", in: M. La Torre, ed., *European Citizenship: an Institutional Challenge*, Dordrecht: Kluwer Law.

Cohen, J. (1999), "Changing Paradigms of Citizenship and the Exclusiveness of the Demos", *International Sociology* 14 (3): 245-268.

Coleman, J. (1990),. *Foundations of Social Theory*. Cambridge: Harvard University Press.

Commission of the European Communities (2001), *European Governance. A White Paper* (*http://europa.eu.int/eur-lex/en/com/cnc/2001/com2001_0428en01.pdf*)

Constant, B. (1819), *De la Liberté Chez les Modernes*, Edited by M. Gauchet, ed. Paris: Pluriel.

Conzelmann, T. (1995), "Networking and the Politics of EU Regional Policy: Lessons from North Rhine-Westphalia, Nord-Pas de Calais and North West England", *Regional & Federal Studies*, 5: 134-172.

Corbett, R., F. Jacobs & M. Shackleton (2005), *The European Parliament*. 6th ed. London: John Harper Publishers.

Cotta, M., P. Isernia & L. Verzichelli, eds. (2005), *L'Europa in Italia. Elite, Opinione Pubblica e Decisioni*. Bologna: Il Mulino.

Couch, C., L. Leontidou & G. Petchel-Held, eds. (2007), *Urban Sprawl in Europe: Landscapes Land Use Change, and Policy*. Blackwell, Oxford

Council of the European Union (2004), "Treaty Establishing a Constitution for Europe", Vol. 47. *Official Journal of the European Union* 2004/C 310/01.

Cowan, J.K., M.B. Dembour & R.A. Wilson, eds. (2001), *Culture and Rights: Anthropological Perspectives,* Cambridge: Cambridge University Press.

Cox, R. (1997), "Democracy in Hard Times: Economic Globalization and the Limits to Liberal Democracy", in A. McGrew, ed., *The Transformation of Democracy? Globalization and Territorial Democracy*. Cambridge: Polity Press.

Craig, P. (1999), "The Nature of the Community: Integration, Democracy, and Legitimacy", in P. Craig & G. de Búrca, eds. (1999), *The Evolution of EU Law*. Oxford: Oxford University Press, 1-54.

Cronin, C. (2003), "Democracy and Collective Identity: In Defence of Constitutional Patriotism", *European Journal of Philosophy*, 11(1): 1-28.

Crouch, C. (1993), *Industrial Relations and European State Traditions*. Oxford: Clarendon Press.

Crouch, C., K. Eder, et al., eds. (2001), *Citizenship Markets and the State*. Oxford: Oxford University Press.

Dagger, R. (1997), *Civic Virtues: Rights, Citizenship and Republican Liberalism*, New York and Oxford: Oxford University Press.

Dahl, R. A. (1989), *Democracy and its Critics*. New Haven, Yale University Press.

Dalton, R. J. & M. P. Wattenberg (2000), *Parties without Partisans. Political Change in Advanced Industrial Democracies*. Oxford: Oxford University Press.

Dalton, R. J. (2004), *Democratic Challenges, Democratic Choices. The Erosion of Political Support in Advanced Industrial Democracies*. Oxford: Oxford University Press.

Dalton, R. J. (2006), *Citizen Politics. Public Opinion and Political Parties in Advanced Industrial Democracies*. Washington DC: CQ Press.

De Búrca, G. (1999), "The Institutional Development of the European Union: A Constitutional Analysis", in P. Craig & G. de Búrca, eds., *The Evolution of EU Law*, Oxford: Oxford University Press, 55-82.

De Greiff, Pablo (2000), "Habermas on Nationalism and Cosmopolitanism." *Ratio Juris*, 15: 418-438.

De Las Casas, Bartolomé (1999) [1543], *Brevísima Relación de la Destrucción de las Indias: Primera Edición Crítica,* ed. by I. Pérez Fernández, O.P. Madrid: Punto Print, S.L.

de Wijk, R. (2003), "European Military Reform for a Global Partnership", *The Washington Quarterly*, 27 (1): 197-210.

Dehousse, R. (1997), "Regulation by Networks in the European Community: the Role of European agencies", *Journal of European Public Policy*, 4: 246-261.

Delanty, G. (1995), *Inventing Europe, Idea, Identity, Reality*. Basingstoke: Macmillan.

Delanty, G. (1996), "Habermas and Post-National Identity: Theoretical Perspectives on the Conflict in Northern Ireland", *Irish Political Studies*, 11: 20-32.

Delanty, G. (2000), *Citizenship in a Global Age*. Buckingham: Open University Press.

209

Della Seta, P. (1978), "Notes on Urban Struggles in Italy", *International Journal of Urban and Regional Research*, 2: 303-29.

Demand, N.H. (1970), *Urban Relocation in Archaic and Classical Greece: Flight and Consolidation*. University of Oklahoma Press, Norman

Derrida, J. & J. Habermas (2003), "Europe: Plaidoyer Pour une Politique Extérieure Commune", *Libération*, 31, (May 2003),: 44-46.

Deutsch, K., S. A. Burrell, R. A. Kann, M. Jr. Lee, M. Lichtermann, F. L. Loewenheim, & R. W. Van Wagenen (1957), *Political Community and the North Atlantic Area*. Princeton, NJ: Princeton University Press.

Donati, P. & I. Colozzi (2004), *Il Privato Sociale Che Emerge: Realtà e Dilemmi*, Bologna: Il Mulino.

Douglass, M. & J. Friedmann, eds. (1998), Cities for Citizens: Planning and the Rise of Civil Society in the Global Age .London: Wiley.

Dowding, K. (1995), "Model or Metaphor? A Critical Review of the Policy Network Approach", *Political Studies*, 43: 36-158.

Doxiadis, K. et al (1976), *Regional Plan and Programme of the Greater Athens Area*, vols I & II. Athens: Ministry of Coordination and Programming. [Δοξιάδης, Κ. & συνεργάτες (1976), Χωροταξικό Σχέδιο και Πρόγραμμα Περιοχής Πρωτευούσης, τόμοι Ι και ΙΙ. Αθήνα: Υπουργείο Συντονισμού και Προγραμματισμού.]

Duchêne, F. (1972), "Europe's Role in World Peace", in R. Mayne, ed., *Europe Tomorrow: Sixteen Europeans Look Ahead*. London: Fontana.

Duchêne, F. (1973), "The European Community and the Uncertainties of Interdependence", in: M. Kohnstamm & W. Hager, eds., *A Nation Writ Large? Foreign-Policy Problems before the European Community*. London: Macmillan.

Eder, K. & B. Giesen, eds. (2001), *European Citizenship: National Legacies and Transnational Projects*, Oxford: Oxford University Press.

Egeberg, M, & J. Trondal. (1999), "Differentiated Integration in Europe: the Case of the EEA Country Norway", *Journal of Common Market Studies* 37(1): 133-42.

Egeberg, M. & H. Sætren (1999), "Identities in Complex Organizations: A Study of Ministerial Bureaucrats", in: M. Egeberg & P. Lægreid, eds., *Organizing Political Institutions*, Oslo: Scandinavian University Press.

Egeberg, M. (1999), "Transcending Intergovernmentalism? Identity and Role Perceptions of National Officials in EU Decision-Making", *Journal of European Public Policy* 6(3): 456-74.

Egeberg, M. (2004), "An Organisational Approach to European Integration: Outline of a Complementary Perspective", *European Journal of Political Research* 43: 199-219.

Egeberg, M., G. Schaefer & J. Trondal (2003), "The Many Faces of EU Committee Governance", *West European Politics*, 26: 19-40.

Ehrenberg, J. (1999), *Civil Society: The Critical History of an Idea*, New York: New York University Press.

Elias, N. (1970), *What is Sociology?*, London: Hutchinson.

Elster, J. (1989), *The Cement of Society. Studies in Rationality and Social Change*. Cambridge: Cambridge University Press.

Esaiasson, P. & S. Holmberg (1996), *Representation from Above. Members of Parliament and Representative Democracy in Sweden*. Aldershot: Darthmouth.

European Commission (2002). *Towards a Reinforced Culture of Consultation and Dialogue - General Principles and Minimum Standards for Consultation of Interested Parties by the Commission.* COM (2002) 704.

European Economic and Social Committee (1991), *The Role and Contribution of Civil Society Organisations in the Building of Europe* (*http://www.eesc.europa.eu/sco/docs/ces851-1999_ac_en.PDF*)

Falk, R. (1996), "Revisioning Cosmopolitanism", in M.C. Nussbaum & J. Cohen, eds., *For Love of Country: Debating the Limits of Patriotism*, Boston:Beacon Press.

Ferguson, A. (2001) [1767], *An Essay on the History of Civil Society*, ed. F. Oz-Salzberger, Cambridge: Cambridge University Press

Ferry, J. M. (1992a), "Une "Philosophie" de la Communauté", *Esprit*, 176: 80-93.

Ferry, J. M. (1992b), "Une "Philosophie" de la Communauté", in J. M. Ferry & P. Thibaud, eds., *Discussion sur l'Europe*. Paris: Calmann-Lévy.

Ferry, J. M. (1992c), "Identité et Citoyenneté Européenne. A propos du Sommet de Maastricht", in: J. Lenoble & N. Dewandre, eds., *L'Europe au Soir du Siècle. Identité et Démocratie.* Paris: Esprit.

Ferry, J. M. (1992d), "Pertinence du Postnational", in:. J. Lenoble & N. Dewandre, eds., *L'Europe au Soir du Siècle. Identité et Démocratie.* Paris: Esprit.

Ferry, J. M. (2000), *La Question de l'Etat Européen*. Paris: Gallimard.

Filippov, M., P. C. Ordeshook, & O. Shvetsova (2004), *Designing Federalism: A Theory of Self-Sustainable Federal Institutions*. Cambridge: Cambridge University Press.

Fine, R. (2003), "Taking the "Ism" out of Cosmopolitanism", *European Journal of Social Theory*, 6 (4): 451-70.

Fitoussi, J.P. (2005), "Les Piètres Performances de la Zone Euro", *Le Monde*, January 2-3, 2005.

Follesdal, A, & S. Hix (2005), "Why There is a Democratic Deficit in the EU: A Response to Majone and Moravcsik." *European Governance Papers* 1, 2.

Follesdal, A. (1998), "Subsidiarity." *Journal of Political Philosophy* 6(2): 231-59.

Follesdal, A. (1999), "Third Country Nationals As Euro-Citizens - the Case Defended " in : D. Smith &. Wright, eds., *Whose Europe? The Turn Towards Democracy*. London: Blackwell.

Follesdal, A. (2000), "The Future Soul of Europe: Nationalism or Just Patriotism? On David Miller's Defence of Nationality", *Journal of Peace Research* 37(4): 503-18.

Follesdal, A. (2001), "Federal Inequality among Equals: A Contractualist Defense", *Metaphilosophy*: 236-55.

Follesdal, A. (2001b), "Union Citizenship: Unpacking the Beast of Burden." *Law and Philosophy* 20: 313-343.

Follesdal, A. (2002), "Constructing a European Civic Society: Vaccination for Trust in a Fair, Multi-Level Europe", *Studies in East European Thought* 54: 303-24.

Follesdal, A. (2003), "Federalism", in: E. N. Zalta, ed., *Stanford Encyclopedia of Philosophy* - http://plato.stanford.edu/entries/federalism/.

Follesdal, A. (2004), "Liberal Contractualism - Partial and Particularist, Impartial and Cosmopolitan", in:. S Caney & P. Lehning, eds., *International Justice*. London: Routledge.

Follesdal, A. (2005), "Towards a *Stable* Federal Finalité? Forms and Arenas of Institutional and National Balances in the Constitutional Treaty for Europe", *Journal of European Public Policy - Special Issue: Towards a Federal Europe?* 12(3): 572-89.

Follesdal, A. (2006), "The Legitimacy Deficits of the European Union." *Journal of Political Philosophy*: 14(4):441-468.

Franck, T. M. (1968), "Why Federations Fail", in: T. M. Franck, ed., *Why Federations Fail: An Inquiry into the Requisites for Successful Federalism*. New York: New York University Press.

211

Frankenfeld, P. (1992), "Technological Citizenship: A Normative Framework for Risk Studies" *Science and Technology and Human Values*, 17(4).

Fried, R. C. (1973), Planning *the Eternal City: Roman Politics and Planning since World War II.* London: Yale University Press.

Friedmann, J. & M. Douglass (1998), " Editors' Introduction", in: M. Douglass. & J. Friedmann, eds., *Cities for Citizens: Planning and the Rise of Civil Society in the Global Age*. London: Wiley.

Friese, H. & P. Wagner (2002), "The Nascent Political Philosophy of the European Polity", *The Journal of Political Philosophy*, 10(3): 342-64.

Gabert, P. (1958), "L'Immigration Italienne à Turin", *Bulletin de l'Association de Géographes Français*, 276-277:. 30-45.

Galtung, J. (1973), *The European Community: A Superpower in the Making*, London: George Allen and Unwin.

Garcia, S. (1993), "Local Economic Policies and Social Citizenship in Spanish Cities. *Antipode*, 25: 191-205.

Garcia, S. ed. (1993), *European Identity and the Search for Legitimacy*. London: Pinter Publishers.

Garret, G. & P. Lange (1991), "Political Responses to Interdependence: What's 'Left' for the Left?", *International Organization*, 45 (4): ⦂ 539-564.

George, M.D. (1966), *London Llife in the Eighteenth Century*. Harmondsworth: Penguin.

Ghirardo, D.A. (1980), The Mezzanotte in the Mezzogiorno: The Urban Problems of Southern Italy. *Journal of Urban History*, 6(2): 221-30.

Giddens, A. (1991), *Modernity and Self-identity: Self and Society in the Late Modern Age*. Oxford: Polity Press.

Giner, S. & T. Montagut (2005), "Cosa Pública, Cosa Privada: Hacia una Teoría del Tercer Sector", in: J.L. García Delgado, ed., *La Economía Social en España*, Madrid: Fundación Once.

Giner, S. (1976), *Mass Society*, London: Martin Robertson; New York: Academic Press.

Giner, S. (1978), "Clase, Poder y Privilegio en la Sociedad Corporativa", *Ensayos Civiles*, Barcelona: Península.

Giner, S. (1985), "Political Economy, Legitimation and the State in Southern Europe', in: R. Hudson & J. Lewis, eds., *Uneven Development in Southern Europe: Studies of Accumulation, Class, Migration and the State*. London: Methuen.

Giner, S. (1994), "Lo Privado Público: Altruyismo y Politeya Democrática", *Doxa*, 15.16: 161-178.

Giner, S. (2000), "Cultura Republicana y Política del Porvenir", in: S. Giner, ed., *La Cultura de la Democrazia*. Barcelona: Ariel.

Giner, S. (2005), "Ciudadanía Pública y Sociedad Civil Republicana", *Documentación Social* 139 (Oct.-Dec.): 13-35.

Gnesotto, N. ed. (2004), *EU Security and Defence Policy: the First five Years (1999-2004)*, Paris: EU Institute for Security Studies.

Goodin, R. E. (1988), *Reasons for Welfare: the Political Theory of the Welfare State*. Princeton N.J.: Princeton University Press.

Goodin, R. E. (1992), *Motivating Political Morality*. Oxford: Blackwell.

Goodin, R. E. (1996), "Institutionalizing the Public Interest: The Defense of Deadlock and Beyond", *American Political Science Review* 90(2): 331-43.

Goodsell, C. T. (1988), *The Social Meaning of Civic Space. Studying Political Authority through Architecture*. Lawrence: University Press of Kansas.

212

Gramsci, A. (1971), *Selections from the Prison Notebooks*. New York: International Publishers.

Gramsci, A. (1994), *Pre-Prison Writings*. Cambridge: Cambridge University Press.

Gray, J. (1996), *After Social Democracy*, London: Demos.

Grimm, D. (1995), "Does Europe Need a Constitution?", *European Law Journal* 1(3): 282-302.

Guild, E. (1996), "The Legal Framework of Citizenship of the European Union", in: D. Cesarani, & M. Fulbrook, eds., *Citizenship, Nationality and Migration in Europe*. London: Routledge.

Gulick, L. (1937), "Notes on the Theory of Organization. With Special Reference to Government", in: L. Gulick & L. Urwick, eds., *Papers on the Science of Administration*, New York: Institute of Public Administration, Columbia University.

Gunsteren, H. van (1988), "Admission to Citizenship." *Ethics*: 731-41.

Haas, P.M. (1992), "Introduction: Epistemic Communities and International Policy Coordination", *International Organization*, 46(1): 1-35.

Habermas, J. (1989), *The New Conservatism. Cultural Criticism and the Historians' Debate*. Boston MA: MIT Press.

Habermas, J. (1990), "Historical Consciousness and Post-Traditional Identity", in: J. Habermas, ed., *The New Conservatism: Cultural Criticism and the Historians' Debate*. Cambridge MA: MIT Press.

Habermas, J. (1992), "Citizenship and National Identity: Some Reflections on the Future of Europe", *Praxis International*, 12(1): 1-19.

Habermas, J. (1993), "Struggles for Recognition in the Democratic Constitutional State." *European Journal of Philosophy* 1 (2): 128-155.

Habermas, J. (1994), "Struggles for Recognition in the Democratic Constitutional State", in A. Gutmann ed., *Multiculturalism: Examining the Politics of Recognition*, Princeton N.J.: Princeton University Press.

Habermas, J. (1996a), "The European Nation-State - its Achievements and its Limits", in: G. Balakrishnan, ed., *Mapping the Nation*. London: Verso.

Habermas, J. (1996b), *Between Facts and Norms: Contributions to a Discourse Theory of Law and Democracy*. Cambridge MA: Polity Press.

Habermas, J. (1998a), "Does Europe Need a Constitution? Remarks on Dieter Grimm ", in: J. Habermas, *The Inclusion of the Other: Studies in Political Theory*. Cambridge, MA.: MIT Press.

Habermas, J. (1998b), "Un Débat sur *Droit et Démocratie*", in: J. Habermas, ed., *L'intégration Républicaine. Essais de Théorie Politique*, Paris: Fayard.

Habermas, J. (1998c), *Die postnationale Konstellation. Politische Essays*, Frankfurt a. M.: Suhrkamp.

Habermas, J. (1998d), *The Inclusion of the Other: Studies in Political Theory*, Cambridge MA: MIT Press.

Habermas, J. (1999), "Citizenship and National Identity. Some Reflections on the Future of Europe", in: R. Beiner ed., *Theorizing Citizenship*, New York: State University of New York Press.

Habermas, J. (2001a), "Why Europe Needs a Constitution", *New Left Review*, 11: 5-26.

Habermas, J. (2001b), *The Postnational Constellation*, Cambridge: Polity Press.

Haine, J. Y. (2004), "ESDP: An Historical Perspective", in: N. Gnesotto ed., *EU Security and Defence Policy: the First five Years (1999-2004)*. Paris: EU Institute for Security Studies.

Hale, J. (1993), "The Renaissance Idea of Europe", in: S. Garcia, ed., *European Identity and the Search for Legitimacy*. London: Pinter Publishers.

Hall, J. A. & F. Trentmann, eds. (2005), *Civil Society :Reader in History ,Theory and Global Politics*, New York: Palgrave Macmillan.

Hall, J. A., ed. (1995), *"Civil Society: Theory, History, Comparison*, Cambridge: Polity.

Hansen, R. & P. Weil (2001), *Towards a European Nationality: Citizenship, Immigration, and Nationality Law in the EU*. London: Palgrave.

Hardoy, J. E. (1973), *Pre-Columbian Cities*. New York: Walker.

Harris, J. (2004), "Nationality, Rights and Virtue: Some Approaches to Citizenship in Great Britain", In: R. Bellamy, D. Castiglione &. E. Santaro,. eds., *Lineages of European Citizenship*. London: Palgrave.

Hasenteufel, P. (1995), "Do Policy Networks Matter? Lifting Descriptif et Analyse de l'Etat en interaction", in: P. Le Galès & M. Thatcher, eds., *Les Réseaux de Politique Publique. Débat Autour des Policy Networks*. Paris: L'Harmattan.

Hayes-Renshaw, F. & H. Wallace (1997), *The Council of Ministers*, New York: St Martin's Press.

Hayward, J., ed. (1996), *Elitism, Populism and European Politics*. Oxford: Clarendon Press.

Heath, J. (1995), "Review Essay: Habermas and Speech-Act Theory", *Philosophy and Social Criticism* 21(4): 141-7.

Heather, D. (1990), *Citizenship: The Civic Ideal in World History*. London: Longman.

Hegel, G. W. F. (1991) [1807], *Phänomenologie des Geistes,* in: *Werke*, vol. 3, ed. by E. Moldenhauer & K.M. Michel. Frankfurt a.M.: Suhrkamp.

Held, D. (1995), *Democracy and the Global Order: From the Modern State to Cosmopolitan Governance*. Cambridge: Polity Press.

Held, D., A. McGrew, D. Goldblatt & J. Perraton (1999), *Global Transformations. Politics, Economics and Culture*. Cambridge: Polity.

Heritier, A. (1993), "Policy-Netzwerkanalyse als Untersuchungsinstrument im europäischen Kontext: Folgerungen aus einer empirischen Studie regulativer Politik", in: A. Heritier, ed., *Policy-Analyse. Politische Vierteljahresschrift*, Sonderheft 24. Opladen: Westdeutscher Verlag.

Hindess, B. (1998), "Divide and Rule: The International Character of Modern Citizenship" *European Journal of Social Theory*, 1(1), 57-70.

Hix, S (1999), "Voters, Party Leaders and the Dimensionality of EU Politics." Paper presented at the workshop on "Multi-level Party Systems: Europeanisation and the Reshaping of National Political Representation", *European University Institute, Florence*, December 16-18.

Hix, S, & C. Lord (1997), *Political Parties in the European Union*. London: Macmillan.

Hix, S. & K. Goetz, eds. (2001), *Europeanised Politics? European Integration and National Political Systems*. London: Frank Cass.

Hobbes, T. (1997) [1651], *Leviathan, or the Matter, Forme, and Power of a Commonwealth, Ecclesiastical and Civil*, ed. by R. E. Flathman & D. Johnston. New York – London: W. W. Norton & Company.

Hooghe, L. & G. Marks (1997), "Contending Models of Governance in the European Union", in: A.W. Cafruny & C. Lankowski, eds., *Europe's Ambiguous Unity. Conflict and Consensus in the Post-Maastricht Era*. Boulder: Lynne Rienner.

Hooghe, L. & G. Marks (2001), *Multi-Level Governance and European Integration*. Lanham MD: Rowman & Littlefield.

Hooghe, L. & G. Marks (2003), "Unravelling the Central State, but How? Types of Multi-Level Governance", *American Political Science Review* 97(2): 233-243.

Hooghe, L. ed. (1996), *Cohesion Policy and European Integration: Building Multilevel Governance*. Oxford: Oxford University Press.

214

Howorth, J. (2003), "Saint Malo plus Five: An Interim Assessment of ESDP", *Notre Europe Policy Paper*, 7, Paris.

Hudson, R. & J. Lewis, eds. (1985), *Uneven Development in Southern Europe: Studies of Accumulation, Class, Migration and the State*. London: Methuen.

Hume, D. (1882) [1754], "Idea of a Perfect Commonwealth", in: D. Hume, *Essays Moral, Political and Literary*. London: Longmans, Green.

Hutchings, K. & R. Dannreuther (1999), *Cosmopolitan Citizenship*. London: Macmillan.

Hyde-Price, A. (2004), "The EU, Power and Coercion: From "Civilian" to "Civilising" Power", *CIDEL Workshop*, Oslo 22-23 October 2004.

Ingram, A. (1996), "Constitutional Patriotism", *Philosophy and Social Criticism* 22 (6): 1-18.

Isin, E. & B. Turner, eds. (2002), *Handbook of Citizenship Studies*. London: Sage.

Isin, E. & P. Wood (1999), *Citizenship and Identity*. London: Sage.

Jachtenfuchs, M. (1997), "Democracy and Governance in the European Union", *European Integration online Papers (EioP)*, 1(2). *http://eiop.or.at/eiop/texte/1997-002a.htm*

Jacobsen, D. (1997), *Rights across Borders: Immigration and the Decline of Citizenship*. Baltimore, MD: Johns Hopkins University Press.

Jacobsson, B. (1999), "Europeiseringen och Statens Omvandling", in: K. Goldmann, J. Hallenberg, B. Jacobsson, U. Mörth & A. Robertson, *Politikens Internationalisering*, Lund: Studentlitteratur.

Janoski, T. (1998). *Citizenship and Civil Society*. Cambridge: Cambridge University Press.

Jeffery, C. & D. Hough (2001), "The Electoral Cycle and Multi-Level Voting in Germany", *German Politics*, Vol. 1082): 73-98.

Jeffery, C. (n.d.): "Equity and Diversity. Devolution, Social Citizenship and Territorial Culture in the UK", *ESRC Devolution Programme*, Institute for German Studies, University of Birmingham.

Jensen-Butler, C., A. Shakhar & J. van den Weesep, eds. (1996), *European Cities in Competition*. Avebury: Aldershot

Jepperson, R., A. Wendt & P. J. Katzenstein (1996), "Norms, Identity and Culture in National Security", in P. J. Katzenstein ed., *The Culture of National Security: Norms and Identities in World Politics*, New York: Columbia University Press.

Joerges, C. & J. Neyer (1997), "Transforming Strategic Interaction into Deliberative Problem-Solving: European Comitology in the Foodstuffs Sector", *Journal of European Public Policy*, 4: 609-625.

Joerges, C., Y.Mény, & J. H. H. Weiler, eds. (2000), "What Kind of Constitution for What Kind of Polity? Responses to Joschka Fischer." *Badia Fiesolana: European University Institute*, http://www.iue.it/RSC/symposium/.

Jones, E. (1990), *Metropolis: The World's Great Cities*. Oxford: Oxford University Press.

Joppke, C. (2005), 'Exclusion in the Liberal State.' *European Journal of Social Theory*, 8 (1): 43-61.

Jørgensen, K. E. (1997), "Western Europe and the Petersberg Tasks", in: K. E. Jørgensen, ed., *European Approaches to Crisis Management*, The Hague: Kluwer Law International.

Kagan, R. (2003), *Of Paradise and Power. America and Europe in the New World Order*. New York: A. Knopf.

Kaika, M. (2005), *City of Flows: Modernity, Nature and the City*. Abingdon: Routledge.

Kant, I (1990), *Foundations of the Metaphysics of Morals*. Second edition, edited by L. White Beck. New York: Prentice Hall

Kant, I. (1912) [1795], *Zum ewigen Frieden. Ein philosophischer Entwurf.* Königsberg, Nicolovius in *Kants Gesammelte Schriften*, Bd. 8, Berlin-Leipzig: W. de Gruyter.

Karapostolis, V. (1995), *Hand-Made City: Athens Between Yes and No.* Athens: Alexandria. [Καραποστόλης, Β. (1995), Χειροποίητη πόλη: Η Αθήνα ανάμεσα στο Ναι και στο Όχι. Αθήνα: Αλεξάνδρεια.]

Karpat, K. H. (1976), *The Geçecondu: Rural Migration and Urbanisation.* Cambridge: Cambridge University Press.

Katz, R. & B. Wessels, eds. (1999), *The European Parliament, the National Parliaments and European Integration.* Oxford: Oxford University Press.

Katz, R. & P. Mair (1992), "The Membership of Political Parties in European Democracies, 1960-1990", *European Journal of Political Research*, 22: 334-7.

Katz, R. & P. Mair (1995), "Changing Models of Party Organization and Party Democracy: The Emergence of the Cartel Party", *Party Politics*, 1(1): 5-28.

Kayser, B., P.Y. Pechoux, & M. Sivignon (1971), *Exode Rural et Attraction Urbaine en Grèce.* Athens: EKKE.

Kearns, G. & C. Philo, eds. (1993), *Selling Places: The City as Cultural Capital, Past and Present.* Oxford: Pergamon Press.

Keating, M. & J. Loughlin, eds. (1997), *The Political Economy of Regionalism.* London: Frank Cass.

Keating, M. (1998), *The New Regionalism in Western Europe. Territorial Restructuring and Structural Change.* Cheltenham: Edward Elgar.

Kerremans, B. (1996), "Do Institutions Make a Difference? Non-Institutionalism, Neo-Institutionalism, and the Logic of Common Decision-Making in the European Union", *Governance*, 9: 217-240.

King, R., P. De Mas & J.M. Beck, eds. (2001), *Geography, Environment and Development in the Mediterranean.* Brighton: Sussex Academic Press.

Kögler, H.-H. (2005), "Constructing a Cosmopolitan Public Sphere: Hermeneutic Capabilities and Universal Values", *European Journal of Social Theory*, 8 (3): 297-320.

Kohler-Koch, B. (1999), Europe in Search of Legitimate Governance. Oslo: *ARENA Working Paper* n. 27.

Kohler-Koch, B. & R. Eising (1999), *The Transformation of Governance in the European Union.* London: Routledge.

Kreher, A. (1997), "Agencies in the European Community – A Step towards Administrative Integration in Europe", *Journal of European Public Policy*, 4: 225-245.

Kreppel, A. (2002), *The European Parliament and the Supranational Party System. A Study in Institutional Development.* Cambridge: Cambridge University Press.

Kymlicka, W. (1995), *Multicultural Citizenship. A Liberal Theory of Minority Rights.* Oxford: Oxford University Press.

Kymlicka, W., & N. Wayne, eds. (2000), *Citizenship in Diverse Societies*, Oxford: Oxford University Press.

Kymlicka, W., & W. Norman (1994), "Return of the Citizen: A Survey of Recent Work on Citizenship Theory." *Ethics* 104: 352-81.

La Torre, M. (1998), "Constitution, Citizenship, and the European Union", in: M. La Torre, ed., *European Citezenship: An Institutional Challenge*, Dordrecht: Kluwer Law.

Laborde, C. (2002), "From Constitutional to Civic Patriotism", *British Journal of Political Science* 32: 591-612.

Laborde, C. (2004), "Republican Citizenship and the Cruisis of Integration in France. In: R. Bellamy, D. Castiglione &. E. Santaro,. eds., *Lineages of European Citizenship*. London: Palgrave.

Lacorne, D. (2001), "European Citizenship: the American Model", in: K. Nicolaidis & R. Howse, eds,. *The FederalVision: Legitimacy and Levels of Governance in the US and the EU*. Oxford: Oxford University Press.

Lacoste, Y. (1997), *Vive la Nation. Destin d'une Iidée Géopolitique*, Paris: Fayard.

Lacroix, J. (2002), "For a European Constitutional Patriotism", *Political Studies*, 50 (5): 944-958.

Lacroix, J. (2004), *L'Europe en Procès. Quel Patriotisme au-delà des Nationalismes?* Paris: Cerf.

Ladeur, K.-H. (1997), "Towards a Legal Theory of Supranationality – The Viability of the Network Concept", *European Law Journal*, 3: 33-54.

Ladeur, K.-H. (1999), "Towards a Legal Concept of the Network in European Standard-Setting", in: C. Joerges, K.-H. Ladeur & E. Vos, eds., *Integrating Scientific Expertise into Regulatory Decision-Making. National Traditions and European Innovations*. Baden-Baden: Nomos.

Laffan, B. (1996), "The Politics of Identity and Political Order in Europe", *Journal of Common Market Studies* 34(1): 81-102.

Lamoureux, D. (1995), "Le Patriotisme Constitutionnel et les Etats Multinationaux", in: F. Blais, G. Laforest & D. Lamoureux, eds., *Libéralismes et Nationalismes. Philosophie et Politique*. Montreal: Presses de l'Université Laval.

Lane, R. E. (1996), "'Losing Touch' in a Democracy: Demands versus Needs", in: J. Hayward, ed., *Elitism, Populism and European Politics*. Oxford: Clarendon Press.

Larmore, C. E. (1996), *The Morals of Modernity*. Cambridge: Cambridge University Press.

Larsen, H. (2002), "A Global Military Actor?" *Cooperation and Conflict*, 37 (3): 282-302.

Le Galès, P. & M. Thatcher, eds. (1995), *Les Réseaux de Politique Publique. Débat autour des Policy Networks*. Paris: L'Harmattan.

Lehmbruch, G. (1982), "Neo-Corporatism in Comparative Perspective", in: G. Lehmbruch & P.C. Schmitter, eds., *Patterns of Corporatist Policy-Making*, London: Sage.

Lehning, P. & A. Weale, eds. (1997), *Citizenship, Democracy and Justice in the New Europe*. London: Routledge.

Leibfried, S. & P. Pierson, eds., (1995), *European Social Policy. Between Fragmentation and Integration*. Washington, D.C.: The Brookings Institution.

Lemco, J. (1991), *Political Stability in Federal Governments*. New York: Praeger.

Leontidou, L. (1989/2001). *Cities of Silence: Working-Class Space in Athens and Piraeus, 1909-1940*. Athens: ETVA (Cultural Technological Foundation of the Hellenic Bank of Industrial Development),& Themelio.

Leontidou, L. (1990/2006), *The Mediterranean City in Transition: Social Change and Urban Development*. Cambridge: Cambridge University Press.

Leontidou, L. (1993), "Postmodernism and the City: Mediterranean Versions", *Urban Studies*, 30(6): 949-65.

Leontidou, L. (1995), "Repolarization in the Mediterranean: Spanish and Greek Cities in Neoliberal Europe, *European Planning Studies*, 3(2): 155-72.

Leontidou, L. (1996), "Athens: Inter-Subjective Facets of Urban Performance", in: C. Jensen-Butler, A. Shakhar & J. van den Weesep, eds., *European Cities in Competition*. Avebury: Aldershot

Leontidou, L. (2001), "Cultural Representations of Urbanism and Experiences of Urbanisation in Mediterranean Europe", in: R. King, P. De Mas, & J.M. Beck, eds., *Geography, Environment and Development in the Mediterranean*. Brighton: Sussex Academic Press.

Leontidou, L. (2004), "The Boundaries of Europe: Deconstructing Three Regional Narratives", *Identities – Global Studies in Culture and Power* 11(4): 593-617. [Λεοντίδου, Λ.(1989/ 2001), Πόλεις της Σιωπής. Εργατικός εποικισμός της Αθήνας και του Πειραιά, 1909-1940. Αθήνα: ΕΤΒΑ και Θεμέλιο.]

Leontidou, L. (2005), *Geographically Illiterate Land: Hellenic Idols in the Epistemological Pathways of European Geography*. Athens: Hellenica Grammata. [Λεοντίδου, Λ. (2005), Αγεωγράφητος χώρα: Ελληνικά Είδωλα στις Επιστημολογικές Διαδρομές της Ευρωπαϊκής Γεωγραφίας. Αθήνα: Ελληνικά Γράμματα.]

Leontidou, L. (2006), "Urban Social Movements: From the 'Right to the City' to Transnational Spatialities and *Flaneur* Activists", *City: Analysis of Urban Trends, Culture, Theory, Policy, Action*, 10(3): 259-268.

Leontidou, L., H. Donnan & A. Afouxenidis (2005), "Exclusion and Difference along the EU Border: Social and Cultural Markers, Spatialities and Mappings", *International Journal of Urban and Regional Research* 29(2): 389-407.

Levi, M. (1998a), *Consent, Dissent and Patriotism*. New York: Cambridge University Press.

Levi, M. (1998b), "A State of Trust", in: V. Braithwaite & M. Levi, eds., *Trust and Governance*. New York: Russell Sage.

Lewis, J. (2000), "The Methods of Community in EU Decision-Making and Administrative Rivalry in the Council's Infrastructure", *Journal of European Public Policy* 7: 261-89.

Linz, J. J. (1999), "Democracy, Multinationalism and Federalism.", in: W. Busch & A. Merkel, eds., *Demokratie in Ost Und West.*. Frankfurt a.M.: Suhrkamp. (page numbers from http://www.march.es/NUEVO/IJM/CEACS/PUBLICACIONES/WORKING%20PAPERS/1997 _103.pdf).)

Locke, J. (1990), *Two Treatises of Government*, ed. by P. Laslett, Cambridge: Cambridge University Press.

Loughlin, J. (1996), "Europe of the Regions and the Federalization of Europe", *Publius: The Journal of Federalism*, 26(4): 141-62.

Loury, G. (1977), "A Dynamic Theory of Racial Income Differences", in: P. A. Wallance & A. Le Mund, eds., *Women, Minorities, and Employment Discrimination*. Lexington MA: Lexington. Books.

Lowi, T.J. (1964), "American Business, Public Policy, Case Studies and Political Theory", *World Politics* 16: 676-715.

Lurry, C. (1993), *Cultural Rights*. London: Routledge.

MacCormick, N. (1995), "Sovereignty, Democracy and Subsidiarity", in: R. Bellamy, V. Bufacchi & D. Castiglione, eds., *Democracy and Constitutional Culture in the Union of Europe*. London: Lothian Foundation.

MacCormick, N. (1996), "Liberalism, Nationalism, and the Post-Sovereign State." *Political Studies* 44, Special issue: 553-67.

MacCormick, N. (1997), "Democracy, Subsidiarity, and Citizenship in the 'European Commonwealth'", *Law and Philosophy* 16(4): 331-56.

Macedo, S. (1990), *Liberal Virtues: Citizenship, Virtue, and Community in Liberal Constitutionalism*. Oxford: Clarendon Press.

Madison, J. (1787), "Vices of the Political System of the United States", *The Papers of James Madison*, Chicago: Chicago University Press.

Madison, J. (1961), "The Federalist No. 62", in: J. Madison, A. Hamilton & J. Jay, eds., *The Federalist*. Cambridge MA: Harvard University Press.

Magnette, P. (1999). "Cittadinanza Europea e Società Civili." *Europa/Europe* 4(3).

Majone, G. (1996), "Temporal Consistency and Policy Credibility: Why Democracies Need Non-Majoritarian Institutions", *EUI Working Paper*, RSC 96/57.

Majone, G. (1998), "State, Market and Regulatory Competition: Lessons for the Integrating World Economy", in: A. Moravcsik, ed., *Centralization or Fragmentation? Europe Facing the Challenges of Deepening, Diversity, and Democracy*. New York: Council on Foreign Relations.

Mann, M. (1987), "Ruling Class Strategies and Citizenship", *Sociology*, 21 (3): 339-54.

Manners, I. & R.G. Whitman (2003), "The 'Difference Engine': Constructing and Representing the International Identity of the European Union", *Journal of European Public Policy* 10 (3): 380-404.

Manners, I. (2002), "Normative Power Europe: A Contradiction in Terms?"' *Journal of Common Market Studies* 40 (2): 235-58.

March, J. G. & H. A. Simon (1993) [1958], *Organizations*. 2nd ed. London: Blackwell.

March, J. G. & J P. Olsen (1989), *Rediscovering Institutions: The Organization Basis of Politics*. New York: The Free Press.

March, J. G. & J. P. Olsen (1976), *Ambiguity and Choice in Organizations*. Bergen: Scandinavian University Press.

March, J. G. (1994), *A Primer on Decision Making. How Decisions Happen*. New York: The Free Press.

Mariani, R, (1976), *Fascismo e 'Città Nuove'*. Milan: Feltrinelli.

Markell, P. (2000), "Making Affect Safe for Democracy? On "Constitutional Patriotism"', *Political Theory* 28 (1): 38-63.

Marks, G, & C. J. Wilson (1999), "National Parties and the Contestation of Europe", in: T. Banchoff & M. Smith, eds., *Legitimacy and the European Union. The Contested Polity*. London: Routledge.

Marks, G. (1993), "Structural Policy and Multilevel Governance in the European Community", in: A. Cafruny & G. Rosenthal, eds., *The State of the European Community. The Maastricht Debates and Beyond*. Boulder: Lynne Rienner.

Marks, G., L. Hooghe & K. Blank (1996), "European Integration from the 1980s: State-Centric v. Multi-Level Governance", *Journal of Common Market Studies*, 43(3): 341-78.

Marschak, J., (1950) "Rational Behavior, Uncertain Prospects, and Measurable Utility", *Econometrica*, 18(2): 111-141.

Marsh, M. & P. Norris, eds. (1997), Political Representation in the European Parliament. Special issue of the *European Journal of Political Research*, 32.

Marshall, T.H. (1973), "Citizenship and Social Class", in: T. H. Marshall, *Class, Citizenship and Social Development*, Westport CT: Greenwood Press.

Marshall, T.H. (1992), *Citizenship and Social Class*. London: Pluto Press.

Marx, K. (1961), *Capital: a Critical Analysis of Capitalist Production*. Moscow: Progress Publishers.

Mason, A. (1999), "Political Community, Liberal-Nationalism, and the Ethics of Assimilation", *Ethics* 109(2): 261-86.

Mason, A. (2000), *Community, Solidarity and Belonging. Levels of Community and their Normative Significance*. Cambridge: Cambridge University Press.

219

Maull, H. (2000), "Germany and the Use of Force: Still a 'Civilian Power'?", *Survival*, 42 (2): 56-80.

Mayntz, R. (1991), "Modernization and the Logic of Interorganizational Networks", *Discussion Paper*, Köln: Max-Planck-Institut für Gesellschaftsforschung.

McCarthy, T. (1999), "On Reconciling Cosmopolitan Unity and National Diversity", *Public Culture* 11 (1): 175-208..

McKay, D. (2001*)*, *Designing Europe - Comparative Lessons from the Federal Experience.* Oxford: Oxford University Press.

McKay, D. (2004), "The EU As a Self-Sustaining Federation: Specifying the Constitutional Conditions", in: L. Dobson & A. Follesdal, eds., *Political Theory and the European Constitution.* London: Routledge.

Meehan, E. (1993), *Citizenship and the European Community.* London: Sage.

Mény, Y. (1993), *Politique Comparée. Les Démocraties: Allemagne, Etats-Unis, France, Grande-Bretagne, Italie.* 4th ed. Paris: Montchrestien.

Mertens, T. (1996), "Cosmopolitanism and Citizenship: Kant against Habermas", *European Journal of Philosophy* 4(3): 328-47.

Michelman, F. (2001), "Morality, Identity and 'Constitutional Patriotism'", *Ratio Juris,* 14 (3): 253-71.

Mill, J. S. (1958) [1861]. *Considerations on Representative Government.* New York: Liberal Arts Press.

Mill, J. S. (1969) [1873], *Autobiography.* Jack Stillinger, ed. Boston: Houghton Mifflin.

Mill, J. S. (1970) [1869]. *The Subjection of Women.* Wendell Robert Carr, ed. Cambridge MA: MIT Press.

Miller, D. (1994), "The Nation-State: a Modest Defence", in: C. Brown, ed., *Political Restructuring in Europe: Ethical Perspectives.* London: Routledge.

Miller, D. (1995), *On Nationality.* Oxford: Oxford University Press.

Miller, D. (2000), *Citizenship and National Identity.* London: Blackwell.

Mitzen, J. (2006), "Anchoring Europe's Civilizing Identity: Habits, Capabilities, and Ontological Security", *Journal of European Public Policy,* 13 (2): 270-85.

Moore, R.I., ed. (1987), *Atlas of World History.* Chicago: Rand McNally & Co.

Moravcsik, A. (1998), *The Choice for Europe: Social Purpose and State Power From Messina to Maastricht.* Ithaca: Cornell University Press.

Moravcsik, A. (2003), "Striking a New Transatlantic Bargain", *Foreign Affairs,* 82 (4): 74-89.

Moreno, L. (2000), *Ciudadanos Precarios.* Barcelona: Ariel.

Morse, R. M. (1976), "The City-Idea in Argentina: A Study in Evanescence," *Journal of Urban History,* 2(3):. 307-30

Mouzelis, N. (1978), *Modern Greece: Facets of Underdevelopment.* London: Macmillan.

Müller, J.W. (2000), *Another Country. German Intellectuals, Unification and National Identity.* New Haven and London: Yale University Press.

Nabulsi, K.,(1999), "Hope and Heroic Action: Rousseau, Paoli, Kosciuszko, and the Republican Tradition of War", in: K. Nabulsi, *Traditions of War.* Oxford: Oxford University Press.

Nentwich, M. (1998), *Political Theory and the European Union. Legitimacy, Constitutional Choice and Citizenship.* London: Routledge.

Newton, K. (1999), "Social and Political Trust in Established Democracies", in: P. Norris, ed., *Critical Citizens: Global Support for Democratic Government.* Oxford: Oxford University Press.

Nicolaidis, K. (2001), "Conclusion: The Federal Vision Beyond the Nation State", in: K. Nicolaidis & R. Howse, eds., *The Federal Vision: Legitimacy and Levels of Governance in the US and the EU*. Oxford: Oxford University Press.

Nicolaidis, K., & R. Howse, eds. (2001), *The Federal Vision: Legitimacy and Levels of Governance in the US and the EU*. Oxford: Oxford University Press.

Nida-Rümelin, J. (1993), *Kritik des Konsequentialismus*. München: Oldenbourg.

Nida-Rümelin, J. (1997), *Economic Rationality and Practical Reason*. Dordrecht: Kluwer.

Nida-Rümelin, J. (2001), *Strukturelle Rationalität*. Stuttgart: Reclam.

Nida-Rümelin, J. (2005), "Why Rational Deontological Action Maximizes Subjective Value", *Protosociology 21*: 174-185.

Norman, W. J. (1994), "Towards a Philosophy of Federalism", in: J. Baker, ed., *Group Rights*. Toronto: University of Toronto Press.

Norman, W. J. (1995), "The Ideology of Shared Values: A Myopic Vision of Unity in the Multi-Nation State", in : J. Carens, ed., *Is Quebec Nationalism Just? Perspectives From Anglophone Canada*. Montreal: McGill-Queens University Press.

Norton, P., ed. (1996), *National Parliaments and the European Union*. London: Frank Cass.

Nussbaum, M. et al (1996), *For Love of Country: Debating the Limits of Patriotism*. Chicago: Chicago University Press.

Offe, C. (2000). "The Democratic Welfare State in an Integrating Europe", in: M. Greven & L. Pauly, eds., *Democracy Beyond the State?: The European Dilemma and the Emerging Global Order*. Toronto: University of Toronto Press.

Olafson, F. A. (1990), "Habermas as a Philosopher." *Ethics* 100: 641-57.

Olsen, J P. (2000), "How, Then, Does One Get There?", in: C. Joerges, Y. Mény & J. H. H. Weiler, eds., *What Kind of Constitution for What Kind of Polity? Responses to Joschka Fischer*. Badia Fiesolana: European University Institute.

O'Neil, S. (1997), *Impartiality in Context. Grounding Justice in a Pluralist World*. New York: State University of New York Press.

O'Neill, O. (1989), *Constructions of Reason*. Cambridge: Cambridge University Press.

Ong, A. (1999), *Flexible Citizenship: The Cultural Logics of Transnationality*. Durham: Duke University Press.

Ostrom, E. (1991), *Governing the Commons: The Evolution of Institutions for Collective Action*. Cambridge: Cambridge University Press.

Parekh, B. (2000), *Rethinking Multiculturalism: Cultural Diversity and Political Theory*. London: Macmillan.

Park, R.E. & E.W. Burgess (1967), *The City*. Chicago: University of Chicago Press.

Peters, G. (1986), *American Public Policy*. Basingstoke: Macmillan.

Peterson, J. (1994), "Policy Networks and European Union Policy Making: A Reply to Kassim", *West European Politics*, 18: 389-407.

Pettit, P. (1997), *Republicanism: A Theory of Freedom and Government*. Oxford: Oxford University Press.

Piattoni, S. (1999), "Trends Towards Personalistic Representation. Some Ideas for the Study of Micro-Politics in Europe." Paper presented at the workshop on "Multi-level Party Systems: Europeanisation and the Reshaping of National Political Representation", *European University Institute, Florence*, December 16-18.

Piattoni, S. (2000a), "Personalistic Politics across Institutional Levels. Political Entrepreneurship in Europe", *European Forum Paper*, March 19.

Piattoni, S. (2000b), "Alcune Riflessioni sulla Personalizzazione della Politica in Italia", paper presented at the panel on "Personalizzazione della politica italiana in prospettiva comparata", *SISP yearly meeting*, Naples, 28-30 September.

Pierson, P. (1998), "Social Policy and European Integration", in: A. Moravcsik, ed., *Centralization or Fragmentation? Europe Facing the Challenges of Deepening, Diversity, and Democracy.* New York: Council on Foreign Relations.

Pirenne, H. (1927), *Les Villes du Moyen Age.* Bruxelles: Maurice Lamertin.

Pitkin, H. F. (1967), *The Concept of Representation.* Berkeley: University of California Press.

Pounds, N. J. G. (1990), *An Historical Geography of Europe.* Cambridge: Cambridge University Press

Preuss, U. K. (1995), "Problems of a Concept of European Citizenship." *European Law Journal* 1(3): 267-81.

Preuss, U. K. (2004), "Citizenship and the German State", In: R. Bellamy, D. Castiglione &. E. Santaro,. eds., Lineages of European Citizenship. London: Palgrave.

Preuss, U. K. (1996), "Two Challenges to European Citizenship", in: R. Bellamy & D. Castiglione, eds.. *Constitutionalism in Transformation: European and Theoretical Perspectives.* Oxford: Blackwell.

Putnam, R. D. (1993), *Making Democracy Work: Civic Traditions in Modern Italy.* Princeton NJ: Princeton University Press.

Putnam, R. D. (1995), "Bowling Alone: America's Declining Social Capital", *Journal of Democracy*: 6 (1): 65-78.

Putnam, R. D. (1999), *Bowling Alone,* New York: Simon and Shuster.

Putnam, R. D. (2001), *Gesellschaft und Gemeinschaft. Sozialkapital im internationalen Vergleich.*Gütersloh: Bertelsmann.

Rawls, J. (1971), *A Theory of Justice.* Cambridge MA: Harvard University Press.

Rawls, J. (1993), *Political Liberalism.* New York: Columbia University Press.

Rawls, J. (1999), *The Law of Peoples.* Cambridge MA: Harvard University Press.

Rawls, J. (2001), *Justice As Fairness: A Restatement.* Ed., Erin Kelly, ed. Cambridge MA.: Harvard University Press.

Reif, K. & H. Schmidt (1980), "Nine Second-Order National Elections: A Conceptual Framework for the Analysis of European Election Results", *European Journal of Political Research*, 8(1): 3-45.

Reif, K. (1997), "Reflections: European Elections as Member State Second-Order Elections Revisited", *European Journal of Political Research*, 31(1): 115-124.

Rhodes, R. A. W. (1997), *Understanding Governance.* Buckingham: Open University Press.

Richardson, J. (1994). "EU Water Policy: Uncertain Agendas, Shifting Networks and Complex Coalitions." *Environmental Politics* 3(4): 139-167.

Ricoeur, P. (1990), *Soi-Même Comme un Autre.* Paris: Seuil

Riedel, M. (1975), "Gesellschaft, bürgerliche", in: O. Brunner, W. Conze & R. Koselleck, eds., *Geschichtliche Grundbegriffe. Historisches Lexikon zur politisch-sozialen Sprache in Deutschland*, vol. II. Stuttgart: Klett.

Risse, T. (2000), "Let's Argue! Communicative Action in World Politics", *International Organization* 54: 1-39.

Risse-Kappen, T. (1996), "Exploring the Nature of the Beast: International Relations Theory and Comparative Policy Analysis Meet the European Union", *Journal of Common Market Studies* 34: 53-80.

222

Rittberger, B. (2005), *Building Europe's Parliament. Democratic Representation Beyond the Nation State*. Oxford: Oxford University Press.

Roche, M. (1992), *Rethinking Citizenship: Welfare, Ideology and Change in Modern Society, Cambridge*: Polity Press.

Rometsch, D. & W. Wessels, eds. (1966), *The European Union and the Members States*. Manchester: Manchester University Press.

Rosecrance, R. (1998), "The European Union: A New Type of International Actor", in: J. Zielonka, ed., *Paradoxes of European Foreign Policy*. The Hague: Kluwer Law International.

Rosmini, A. (1993) [1841-1843]), *The Philosophy of Right*, vol. 2: *Rights of the Individual*, Transl. by D. Cleary & T. Watson. Durham: Rosmini House.

Rothstein, B. (1998), *Just Institutions Matter: The Moral and Political Logic of the Universal Welfare State*. Cambridge: Cambridge University Press.

Rothstein, B. (1999), "Trust, Social Dilemmas, and the Strategic Construction of Collective Memories." Paper can be downloaded form: http://www.russellsage.org/publications/workingpapers/Trust%20Social%20Dilemmas%20and%20the%20Strategic%20Construction%20of%20Collective%20Memories/document

Rousseau, J. J. (1964) [1762], "Du Contrat Social", in: B. Gagnebin & M. Raymond, eds., *Œuvres Complètes*, vol. 3. Paris: Gallimard.

Rousseau, J. J. (1972) [1772]. *The Government of Poland*. New York: Bobbs-Merrill.

Rousseau, J. J. (1978) [1762]. *On the Social Contract*. New York: St. Martin's Press.

Rousseau, J. J. (1993) [1762]. *Emile: a Treatise on Education*. New York: Everyman.

Rummel, R. (2002), "From Weakness to Power with the ESDP", *European Foreign Affairs Review*, 7: 453-71.

Rutten, M. (2001), "From St-Malo to Nice. European Defence: Core Documents", *Chaillot Paper*, 47, Paris: Institute for Security Studies of WEU.

Ruzza, Carlo (2004), *Europe and Civil Society. Movement Coalitions and European Governance*. Manchester: Manchester University Press.

Sabatier, P.A. (1988), "An Advocacy Coalition Framework of Policy Change and the Role of Policy-Oriented Learning Therein", *Policy Sciences* 21: 129-168.

Salcedo, J. (1977), Madrid *Culpable: Sobre el Espacio y la Población en las Sciencias Sociales*. Madrid: Tecnos.

Sartori, G. (1970), "Concept Misformation in Comparative Politics", *American Political Science Review*, 64(4): 1033-1053.

Saunders, P. (1986), *Socia Theory and the UrbanQquestion*. 2nd edn. Hutchinson, London

Sbragia, A. (2002), "The Dilemma of Governance with Government", *Jean Monnet Working Paper* 3/02, NYU School of Law.

Scanlon, T. M. (1982), "Contractualism and Utilitarianism", in: A. K. Sen & B. Williams, eds., *Utilitarianism and Beyond*. Cambridge: Cambridge University Press.

Scanlon, T. M. (1998), *What We Owe to Each Other*. Cambridge MA: Harvard University Press.

Schaefer, G.F. (1996), "Committees in the EC Policy Process: A First Step Towards Developing a Conceptual Framework", in: R.H. Pedler & G.F. Schaefer, eds., *Shaping European Law and Policy. The Role of Committees and Comitology in the Political Process*. Maastricht: European Institute of Public Administration.

Scharpf, F. W. (1988), "The Joint Decision Trap: Lessons from German Federalism and European Integration.", *Public Administration* 66(3): 239-78.

Scharpf, F. W. (1997a), "Economic Integration, Democracy and the Welfare State", *Journal of European Public Policy* 4(1): 18-36.

Scharpf, F. W. (1997b), *Games Real Actors Play: Actor-Centered Institutionalism in Policy Research*. Boulder CO: Westview Press.

Scharpf, F. W. (1999), *Governing in Europe: Effective and Democratic?* Oxford: Oxford University Press.

Scharpf, F.W., ed. (1993), *Games in Hierarchies and Networks. Analytical and Empirical Approaches to the Study of Governance Institutions*, Frankfurt a. M.: Campus Verlag/Westview Press.

Schattschneider, E. E. (1975), *The Semisovereign People*. Hinsdale Il: The Dryden Press.

Schmitt, B. (2004), "European Capabilities – How many Divisions", in: N. Gnesotto, ed., *EU Security and Defence Policy: the First five Years (1999-2004)*, Paris: EU Institute for Security Studies.

Schmitt, C. (1963), *Der Begriff des Politischen*. Berlin: Duncker & Humblot.

Schmitt, H. & J. Thomassen, eds. (1999), *Political Representation and Legitimacy in the European Union*. Oxford: Oxford University Press.

Schmitter, P.C. (1979), "Still the Century of Corporatism?", in: P.C. Schmitter & G. Lehmbruch, eds., *Trends Toward Corporatist Intermediation*. London: Sage.

Schnapper, D. (2004), "Citoyenneté Européenne et Démocratie Providentielle", in: P. Savidan, ed., *La République ou l'Europe?* Paris: Livre de Poche.

Schorske, C.E. (1998), *Thinking with History: Explorations in the Passage to Modernism*. Princeton NJ: Princeton University Press.

Schuman, R. (1950), "Declaration of May 9." http://www.robert-schuman.org/anglais/robert-schuman/declaration.htm.

Scott, W.R. (1981), *Organizations: Rational, Natural, and Open Systems*. New Jersey: Prentice-Hall.

Sedelmeier, U. (2004), "Collective Identity", in: W. Carlsnaes, H. Sjursen & B. White, eds., *Contemporary European Foreign Policy*. London: SAGE Publishers.

Sen, A. K. (1967), "Isolation, Assurance and the Social Rate of Discount", *Quarterly Journal of Economics* 81: 112-24.

Sen, A. K. (2001), "Choice, Orderings and Morality", in: S. Körner, ed., *Practical Reason*. New Haven: Yale University Press..

Seneca, L. A. (1969), *Ad Lucilium Epistulae Morales*, ed. by L.D. Reynolds. Oxford: Clarendon.

Shapiro, M. (1997), "The Problems of Independent Agencies in the United States and the European Union", *Journal of European Public Policy* 4: 276-291.

Shaw, J. (1997a), "Citizenship of the Union: Towards Post-National Citizenship?", *Harvard Jean Monnet Chair Paper 6/97*.

Shaw, J. (1997b), "European Citizenship: The IGC and Beyond", *European Integration Online Papers* 1, 3.

Sim, B. and H. Skjeie (2004), "The Scandinavian Model of Citizenship", In: R. Bellamy, D. Castiglione &. E. Santaro,. eds., *Lineages of European Citizenship*. London: Palgrave.

Simeon, R., & D. P. Conway (2001), "Federalism and the Management of Conflict in Multinational Societies", in: A. G. Gagnon & J. Tully, eds., *Multinational Democracies*. Cambridge: Cambridge University Press.

Simon, H.A. (1965), *Administrative Behavior,* New York: The Free Press.

Singer, P. (2003), *One World: The Ethics of Globalization*. New Haven: Yale University Press.

Sjursen, H. (2006), "The EU as a 'Normative' Power: How Can This Be?", *Journal of European Public Policy,* Special Issue, 13 (2): 235-51.

Skelcher, C. (2005), "Jurisdictional Integrity, Polycentrism and the Design of Democratic Governance", *Governance,* 18(1): 89-111.

Smismans, S. (2005), "How to be Fundamental with Soft Procedures? The Open Method of Coordination and Fundamental Social Rights", in: G. de Búrca & B. de Witte, eds., *The Protection of Social Rights in Europe: Changes and Challenges.* Oxford: Oxford University Press.

Smismans, S. (2007), „New Governance – The Solution for Active European Citizenship, or the End of Citizenship?', *Columbia Journal of European Law*, Vol. 13 (3).

Smith, A. (1995), "Réintroduire la Question du Sens dans les Réseaux d'Action Publique", in: P. Le Galès & M. Thatcher, eds., *Les Réseaux de Politique Publique. Débat Autour des Policy Networks,* Paris: L'Harmattan.

Smith, K. E. (2005), "Still Civilian Power EU?", *European Foreign Policy Unit Working Paper,* 1.

Solana, J. (2004), "Preface", in: N. Gnesotto, ed, *EU Security and Defence Policy: the First five Years (1999-2004)*, Paris: EU Institute for Security Studies.

Somers, M. (1995), "Narrating and Naturalizing Civil Society and Citizenship Theory: The Place of Political Culture and the Public Sphere", *Sociological Theory* 13 (3): 229-74.

Soysal, Y. (1994), *Limits of Citizenship: Migrants and Postnational Membership in Europe.* Chicago: Chicago University Press.

Spengler, O. (1926), *The Decline of the West.* Authorized translation with notes by C. F. Atkinson. New York: A.A. Knopf.

Stavridis, S. (2001), "'Militarising" the EU: the Concept of Civilian Power Europe Revisited", *The International Spectator*, 31 (4): 43-50.

Stepan, A. (1999), "Federalism and Democracy: Beyond the U.S. Model", *Journal of Democracy* 10: 19-34.

Stevenson, N., ed. (2000), *Culture and Citizenship.* London: Sage.

Stinchcombe, A. L. (1986), "Reason and Rationality", *Sociological Theory* 4(Fall): 151-66.

Streeck, W. (1996), "Neo-Voluntarism: a New European Social Policy Regime?", in: G Marks, F. W. Scharpf, P. Schmitter & W. Streeck, eds., *Governance in the European Union.* London: Sage.

Stuurman, S. (2004), "Citizenship and Cultural Difference in France and the Netherlands", in: R. Bellamy, D. Castiglione & E. Santoro, eds. (2004), *Lineages of European Citizenship: Rights, Belonging and Participation in Eleven Nation-States.* London: Palgrave.

Sunstein, C.R. (1988), "Beyond the Republican Revival", *Yale Law Journal* 97: 1539-1694.

Tamir, Y. (1993), *Liberal Nationalism.* Princeton NJ: Princeton University Press.

Tassin, E. (1994), "Identité Nationales et Citoyenneté Politique", *Esprit* 198: 97-111.

Taylor, C. (1995), "Invoking Civil Society", in: C. Taylor, *Philosophical Argument.* Cambridge MA: Harvard University Press.

Taylor, M. (1969), "Proof of a Theorem on Majority Rule", *Behavioral Science* 14(3): 228-31.

Taylor, M. (1987), *The Possibility of Cooperation.* Cambridge: Cambridge University Press.

Telò, M. (2005), *Europe a Civilian Power? European Union, Global Governance, World Order.* Basingstoke: Palgrave.

Thatcher, M. (1995), "Les Réseaux de Politique Publique: Bilan d'un Sceptique", in: P. Le Galès & M. Thatcher, eds., *Les Réseaux de Politique Publique. Débat Autour des Policy Networks.* Paris: L'Harmattan.

Thibaud, P. (1992), "L'Europe Par les Nations (et Réciproquement)", in: J.M. Ferry & P. Thibaud, *Discussion sur l'Europe*. Paris: Calmann-Lévy.

Thompson, D. F., & A. Gutmann (1996), *Democracy and Disagreement*. Cambridge MA: Harvard University Press.

Tocqueville, A. (1990) [1835-1840], *De la Démocratie en Amérique*, ed. by E. Nolla. Paris: Librairie Philosophique J. Vrin.

Touraine, A. (2000), *Can We Live Together? Equal and Different*. Cambridge: Polity Press.

Toynbee, A., ed. (1967), *Cities of Destiny*. London: Thames and Hudson.

Trenz, H. J. & K. Eder (2004), "The Democratizing Dynamics of a European Public Sphere", *European Journal of Social Theory*, 7 (1): 5-25.

Trondal, J. & F. Veggeland (2003), "Access, Voice and Loyalty. The Representation of Domestic Civil Servants in the EU Committees", *Journal of European Public Policy*, 10: 59-77.

Trondal, J. (2000), "Multiple Institutional Embeddedness in Europe: The Case of Danish, Norwegian, and Swedish Government Officials", *Scandinavian Political Studies* 23(4): 311-41.

Trondal, J. (2001a), *Administrative Integration across Levels of Governance. Integration through Participation in EU Committees*. Dissertation submitted to the Department of Political Science, University of Oslo.

Trondal, J. (2001b), "Is There Any Social Constructivist-Institutionalist Divide? Unpacking Social Mechanisms Affecting Representational Roles Among EU Decision-Makers", *Journal of European Public Policy*, 8: 1-23.

Turner, B. (1986), *Citizenship and Capitalis.* London: Allen Unwin

van den Berg, L., R. Drewett, L.H. Klaasen, A.Rossi, A. & C.H.T. Vijverberg (1982), *Urban Europe: A Study of Growth and Decline*. Oxford: Pergamon Press.

van der Eijk, C. & M. N. Franklim, eds. (1996), *Choosing Europe? The European Electorate and National Politics in the Face of Union*. Ann Arbor: Michingan University Press.

Vertovec, S. & R. Cohen, eds. (2002), *Conceiving Cosmopolitanism*. Oxford: Oxford University Press.

Vervaele, J. A. E. (1999), "Shared Governance and Enforcement of European Law: From Comitology to a Multi-level Agency Structure?", in: C. Joerges, K.-H. Ladeur & E. Vos, eds., *Integrating Scientific Expertise into Regulatory Decision-Making. National Traditions and European Innovations*. Baden-Baden: Nomos.

Viroli, M. (1995), *For Love of Country. An Essay on Patriotism and Nationalism*, Oxford: Oxford University Press.

von Neumann, J. & O. Morgenstern (1944), *Theory of Games and Economic Behavior*, Princeton NJ: Princeton University Press.

Waldron, J. (1993), "Special Ties and Natural Duties", *Philosophy and Public Affairs* 22(1): 3-30.

Waldron, J. (2000), "Cultural Identity and Civic Responsibility", in: W. Kymlicka & W. Norman, eds., *Citizenship in Diverse Societies*. Oxford: Oxford University Press.

Waldron,J.(1987) "Theoretical foundations of liberalism", Reprinted in: Waldron (1993). "Theoretical Foundations of Liberalism" *Philosophical Quarterly* 1987; 37127-50.

Walker, N. (2004), "The Legacy of Europe's Constitutional Moment", *Constellations* 11 (3): 368-371.

Wallace, H. &W. Wallace, eds. (2000), *Policy-Making in the European Union*. New York: Oxford University Press.

Walzer, M. (1983), *Thick and Thin: The Moral Argument at Home and Abroad*. New York: Basic Books.

Walzer, M. (1994), "Spheres of Affection", *Boston Review*, 19 (5), 29.

Walzer, M. (1998), "Citizenship." *Democrazia e Diritto* 28(2-3): 43-52.

Ward, D. (1973), "The Making of Immigrant Ghettoes 1840-1920", in: A. N. Callow Jr., ed., *American Urban History: an Interpretative Reader with Commentaries,* 2nd edn. New York: Oxford University Press.

Warleigh, A. (2000), "The Hustle: Citizenship Practice, NGOs and "Policy Coalitions" in the European Union - the Cases of Auto Oil, Drinking Water and Unit Pricing." *Journal of European Public Policy* 7(2): 229-243.

Warleigh, A. (2001), "Europeanizing Civil Society: NGOs as Agents of Political Socialization in the European Union." *Journal of Common Market Studies* 39(4): 619-639.

Weale, A. (1999), *Democracy.* Basington: Palgrave.

Weale, A. (2005), *Democratic Citizenship and the European Union.* Manchester: Manchester University Press.

Weber, M. (1966), *The City.* The Free Press: New York

Weiler, J. H. H. (1996), "The Selling of Europe: The Discourse of European Citizenship in the IGC 1996", *Harvard Jean Monnet Working Paper 3/96.*

Weiler, J. H. H. (1999), *The Constitution of Europe.* Cambridge: Cambridge University Press.

Weiler, J. H. H. (2001), "Federalism and Constitutionalism: Europe's Sonderweg.", in: K. Nicolaidis & R. Howse, eds., *The Federal Vision: Legitimacy and Levels of Governance in the US and the EU.* Oxford: Oxford University Press.

Weiler, J. H. H., U. Haltern & F. Mayer (1995), "European Democracy and Its Critique: Five Uneasy Pieces", *EUI Working Paper RSC No 95/11, and Harvard Jean Monnet Working Paper 1/1995.*

Wendt, A. (1999), *Social Theory of International Politics.* Cambridge: Cambridge University Press.

Wessels, B. & U. Diedrichs (1999), "The European Parliament and EU Legitimacy", in: T. Banchoff & M. Smith, eds., *Legitimacy and the European Union. The Contested Polity.* London: Routledge.

Wessels, W. (1999), "Comitology as a Research Subject: a New Legitimacy Mix?", in: C. Joerges & E. Vos, eds., *EU Committees: Social Regulation, Law and Politics.* Oxford: Hart.

White, M. & L. White (1977), *The Intellectual Versus the City: From Thomas Jefferson to Frank Lloyd Wright.* Oxford: Oxford University Press.

White, P. (1984), *The West European City: A Social Geography.* London: Longman.

Whitman, R. (1998), *From Civilian Power to Superpower? The International Identity of the European Union.* London: Macmillan.

Whitman, R. (2002), "The Fall, and Rise, of Civilian Power Europe?", *National Europe Centre Paper*, Australian National University, 16.

Wiener, A. (1998), *European Citizenship Practice: Building Institutions of a Non-State.* Boulder CO: Westview.

Wiener, M. J. (1985), *English Culture and the Decline of the Industrial Spirit 1850-1980.* Harmondsworth: Pelican.

Williams, R. (1973), *The Country and the City.* London: Chatto & Windus.

Wimmer, A. (2002), *Nationalist Exclusion and Ethnic Conflict: Shadows of Modernity.* Cambridge: Cambridge University Press.

Wirth, L. (1938), "Urbanism as a Way of Life", *American Journal of Sociology*, 44(1): 1-24.

Wolff, C. (1972) [1750], *Jus gentium. Prolegomena,* ed. M. Thomann, Hildesheim: Georg Olms Verlag.

Wynn, M. (1984), *Planning and Urban Growth in Southern Europe*. Mansell: London.

Young, I. M. (1990), *Justice and the Politics of Difference*. New Haven: Princeton University Press.

Zeitlin, F .I. (1996), *Playing the Other: Gender and Society in Classical Greek literature*. Chicago: University of Chicago Press.

Zielonka, J. (1998), *Explaining Euro-Paralysis*. London: Macmillan.

Ziller, J. (2001), "European Models of Government: A Patchwork with Missing Pieces?", *Parliamentary Affairs,* 54: 102-119.

Zimmerman, A. (1995), "Toward a More Democratic Ethics of Technological Governance", *Science, Technology and Human Values,* 20 (1): 86-107.

Zolo, D. (1997), *Cosmopolis: Prospects for World Government*. Cambridge: Polity Press.

228

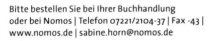